Wittgenstein

and the *Philosophical Investigations*

'The movement of Wittgenstein's thought, how the different topics
hang together, why they come in the order they do – are all made
clearer than in any other discussion I know. It assumes some basic
knowledge of philosophy, but not much beyond that ... anyone
interested in Wittgenstein could read it with advantage.'

(*Jane Heal, St John's College, Cambridge*)

Wittgenstein is one of the small number of twentieth-century philosophers who is well known outside philosophical circles. This may be due
to his exceptional life and personality and the number of biographies and
memoirs written about him. However, it is also because his writing has
the power to interest the non-specialist reader in a way that other works
of philosophy do not.

This GuideBook gives students a clear and concise reading of
Wittgenstein's most important work – the *Philosophical Investigations*.
McGinn argues that the unique style of the *Investigations* makes it an
exceptional work of literature as well as philosophy. *Wittgenstein and the*
Philosophical Investigations will take the student through the text without getting bogged down in scholarly detail. This book is ideal for
students who want to understand the text, the context of the work and the
philosopher.

Marie McGinn lectures in philosophy at the University of York. She is
the author of *Sense and Certainty: The Dissolution of Scepticism* (1989).

**Routledge
Philosophy
GuideBooks**

Edited by Tim Crane and Jonathan Wolff
University College London

Locke on Government
D. A. Lloyd Thomas

Locke on Human Understanding
E. J. Lowe

Plato and the *Republic*
Nickolas Pappas

Heidegger and *Being and Time*
Stephen Mulhall

**Spinoza and the
*Ethics***
Genevieve Lloyd

LONDON AND NEW YORK

Routledge Philosophy GuideBook to

Wittgenstein

and the *Philosophical Investigations*

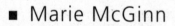 Marie McGinn

First published 1997
by Routledge
11 New Fetter Lane
London EC4P 4EE

Simultaneously published in the
USA and Canada
by Routledge
29 West 35th Street
New York, NY 10001

© 1997 Marie McGinn

Typeset in Times and Frutiger by
Florencetype Ltd, Stoodleigh, Devon

Printed and bound in Great Britain by
Clays Ltd, St. Ives PLC

*British Library Cataloguing in
Publication Data*
A catalogue record for this book is
available from the British Library

*Library of Congress Cataloging in
Publication Data*
McGinn, Marie.
Routledge philosophy guidebook to
Wittgenstein and the Philosophical
investigations / Marie McGinn.
p. cm. – (Routledge philosophy
guidebooks)
Includes bibliographical references and
index.   1. Philosophy.
2. Languages and languages –
Philosophy
3. Semantics (Philosophy)
I. Wittgenstein, Ludwig, 1889–1951.
Philosophische Untersuchungen.
II. Title.   III. Series.
B3376. W563P53255 1996
192–dc20   96–27227
                                           CIP

ISBN 0–415–11190–0 (hbk)
ISBN 0–415–11191–9 (pbk)

To Mark, Sam and Guy

'Stupidity consists in wanting to reach conclusions. We are a thread, and we want to know the whole cloth ... What mind worthy of the name, beginning with Homer, ever reached a conclusion? Let's accept the picture. That's how things are. So be it ...'

(Gustave Flaubert)

Contents

6 Seeing and seeing aspects
Philosophical Investigations, 398–401:
Part II, section xi **177**

Acknowledgements

I would like to thank a number of people for the help they have given me in writing this book. My main debt is to my student, Beth Savickey, with whom I have discussed every aspect of the book and from whose knowledge and understanding of Wittgenstein I have continually benefited. She is exactly the sort of sympathetic and well-informed interlocutor that every author dreams of, and I am indebted to her for the numerous insights that emerged in our two-year-long conversation. I would also like to thank my husband, Mark Rowe, both for continual encouragement and for patiently reading and commenting on draft after draft of text. I would like to thank Tim Crane for asking me to write the book, and for his detailed comments on an earlier draft; and Stephen Mulhall and Jim Hopkins for their vigorous criticism of a draft of chapter 4. I would also like to thank the numerous students at York, and particularly Jonathan Coles, who have taken courses on Wittgenstein with me over the years, and who have repeatedly drawn my attention to details of Wittgenstein's re-marks, or to alternative ways of reading them, that I had missed. I am grateful to Mary Dortch for her skilled and professional work on the index. Finally, I would like to thank the University of York for giving me two research terms without which the book could not have been written.

Abbreviations

Works by Wittgenstein referred to, in order of composition:

TLP   *Tractatus Logico-Philosophicus*, tr. D. F. Pears and B. F. McGuinness (London: Routledge & Kegan Paul, 1961).

CV   *Culture and Value*, ed. G. H. von Wright in collaboration with H. Nyman, tr. P. Winch (Oxford: Blackwell, 1980).

WL   'Wittgenstein's Lectures 1930–33', notes by G. E. Moore, published in *Ludwig Wittgenstein: The Man and His Philosophy*, ed. K. T. Fann (Hassocks: Harvester Press, 1978).

P   'Philosophy', taken from TS 213 ('The Big Typescript'), published in *PO*.

RFGB   'Remarks on Frazer's "The Golden Bough" ', ed. R. Rhees, published in *PO*.

BB   *The Blue and Brown Books* (Oxford: Blackwell, 1958).

LSDPE   'The Language of Sense Data and Private Experience', notes taken by R. Rhees of Wittgenstein's lectures in 1936, published in *PO*.

WLFM   *Wittgenstein's Lectures on the Foundations of Mathematics, Cambridge 1939*, notes by R. G. Bosanquet,

N. Malcolm, R. Rhees and Y. Smythies, ed. Cora Diamond (Hassocks: Harvester Press, 1976).

PI *Philosophical Investigations*, ed. G. E. M. Anscombe and R. Rhees, tr. G. E. M. Anscombe (Oxford: Blackwell, 1963).

RPP 1 *Remarks on the Philosophy of Psychology*, vol. 1, ed. G. E. M. Anscombe and G. H. von Wright, tr. G. E. M. Anscombe (Oxford: Blackwell, 1980).

WLPP *Wittgenstein's Lectures on Philosophy of Psychology 1946–7*, notes by P. T. Geach, K. J. Shah and A. C. Jackson, ed. P. T. Geach (Hassocks: Harvester Press, 1988).

Z *Zettel*, ed. G. E. M. Anscombe and G. H. von Wright, tr. G. E. M. Anscombe (Oxford: Blackwell, 1967).

LWPP 2 *Last Writings on the Philosophy of Psychology*, vol. 2, ed. G. H. von Wright and H. Nyman, tr. C. G. Luckhardt and M. A. E. Aue (Oxford: Blackwell, 1992).

PO *Philosophical Occasions 1912–1951*, ed. J. Klagge and A. Nordmann (Indianapolis, Ind. and Cambridge: Hackett, 1993).

Note: All quotations apart from short phrases from Wittgenstein's texts preserve his punctuation exactly. Where a sentence quoted occurs in the original text within quotation marks I have included these within my own quotation marks.

Introduction

Ludwig Wittgenstein was born in Vienna on 26 April 1889 and died on 29 April 1951 in Cambridge. His claim to be one of the most outstanding philosophers of the twentieth century is now well established. The power and originality of his thought show a unique philosophical mind and many would be happy to call him a genius. The extraordinarily compelling nature of both the man and his thought is shown by the large number of memoirs that have been written by his pupils and others who knew him, as well as by the vast secondary literature that his work has inspired. The memoirs all confirm the picture of a man of exceptional intellectual penetration and unremitting integrity, who possessed great practical skills and who was an exciting and loyal, though often demanding, friend. By contrast, the philosophical responses to his work present no similarly coherent picture, but rather display wide discrepancies in both the interpretation and assessment of his work.

Born into a wealthy, industrialist family with wide cultural interests, Wittgenstein first came to

1

England in 1908, to the College of Technology in Manchester, where he enrolled as a research student in the department of engineering. While he was working on the design of a jet propeller, he became more and more interested in the mathematical problems that it raised. In 1911 he moved to Cambridge to study philosophy of mathematics with the philosopher Bertrand Russell. By 1912, Russell was sufficiently convinced of Wittgenstein's genius to encourage him to give up aeronautics and devote himself to the study of philosophy. In 1912 he presented his first paper to the Cambridge Moral Sciences Club. The subject was 'What is philosophy?', and it shows that from the very beginning Wittgenstein recognized the importance of understanding the nature of philosophical problems and of reflecting on the appropriate methods for approaching them. This concern with diagnosis and method remains characteristic of Wittgenstein throughout his philosophical development.

Up until the outbreak of the First World War Wittgenstein continued to work on logic and the foundation of mathematics. Much of his work was done in Norway, where Wittgenstein went to escape what he felt to be the superficial cleverness of much of the intellectual discussion that went on in Cambridge. During this period he made most of the discoveries about logic and language that were to form the basis for his first book, the *Tractatus Logico-Philosophicus* (1922). This was the only major work of philosophy that he published in his lifetime; his second major work – the *Philosophical Investigations* – was worked on for publication from about 1937 to 1945 but was published only posthumously in 1953. Both of these works are in their own way unique. At first glance, one is struck by the contrast between them. Although they both take language as their central topic, the early work is highly abstract, theoretical, precise and dogmatic, while the later work is concrete, descriptive and somewhat rambling, and its philosophical purpose seems elusive and veiled. They are both clearly by the same author, but one whose conception of his philosophical task undergoes a profound change.

Wittgenstein's work in Norway was interrupted by the outbreak of the First World War, when he returned to Vienna and enlisted in the Austrian army. Despite seeing active service in Galatia and Italy, Wittgenstein continued to work on his ideas about logic and language.

When he became a prisoner of war in Italy in 1918, the manuscript of the *Tractatus* was found in his knapsack. The war and the completion of his great work of philosophy left Wittgenstein intellectually and spiritually exhausted. He felt that his work in philosophy was finished and, after taking great pains to divest himself of the fortune he had inherited from his father, he began training as a school teacher. The next few years were a time of great isolation and strain. Although he believed himself to be finished with philosophy, he was anxious to see the fruits of seven years' intense intellectual labour published. But the strange form in which the *Tractatus* is written, and the brevity and obscurity of the work, meant that publishers were reluctant to take the financial risk of publishing it; even those he most admired – Gottlob Frege and Bertrand Russell – had difficulty in understanding it. Eventually, however, Russell was able to use his influence with Kegan Paul (later Routledge and Kegan Paul) to get the work published, on condition that Russell himself provided an Introduction.

In 1920, Wittgenstein completed his training as an elementary school teacher and went to work at a primary school in Lower Austria, where he continued to work as a teacher until 1926. He had been trained in the methods of the Austrian School Reform Movement, which rejected rote learning and focused, instead, on developing the child's curiosity, on encouraging independent thought and on using practical exercises to allow the child to make its own discoveries. Wittgenstein was enthusiastic and inventive in applying these principles, and his gifts as a teacher led to considerable success. However, the difference in Wittgenstein's background, education and temperament from the Austrian farmers whose children he taught led to the latters' deep suspicion of him, and eventually to a profound alienation and sense of failure on Wittgenstein's part. In 1926 he gave up teaching for good, and returned to Vienna, where he worked, first, as a gardener, and later, as an architect on a house designed by Paul Engelman for his sister, Mrs Margaret Stonborough.

Although he had done no new work on philosophy during this period, Wittgenstein continued to have contact with philosophers and to discuss the ideas of the *Tractatus* with them. The Cambridge philosopher, Frank Ramsey, undertook a detailed study of the work and travelled to Austria several times to work on it with Wittgenstein.

3

Moritz Schlick, Professor of Philosophy at the University of Vienna and a leading member of the Vienna Circle, also studied and greatly admired Wittgenstein's work. In 1927, Schlick persuaded Wittgenstein to attend regular meetings with him and other members of the Circle, including Friedrich Waismann, Rudolf Carnap and Herbert Feigl. The meetings were not entirely successful, as it gradually became apparent that the members of the Vienna Circle had misread the *Tractatus* as putting forward a version of their own positivist philosophy. In fact Wittgenstein did not share their attitude to metaphysics, their commitment to science, or their views on philosophy and ethics, and his own manner of doing philosophy – which Carnap thought closer to that of a creative artist than a scientist – meant that possibilities for co-operation were limited. The most fruitful discussions were on logic and the foundations of mathematics, and they mark both the return of Wittgenstein to full-time philosophy and the first changes and developments of the views that he had held in the *Tractatus*.

In 1929 Ramsey persuaded Wittgenstein that he should return to Cambridge and work with him on developing ideas on the foundations of mathematics that were no more than sketched in the *Tractatus*. Sixteen years later, in preparing a Preface for the *Investigations*, Wittgenstein writes:

> [S]ince beginning to occupy myself with philosophy again, sixteen years ago, I have been forced to recognize grave mistakes in what I wrote in that first book. I was helped to realize these mistakes – to a degree which I myself am hardly able to estimate – by the criticism which my ideas encountered from Frank Ramsey, with whom I discussed them in innumerable conversations during the last two years of his life.
>
> (*PI*, p. viii)

These mistakes, Wittgenstein came to believe, lay not only in the details of the theories about logic and language that he put forward, but in the whole style of thought that the *Tractatus* expresses. Although there are undoubtedly continuities between the early and the later work – in particular, the conviction that '[m]ost of the propositions and questions of philosophers arise from our failure to understand the logic of our language' (*TLP* 4.003) – Wittgenstein's manner of approaching the task of resolving philosophical confusion gradually undergoes a fundamental shift of focus. Where the *Tractatus* attempts to set a limit to what can be thought by means of an abstract theory that sets precise and exact limits to what can be said, the later Wittgenstein moves more and more towards a concern with the detailed workings of the concrete, complex, multifarious and indeterminate phenomenon of language-in-use. Instead of trying to resolve the confusions about the logic of our language – which he believes to be the root of philosophical problems – by means of a clear theory of what the essence of language consists in, Wittgenstein gradually develops a number of techniques for countering these misunderstandings by means of a clarified view of how language actually functions within the everyday lives of speakers.

Wittgenstein first returned to Cambridge as a research student, but after being awarded the degree of Ph.D. – for which he submitted the *Tractatus* – he was appointed as a university lecturer. There then began a series of lecture courses which he used to work out his new ideas and which form the basis of much of the now published work. Norman Malcolm, who first attended Wittgenstein's lectures in 1939, gives the following account of what went on in them:

> His lectures were given without preparation and without notes. He told me that once he had tried to lecture from notes but was disgusted with the result; the thoughts that came out were 'stale', or, as he put it to another friend, the words looked like 'corpses' when he began to read them. In the method that he came to use his only preparation for the lecture, as he told me, was to spend a few minutes before the class met, recollecting the course that the inquiry had taken at the previous meetings. At the beginning of the lecture he would give a brief summary of this and then he would start from there, trying to advance the investigation with fresh thoughts. He told me that the only thing that made it possible for him to conduct his lecture classes in this extemporaneous way was the fact that he had done and was doing a vast amount of thinking and writing about all the problems under discussion. This is undoubtedly true; nevertheless, what occurred in these class meetings was largely *new* research.
> (Malcolm, 1984, pp. 23–4)

During these years at Cambridge – he was elected Professor there in 1939 – Wittgenstein lectured on language, logic, the foundation of mathematics and the philosophy of psychology. Some of this lecture material is now published in the form both of Wittgenstein's own notes for lectures and of lecture notes taken by his students. During this period Wittgenstein constantly wrote down his ideas in manuscripts that provide almost a day-to-day diary of the development of his thought. Most of these are now published. In addition, he dictated three sets of remarks to his pupils, published as the *Yellow Book* (1933–4), the *Blue Book* (1933–4) and the *Brown Book* (1934–5). Wittgenstein himself used all this material in the preparation of a number of typescripts, including a typescript of the *Philosophical Investigations* (1937–45) and *Zettel* (1945–8). In 1947 Wittgenstein retired from the Chair at Cambridge and went to live in an isolated hut on the coast of Galway, in the west of Ireland, where he continued to work on philosophy. His thought in these last years of his life had lost none of its power or originality and he produced important new work on the philosophy of psychology, knowledge and scepticism, and colour; and although he was sometimes too ill to work, he continued to produce original thoughts up until the last few days before his death.

Writing about Wittgenstein's influence, his pupil G. H. von Wright observes:

[Wittgenstein] thought that his influence as a teacher was, on the whole, harmful to the development of independent minds in his disciples. I am afraid that he was right. And I believe that I can partly understand why it should be so. Because of the depth and originality of his thinking, it is very difficult to understand Wittgenstein's ideas and even more difficult to incorporate them into one's own thinking. At the same time the magic of his personality and style was most inviting and persuasive. To learn from Wittgenstein without coming to adopt his forms of expression and catchwords and even to imitate his tone of voice, his mien and gestures was almost impossible. The danger was that the thoughts should deteriorate into jargon. The teaching of great men often has a simplicity and naturalness which makes the difficult appear easy to grasp. Their disciples usually become, therefore, insignificant epigones. The historical significance of such men does not manifest itself in their disciples but through influences of a more indirect, subtle, and often unexpected kind.

(in Malcolm, 1984, p. 17)

To some extent this assessment of Wittgenstein's influence as problematic remains true. There are individual philosophers, such as G. E. M. Anscombe, G. H. von Wright, Peter Winch, Anthony Kenny and John McDowell, who have developed their own thoughts along distinctly Wittgensteinian lines. There is, moreover, both a vast amount of scholarly work and interpretation and ubiquitous evidence of his indirect influence on contemporary philosophical thought. Yet one's overall sense is that he remains an isolated thinker, whose distinctively intense and individual voice is ultimately inimitable. Indeed, this seems to echo Wittgenstein's own sense of the matter:

Am *I* the only one who cannot found a school or can a philosopher never do this? I cannot found a school because I do not really want to be imitated. Not at any rate by those who publish articles in philosophical journals.

(*CV*, p. 61)

Even in the philosophy of the mind, where his influence has perhaps been the greatest, there is a sense that something is lost whenever his ideas are transplanted from their native soil. While his writings have been a source of numerous philosophical insights that are familiar to every student of philosophy, it is not, in the end, merely the ideas that compel, but the unique style of thought that his writing presents.

In the interpretation of the *Philosophical Investigations* that follows, I have not attempted to imitate this style of thought, but merely to set down, as clearly as I can, its characteristic way of diagnosing and countering what Wittgenstein saw as philosophical misunderstandings. By following the line of his thought, in this way, I have tried to convey, not only its distinctive rhythms, but also its peculiar precision and integrity. The lessons that emerge from the work are not, I believe, unique to Wittgenstein. The idea that language can only be understood from the perspective of language-in-use; the denial of a private inner realm of phenomena; the emphasis on the body as the objectification of the human soul; the replacing of the division between matter and mind with a division between the living and the non-living; the emphasis on the idea of form; the appeal to a pre-epistemic relation to other human subjects which is rooted in our immediate responsiveness to them: all of these ideas are familiar in the phenomenological tradition of Husserl, Heidegger and Merleau-Ponty. It is Wittgenstein's sense that these insights must not be made the ground of a positive philosophy, and thus his whole approach to persuading us of their truth, that is unique, and which constitutes his original contribution to philosophy. It is Wittgenstein's distinctive approach to the problems of philosophy – and not simply the lessons that can be extracted from it – that I have tried to reveal in my exposition of the text.

References and further reading

Bartley, W. W., *Wittgenstein* (London: Quartet, 1977)

Engelmann, P., *Letters from Ludwig Wittgenstein with a Memoir* (Oxford: Blackwell, 1967).

Fann, K. T., ed., *Ludwig Wittgenstein: The Man and his Philosophy* (Hassocks: Harvester Press, 1978).

Janik, A. and Toulmin, S., *Wittgenstein's Vienna* (London: Weidenfeld and Nicolson, 1973).

Malcolm, N., *Ludwig Wittgenstein: A Memoir With a Biographical Sketch by George Henrik von Wright* (Oxford: Oxford University Press [1958], 1984).

McGuiness, B., *Wittgenstein: A Life. Young Ludwig 1889–1921* (London: Duckworth, 1988).

Monk, R., *Ludwig Wittgenstein: The Duty of Genius* (London: Jonathan Cape, 1990).

Redpath, T., *Ludwig Wittgenstein: A Student's Memoir* (London: Duckworth, 1990).

Rhees, R., ed., *Ludwig Wittgenstein: Personal Recollections* (Oxford: Blackwell, 1981).

Chapter 1

Style and method
Philosophical Investigations 89–133

Introduction

Wittgenstein's *Philosophical Investigations* is concerned with two principal topics: the philosophy of language and philosophical psychology. As soon as we open the book it is apparent that Wittgenstein's way of treating these topics is quite unlike that of any other philosopher. First of all, the form of the book is quite unique. Instead of the usual chapters with titles indicating the topics to be discussed, we get a first part of 693 distinct, numbered remarks, varying in length from one line to several paragraphs, and a second part of fourteen sections, half a page to thirty-six pages long, each of which is composed of separate remarks which are not numbered. Moreover, instead of presenting arguments and clearly stated conclusions, these remarks reflect on a wide range of topics – many of which recur throughout the work – without ever producing a clear, final statement on any of them. The punctuation that Wittgenstein uses is complex and

distinctive; many of the remarks take the form of a conversation between Wittgenstein and an interlocutor, and it is not always clear whether we are to take the words on the page as an assertion of Wittgenstein's, or of his interlocutor, or simply as the expression of a thought to be considered. Remarks often include questions for which Wittgenstein appears to provide no answer, or analogies whose point we cannot immediately see. Many more remarks include descriptions of concrete examples, both real and imaginary, which are quite unlike the examples in other works of philosophy, and which Wittgenstein never seems to use as the basis of a generalization.

It is Wittgenstein's unique way of treating the topics he deals with that makes the *Investigations* so difficult to understand. It is not that his style is technical or abstract, rather that it is just not possible to see, in the style of the book, what Wittgenstein's method is or how it is supposed to work. Yet understanding Wittgenstein's method and its connection with the form of the text is the key to understanding the *Investigations*. This is so not merely because it is only by means of such understanding that we can know how to read the remarks that make up the work, but because Wittgenstein himself emphasizes over and over again that it is a method or a style of thought, rather than doctrines, that characterizes his later philosophy. It is, moreover, his insistence that his philosophical aims do not involve him in putting forward 'any kind of theory' (*PI* 109) that makes the question of method, and of how to read his remarks, such a difficult one, for it suggests that we cannot approach the book in the usual way, with a view to finding and extracting the views which are expressed in it.

Wittgenstein himself is alive to the difficulty involved in understanding the remarks that make up the *Investigations*. In the Preface to the book, he expresses pessimism as to its being understood, and he frequently speaks of our being somehow *resistant* to thinking or approaching problems in the way he directs us to:

> I am trying to recommend a certain sort of investigation ... [T]his investigation is immensely important and very much *against the grain* of some of you.
>
> (*WLFM*, p. 103)

One difficulty was that [his method] required a 'sort of thinking' to which we are not accustomed and to which we have not been trained – a sort of thinking very different from what is required in the sciences.

(*WL*, p. 44)

We should not be surprised, therefore, if on first reading the book we cannot see the point of Wittgenstein's remarks, or if we cannot see how we are supposed to make use of the examples he constructs. At first sight, the book may well seem fragmentary and diffuse, so that it remains obscure precisely how Wittgenstein's observations are to be brought to bear on the sort of problems about language and subjectivity which we are familiar with in traditional philosophy. The same sense of difficulty and disorientation is described by students who attended his lectures, in which the pattern of discussion closely mirrored the form of Wittgenstein's written remarks:

The considerable difficulty in following the lectures arose from the fact that it was hard to see where all this often rather repetitive concrete detailed talk was leading to – how the examples were interconnected and how all this bore on the problems which one was accustomed to put oneself in abstract terms.

(Gasking and Jackson, 1978, p. 51)

Faced with these difficulties, it may be tempting to treat the apparent fragmentariness of the text as a defect which we must overcome by discerning behind the individual remarks an implicit or burgeoning theory of how language functions, or of how our psychological concepts work. The price of this is that we must then assume that the form which Wittgenstein is so careful to give to his work is irrelevant to his philosophical aims, and reflects nothing more than his own inability to present his views in a more conventional format. Such an approach also means that we are no longer able to make sense of the large number of remarks in which Wittgenstein insists that 'we may not advance any kind of theory' (*PI* 109), that philosophy 'neither explains nor deduces anything' (*PI* 126), that 'we must do away with all *explanation* and description alone must take its place'

(*PI* 109). Some interpreters have clearly been willing to pay this price. For example, A. C. Grayling expresses the following view:

> Wittgenstein's writings seem to me not only summarizable but in positive need of summary . . . Nor is it true that Wittgenstein's writings contain no systematically expressible theories, for indeed they do. It is the difference between what Wittgenstein says and the way he says it which is relevant here; the fact that his later writings are unsystematic in style does not mean that they are unsystematic in content.
>
> (Grayling, 1988, pp. v–vi)

I shall, however, take the opposite view, and assume that any convincing interpretation must succeed in making sense of both the form of the *Investigations* and of Wittgenstein's remarks on the nature of his philosophical method; any other approach is completely at odds with his well attested care both in writing and in arranging his remarks.

The idea of grammatical investigation

Wittgenstein himself is, as I've remarked, perfectly aware of the difficulty that faces us in understanding his work, and even of our resistance to his way of thinking. He sees this difficulty 'not [as] the intellectual difficulty of the sciences, but the difficulty of a change of attitude' (P, p. 161). He wants us to undertake a new sort of investigation, one that directs itself, not to the construction of new and surprising theories or elucidations, but to the examination of language. For he believes that the problems that confront us in philosophy are rooted in 'a misunderstanding of the logic of our language' (*PI* 93); they are 'not empirical problems', but are misunderstandings that 'are solved . . . by looking into the workings of our language, and that in such a way as to make us recognize those workings: *in despite of* an urge to misunderstand them' (*PI* 109). Language is, for Wittgenstein, both the source of philosophical problems and the means to overcome them:

> Philosophy is a battle against the bewitchment of our intelligence by means of language.
>
> (*PI* 109)

We are struggling with language.
We are engaged in a struggle with language.

(CV, p. 11)

Philosophy, as we use the word, is a fight against the fascina-
tion which forms of expression exert on us.

(BB, p. 27)

Thus the power of language to mislead through false analogies and
misleading, surface similarities must be countered by our coming to
see more clearly into the actual workings of language, i.e. into how
the concepts that make up the different regions of our language actually function. Wittgenstein sometimes speaks of the philosophical
misunderstandings that have arisen in connection with a particular
concept as a 'fog' *(PI* 5). He believes that the 'fog' is dispersed by
our coming to command a clear view of how our concepts function,
which we achieve through a careful study of a range of particular,
concrete cases (some of them imaginary) in which our concepts are
used.

In *PI* 90, he describes the kind of investigation he is engaged
in, by which philosophical problems are solved through the clarification of our use of language, as 'a grammatical one'. This idea of
'a grammatical investigation' is central to Wittgenstein's later philosophy, and it is the key to understanding his work. The *Investigations*
can be seen as a large collection of particular grammatical investigations, each one of which examines the detailed workings of an area
of our language that has become a focal point for philosophical myth
and confusion. These investigations of how a part of our language
works are invariably subtle and complex, and how Wittgenstein uses
them as a means to unravel philosophical problems can only properly be understood by looking at how his method works in practice.
One of the principal aims of my exposition of the *Investigations* is
to follow the line of Wittgenstein's particular grammatical investigations very closely, in an attempt to show exactly how his grammatical
method both diagnoses, and attempts to counter, philosophical
confusion through coming to command a clear view of our use of
words. The general remarks on the grammatical method that follow
are, therefore, intended to provide no more than a general indication

of how Wittgenstein approaches philosophical problems, and of the way his approach confronts traditional philosophy.

Wittgenstein describes a grammatical investigation as one in which 'we remind ourselves . . . of the *kind of statement* that we make about phenomena' (*PI* 90). This should not be taken to express an interest simply in what constitutes a syntactically well-formed sentence; Wittgenstein's use of the concept of 'grammar' is, to this extent, different from the traditional one. His use of the concept of 'grammar' relates, not to language considered as a system of signs, but to our *use* of words, to the structure of our *practice of using* language. The concept of 'our practice of using language' is here intended to invoke the idea of language, not as 'some non-spatial, non-temporal phantasm', but as a 'spatial and temporal phenomenon' (*PI* 108), i.e. as the phenomenon of *language-in-use*. Wittgenstein's grammatical method is one in which 'we remind ourselves' of the details of the distinctive patterns of use that constitute what he calls 'the grammar of our concepts'. The techniques which Wittgenstein uses to describe the grammar of our concepts – i.e. our use of words – are various. They include imagining a variety of circumstances in which we would use a given concept or expression, asking how we would teach it to a child, asking how we would verify that it applies in a particular concrete case, looking at the role of disagreement and the nature of the certainty that is possible in connection with it, asking whether it would still be usable if certain facts of nature were different, imagining what we would say in a variety of peculiar cases, comparing our use of an expression with an example that Wittgenstein makes up, and so on. By using these techniques he attempts, not a systematization of the rules that govern our use of words, but an evocation of the distinctive patterns of use that characterize our employment of them; it is by making ourselves aware of these distinctive patterns of use that we clarify the grammar of our concepts.

The purpose of Wittgenstein's evocation of the details of our practice of using the different expressions of our language is twofold. On the one hand, he uses it to make us aware of the clash between our philosophically reflective idea of how a concept works and the way it actually functions, and on the other, he uses it to draw our attention to the profound differences in the patterns of use that characterize the different regions of our language. Wittgenstein labels the latter differences in use 'grammatical differences'; making us aware of these differences is central to his grammatical method. When he speaks of our need to '*command a clear view* of the use of our words', he is thinking both of our need to uncover the conflict between our philosophical notions and the way our concepts actually function, and of our need to become aware of the grammatical differences in how the concepts in the different regions of our language are used. However, while he believes that it is only by achieving this sort of clarity concerning our use of expressions that philosophical problems are diagnosed and overcome, he also recognizes that it is difficult for us to accept this switch of attention away from the construction of theories towards describing the details of our ordinary practice of employing language. We have certain intellectual habits that stand in the way of our undertaking the detailed, grammatical investigations that he is recommending, for we simply cannot see the *point* of describing how the words of our language are used:

> We are not at all *prepared* for the task of describing the use of the word 'to think'. (And why should we be? What is such a description useful for?)
>
> (Z 111)

> One cannot guess how a word functions. One has to *look at* its use and learn from that.
>
> But the difficulty is to remove the prejudice which stands in the way of doing this. It is not a *stupid* prejudice.
>
> (*PI* 340)

Wittgenstein is also aware that his attack on the construction of philosophical theories and his insistence that we concern ourselves exclusively with describing how we use words will create a sense of dissatisfaction and frustration:

> Where does our investigation get its importance from, since it seems only to destroy everything interesting, that is, all that is great and important? (As it were all the buildings, leaving behind only bits of stone and rubble.)
>
> (*PI* 118)

The very idea that 'we must do away with all *explanation*, and description alone must take its place' (*PI* 109), or that 'philosophy leaves everything as it is' (*PI* 124), seems to impose a quite unwarranted intellectual constraint on us, which we must, at least in the first instance, find unsatisfactory and chafing. Surely, we feel, language and mental states are phenomena that cry out for explanation. There must, for example, be some explanation of what language's ability to represent the world consists in, of what our understanding of our language consists in, of what thinking is, of what an intention, or a sensation, is, and so on. How could it possibly be wrong or inappropriate to try to elucidate these phenomena, to say what they consist in, or to offer some sort of explanatory account of them?

Here we come to the nub of our resistance to entering into and understanding the sort of investigation that Wittgenstein wants us to engage in; we've come to the exact point at which his style of thinking 'goes against the grain'. For we simply don't see how what appear to be completely unexceptional questions – 'What is meaning?', 'What is thought?', 'What does understanding consist in?' – could possibly be answered by anything other than a theory which explains or elucidates these phenomena. We feel that it is only by means of elucidations which offer us some sort of account of these phenomena that our urge to understand them more clearly could possibly be met. To suggest that such elucidations cannot, or should not, be given, or that it is not the task of philosophy to give them, can amount, we feel, to nothing less than the absurd suggestion that these phenomena cannot be explained, that they are *sui generis*, or even that they are in some way mysterious or occult. It might be helpful to identify the attitude that makes us so resistant to Wittgenstein's idea that we must concern ourselves with describing language-in-use by a special name, since it is of central importance in the underlying dialectic of Wittgenstein's later philosophy. I shall call it the *theorizing* or *theoretical attitude*. It is this attitude that Wittgenstein means to characterize when he says that 'we feel as if we had to *penetrate* phenomena' (*PI* 90). It is vital to our coming to understand Wittgenstein's later philosophy that we come to see the significance of this attitude and the nature of Wittgenstein's opposition to it.

The rejection of philosophical theories

It is clear that Wittgenstein himself sees the theoretical attitude, which is associated with our idea of the methods and aims of science, as a major obstacle to our achieving the understanding we seek when we ask questions like 'What is meaning?', 'What is thought?', 'What does our understanding of our language consist in?' He writes:

> Philosophers constantly see the method of science before their eyes, and are irresistibly tempted to ask and to answer questions in the way science does. This tendency is the real source of metaphysics and leads philosophers into complete darkness.
>
> (*BB*, p. 18)

> The existence of the experimental method [in psychology] makes us think we have the means of solving the problems which trouble us; though problems and method pass one another by.
>
> (*PI*, p. 230)

> (One of the greatest impediments for philosophy is the expectation of new, deep//unheard of//elucidations.)
>
> (P, p. 179)

Wittgenstein does not intend here to express any general opposition to science. It is rather that the methods of science, or more particularly the way of asking and answering questions in science, are misleading and inappropriate when applied to questions like 'What is meaning?', 'What is thought?', and so on. There is the suggestion that when we interpret these questions as requests for *explanations*, or as the expression of a need to *discover* something, on analogy, say, with the question 'What is the specific gravity of gold?', then we set out on a path that will lead, not to an understanding of these phenomena, but to 'complete darkness'.

In *PI* 89, Wittgenstein picks out those questions which we misunderstand when we take them as requests for explanations as follows:

> Augustine says in the *Confessions* "quid est ergo tempus? Si nemo ex me quaerat scio; si quaerenti explicare velim, nescio."

["What, then, is time? If nobody asks me, I know well enough what it is; but if I am asked what it is and try to explain, I am baffled."] – This could not be said about a question of natural science ("What is the specific gravity of hydrogen?" for instance). Something that we know when no one asks us, but no longer know when we are supposed to give an account of it is something we need to *remind* ourselves of. (And it is obviously something of which for some reason it is difficult to remind oneself.)

The things which we are doomed to misunderstand when we take up a theoretical attitude towards them are, then, just those things 'that we know when no one asks us, but no longer know when we are supposed to give an account of [them]'. Wittgenstein offers the following account of these characteristically philosophical questions:

(Questions of different kinds occupy us, for instance "What is the specific weight of this body", "Will the weather stay nice today", "Who will come through the door next", etc. But among our questions there are those of a special kind. Here we have a different experience. The questions seem to be more fundamental than the others. And now I say: if we have this experience, then we have arrived at the limits of language.)

(P, p. 167)

What we are concerned with when we ask questions of the form 'What is time?', 'What is meaning?', 'What is thought?' is the nature of the phenomena which constitute our world. These phenomena constitute the form of the world which we inhabit, and in asking these questions we express a desire to understand them more clearly. Yet in the very act of framing these questions, we are tempted to adopt an attitude towards these phenomena which, Wittgenstein believes, makes us approach them in the wrong way, in a way which assumes that we have to uncover or explain something. When we ask ourselves these questions, we take up a stance towards these phenomena in which they seem suddenly bewilderingly mysterious, for as soon as we try to catch hold of them in the way that our questions seem to require, we find we cannot do it; we find that we 'no longer know'. This leads us deeper and deeper into a state of frustration and philosophical confusion. We think that the fault lies in our explanations and that we need to construct ever more subtle and surprising accounts. Thus, we 'go astray and imagine that we have to describe extreme subtleties, which in turn we are after all quite unable to describe with the means at our disposal. We feel as if we had to repair a torn spider's web with our fingers' (*PI* 106). The real fault, Wittgenstein believes, is not in our explanations, but in the very idea that the puzzlement we feel can be removed by means of a discovery. What we really need is to turn our whole enquiry round and concern ourselves, not with explanation or theory construction, but with description. The nature of the phenomena which constitute our world is not something that we discover by 'digging', but is something that is revealed in 'the kind of statement we make about phenomena', by the distinctive forms of linguistic usage which characterize the different regions of our language. The method we really need is one that 'simply puts everything before us, and neither explains nor deduces anything. – Since everything lies open to view there is nothing to explain' (*PI* 126). It is by attending to the characteristic structures of what already lies open to view in our use of language that we will overcome our sense of philosophical perplexity and achieve the understanding we seek; the difficulty lies only in the fact that we are so unwilling to undertake, and so unprepared for, this task of description: 'The aspects of things that are most important for us are hidden because of their simplicity and familiarity. (One is unable to notice something – because it is always before one's eyes.)' (*PI* 129).

One of the difficulties in understanding the *Investigations* is that this switch from looking towards the construction of a model or a theory, back towards a concern with the details of particular cases of our ordinary practice of employing language, is so difficult to accept. The style of thought involved in undertaking a grammatical enquiry seems to go in quite the wrong direction, for its direction is the very opposite from the one that the theoretical attitude makes us want to go in. For while we feel that our question can only be answered by the construction of an account that explains what a given phenomenon consists in, Wittgenstein wants us to look at the intricate details of concrete instances of our practice of using language. Wittgenstein expresses this idea that his method tries to turn us in a direction that we are unwilling to follow at a number of points:

> It is as if a man is standing in a room facing a wall on which are painted a number of dummy doors. Wanting to get out, he fumblingly tries to open them, vainly trying them all, one after the other, over and over again. But of course it is quite useless. And all the time, although he doesn't realize it, there is a real door in the wall behind his back and all he has to do is turn round and open it. To help him get out of the room all we have to do is to get him to look in a different direction. But it's hard to do this, since, wanting to get out he resists our attempts to turn him away from where he thinks the exit must be.
>
> (Gasking and Jackson, 1978, p. 52)

> A man will be *imprisoned* in a room with a door that is unlocked and opens inwards; as long as it does not occur to him to pull rather than push it.
>
> (*CV*, p. 42)

The idea that Wittgenstein is opposed to the whole style of thinking that would approach, for example, the problem of understanding how language functions by trying to construct a theory that elucidates what the meaning of expressions consists in goes against the idea that he is merely out to oppose a *particular account* of meaning. Equally, it is contrary to this idea to suggest that Wittgenstein is in the business of replacing a rejected theory of what meaning consists in with a new theory of his own. The book is more radical than the idea that it is attacking particular doctrines about meaning which were held, for example, by the early Wittgenstein, or by Russell or Frege, suggests. The philosophical doctrines and pictures of how language works that Wittgenstein looks at, some of which may be identified with the views of particular philosophers, are really of interest to him insofar as they represent a *style of thought* which he believes makes misunderstanding and confusion inevitable. He is, moreover, interested in the philosophical confusions that this style of thought throws up at the very first moment of their genesis, in the first false steps which take us down paths that lead us, he believes, further and further away from understanding. By a careful examination of the roots of our approach to language, and of the pictures of language and understanding that it has thrown up, Wittgenstein hopes gradually to reveal the darkness into which our sense of a need 'to *penetrate* phenomena' has led us. What he opposes to the misunderstandings and false pictures that he examines is not an alternative explanation or theory of how language functions, but a different style of thought which, by its attention to the characteristic structures of our concrete practice of using language, gradually reveals 'that nothing out of the ordinary is involved' (*PI* 94), that 'everything lies open to view [and] there is nothing to be explained' (*PI* 126).

Thus what we see in the specific doctrines and pictures that form the focus of Wittgenstein's critical remarks are the phantasms, myths, superstitions and chimeras that he believes are spawned by our adopting a theoretical attitude in response to the questions 'What is meaning?', 'What does understanding consist in?', and so on. He does not see the temptation to ask these questions in the way that we do, or the temptation to adopt particular false pictures, as a sign of a defective intellect, but as something that has its roots in the forms of our language. Language itself invites the move from unself-conscious employment of it to an attitude of reflecting on it, and once we take up the reflective attitude, language itself presents a series of traps for the understanding:

> Language contains the same traps for everyone; the immense network of well-kept //passable// false paths. And thus we see one person after another walking the same paths and we know already where he will make a turn, where he will keep on going straight ahead without noticing the turn, etc., etc.
>
> (P, p. 183)

The confusions arising from the theoretical attitude are not, therefore, mere mistakes. They are misunderstandings which, when we become reflective about it, language itself has the power to draw us into. Wittgenstein sometimes suggests that philosophical confusion shares these roots in language both with forms of human mental disturbance and with primitive styles of thought. The problems created by language are *deep* problems that arise in situations of reflection or withdrawal from a practical engagement in human life, 'when language is like an engine idling, not when it is doing work' (*PI* 132):

> The problems arising through a misinterpretation of our forms of language have the character of *depth*. They are deep disquietudes; their roots are as deep in us as the forms of our language and [whose] significance is as great as the importance of our language.
>
> (*PI* 111)

In challenging the pictures we construct in reflecting on how language functions, Wittgenstein does not see himself as out to refute doctrines, but as attempting to release us both from a particular style of thought and from the monsters of the intellect that it has allowed to control our philosophical imagination. To achieve this, Wittgenstein does not challenge outright our desire to follow a particular path, or adopt a particular picture, but allows our inclination a free rein. We are encouraged to explore, or to apply, the accounts and pictures which inexorably draw us, so that we find out for ourselves that they represent 'dummy doors', that they offer no solution to the problems of understanding which confront us. Woven in with remarks that attempt to guide us in this process of discovering the emptiness or inapplicability of the pictures we construct are remarks in which Wittgenstein tries to draw our attention towards the neglected details of our concrete practice of using language. Simply by putting these details together in the right way, or by using a new analogy or comparison to prompt us to see our practice of using language in a new light, we find that we achieve the understanding that we thought could come only with the construction of a theory:

> I think one reason why the attempt to find an explanation is wrong is that we have only to put together in the right way what we *know*, without adding anything, and the satisfaction we are trying to get from the explanation comes of itself.
>
> (RFGB, p. 30)

Philosophy as therapy

Wittgenstein's preferred description of the above process is 'therapy' (*PI* 133) or the 'treatment of an illness' (*PI* 254). This description is apt for a number of reasons. First of all, it conveys the idea that our concern with the construction of elucidations or models is in some way itself an *obstacle* to our progress, something that holds or arrests us and prevents us from moving on. Secondly, it captures the fact that Wittgenstein's method is aimed, not at producing new, stateable conclusions, but at working on us in such a way as to change our whole style of thinking or way of approaching problems. The concept of therapy emphasizes that Wittgenstein's philosophical method aims to engage the reader in an active process of working on himself; it also underlines the fact that the reader's acknowledgement of Wittgenstein's diagnoses of philosophical error is a vital part of his method, for 'we can only convict someone else of a mistake if he acknowledges that this really is the expression of his feeling' (P, p. 165). If the reader is to be liberated from the style of thought and the false pictures which Wittgenstein believes to lie at the root of philosophical confusion, then he must first of all acknowledge that Wittgenstein has identified 'the source of his thought' (P, p. 165). Finally, the concept of therapy recognizes that this process is in its nature protracted. Therapy is essentially a slow process in which the patient is brought by degrees to a new understanding of the nature of the problems that trouble him, one which allows him to recognize that he had been seeking satisfaction in the wrong way, and thereby brings him peace. Wittgenstein's use of an interlocutor's voice allows him to present this therapeutic process, not as a series of exchanges between a therapist and a patient, but in the form of an internal dialogue, in which Wittgenstein both gives expression to the temptations to misunderstand which our language presents to us and struggles to resist these misunderstandings. Thus, the interlocutor's voice (which is introduced both indirectly in remarks beginning 'We want to say . . .', 'One would like to say . . .' and directly through the use of double quotation marks) expresses our desire for explanation and succumbs to the traps that our language presents, while the therapeutic voice works against these inclinations by examining concrete examples as a means to achieving a new way of looking at things.

If all this is correct, then we should not look in Wittgenstein's text for the familiar structure of thesis–refutation–counterthesis (e.g. we should not look for a precise theory of how language represents that Wittgenstein is opposing, for his objections to it, or for his alternative theory of how language functions). We should discern a rhythm of an altogether different kind. Given that we are, at the outset at least, in the grip of the theoretical attitude, our first response to questions like 'What is meaning?', 'What is thought?', and so on, will be to try to model or explain what meaning, thought, etc. actually consist in. The focus of Wittgenstein's interest is, as I remarked earlier, on the very first moves that we make in response to these questions, where the pattern for our future approach is laid down, and a whole series of mistakes is made inevitable. He wants to uncover the point of origin of our philosophical false leads, where their roots in the forms of our language can be more clearly seen and diagnosed. He believes that many of the ideas that we use as the basis for our philosophical accounts are ones that already occur as metaphors or pictures within our everyday discourse. For example, the idea that natural language can be compared with a complex system of rules, or that meaning can be pictured as a word's standing for something, or that pain is inner and pain-behaviour outer, all occur to us quite naturally. However, when we are intent on constructing an explanatory account of meaning or sensations, we try to give these ideas a literalness and explanatory force which we never attempt to give them in ordinary life; we try to transform what is really no more than a way of looking at things – an 'object of comparison' (*PI* 131) – into a theoretical account of the essence of these phenomena; our object of comparison becomes 'a preconceived idea to which reality *must* correspond' (*PI* 131), even though we cannot immediately see just how it does so. As I suggested just now, Wittgenstein adopts two different approaches in response to our sense that these pictures somehow give us the essence of a phenomenon.

The first response that he adopts is to attempt, by a number of characteristic techniques, to reveal the emptiness of the explanatory accounts that we're inclined to offer, or of the pictures and models that we construct. We think that we are putting forward clear, explanatory models of what a given phenomenon consists in that will satisfy our urge to understand. However, when Wittgenstein calls on us to examine these models more carefully, or to connect them with what actually goes on in our practice of employing language, we find that they crumble to dust in our hands. We come to see that the pictures and models that initially seem to us so straightforward and explanatory actually make no connection with the phenomena they are designed to illuminate. Thus we come to see that there is nothing in our actual practice of using language that is explained by the image of our manipulating a system of rules; that the idea that the meaning of a word consists in its standing for an object is a vast oversimplification which is entirely lacking in explanatory power; that the picture of pain as inner and pain-behaviour as outer does not explain the distinction between pain and pain-behaviour which we're trying to make; and so on.

The second response that Wittgenstein makes is directed at evoking an appreciation of the neglected details of concrete examples of 'the spatial and temporal phenomenon of language'. By getting us, again through a variety of techniques, to see the way our concepts actually function on particular occasions, he brings about an understanding of the conceptual differences that both lie at the root of our philosophical puzzlement and provide the means of escape from it. It is through the appreciation of the differences in the way the different regions of our language function that he believes we can escape from philosophical confusion, and find that 'the satisfaction we are trying to get from [an] explanation comes of itself' (RFGB, p. 30). For our puzzlement concerned the nature or essence of particular phenomena – meaning, thought, sensations – and this puzzlement is removed, 'not by giving new information, but by arranging what we have always known' (*PI* 109). What we find is that everything needed to understand how language functions, what the nature of understanding is, what sensations are, is already there before our eyes in the distinctive structures of the concrete phenomenon of language-in-use. Wittgenstein sometimes captures the idea that the essence of phenomena lies open to view in the metaphor of a surface: we do not need to make a discovery in order to remove the puzzlement we feel when we reflect on those things 'that we know when no one asks us, but no longer know when we are supposed to give an account', but to attend to what lies on the surface, in the characteristic forms of our practice of using language. Thus:

> A philosophical problem has the form: 'I don't know my way about.'
>
> (*PI* 123)

> I am showing my pupils the details of an immense landscape which they cannot know their way around.
>
> (*CV*, p. 56)

> God grant the philosopher insight into what lies in front of everyone's eyes.
>
> (*CV*, p. 63)

Both of the above responses are properly called 'grammatical investigations'. The grammatical investigation associated with the first response has a purely negative purpose. It reveals the emptiness of the words or pictures that the philosopher uses in his attempt to provide elucidations of phenomena. The grammatical investigation associated with the second response has a much more positive aim: it uses the grammatical investigation of particular concrete cases in order to reveal that everything we need to understand the way language functions, what understanding, sensations, and so on are, is already there before our eyes, in the concrete details of our practice of using language. In *PI* 122, Wittgenstein introduces the notion of a 'perspicuous representation' in connection with this task of achieving 'a clear view' of our practice of using words. There is no suggestion that the clear view of our use of words is something that Wittgenstein intends to use to curb the philosopher's linguistic excesses. Rather, the clear view of our use of words that Wittgenstein's investigation aims at is associated with 'the understanding that consists in "seeing connexions"'. Wittgenstein's grammatical enquiry aims to produce a kind of understanding which consists in seeing a pattern or form in what is there before our eyes, but which we had previously neglected or overlooked. It is through an emerging sense of this form that the essence of language, meaning, understanding, etc. is gradually revealed and understood. We gradually come to see that 'nothing out of the ordinary is involved' (*PI* 94), that no further (deeper) explanation is needed, that the essence 'lies open to view' (*PI* 126). The particular examples that Wittgenstein examines are not seen as the basis for formulating general claims or theories, but are used as a means, both of exposing the emptiness of the philosopher's accounts, and of showing that everything that we need to understand is already there and only needs to be arranged correctly. It is through the examination of the particular cases themselves, and not through the construction of a general theory based on them, that we both overcome our urge to misunderstand and gradually achieve the understanding we seek.

'. . . the philosophical problems should *completely* disappear'

It is clear that Wittgenstein does not conceive of the task of providing a perspicuous representation of language-in-use to be one that is to be undertaken systematically, as an intellectual end in itself. It is clear, moreover, that he does not conceive of such a perspicuous representation to be something that could be expressed in the form of a systematic description. One might, however, wonder *why* Wittgenstein is so against the idea of a systematic description of the grammar of our language. If a grammatical investigation is one that goes in the opposite direction from theory construction, why shouldn't it take us in that direction systematically? The answer to this question lies, at least in part, in the essential *responsiveness* of Wittgenstein's philosophical method. Thus, the anti-systematic nature of Wittgenstein's philosophy is linked with the idea that a grammatical investigation is one that 'gets its light, that is to say its purpose, from the philosophical problems' (*PI* 109). The self-conscious awareness of the forms of our human practice of employing language that a grammatical investigation results in does not represent an increase in our knowledge of the kind we associate with science; it merely 'reminds us' of something which, insofar as we are masters of the practice of using language, we already know. Bringing this knowledge to self-consciousness does not increase or improve our mastery of this practice, but it gives us a kind of understanding which 'consists in "seeing connexions"', and which frees us from both false pictures and the inappropriate urge to explain the phenomena that puzzle us.

In *PI* 132, Wittgenstein remarks: 'we want to establish an order in our knowledge of the use of language', but he makes it clear that this order is merely 'an order with a particular end in view; one of many possible orders; not *the* order'. The primary purpose of Wittgenstein's drawing our attention to neglected aspects of our practice of using language, through the careful description of particular concrete cases, is not to build up a general or systematic description of that practice. Rather, in response to each specific false picture, or each impulse to misunderstand, Wittgenstein evokes a particular concrete case, or range of cases, in which we see our concepts functioning. What we are gradually brought to realize is, not only that our philosophical pictures make no contact with the phenomena they are intended to explain, but that it is the distinctive ways in which our various concepts function that show us the nature of the phenomena that these concepts describe, that is, that show us what meaning, understanding, sensations, and so on, are. Through the constant repetition of this therapeutic process, Wittgenstein works to bring about a gradual shift in our style of thought. The cumulative effect is that we see things differently. What before had looked like an explanation is now seen to be no more than an empty construction; what before cried out for elucidation is now accepted just as it is, without our feeling a need to give it further foundations or support.

Thus we will miss the whole point of Wittgenstein's philosophical method if we attempt to extract from his remarks a series of philosophical claims about what constitutes meaning, understanding, sensations, and so on. Not only is Wittgenstein not concerned with the construction or elaboration of philosophical theories, but whatever claims we might extract from his remarks are not to be understood as the *point* of the work. Thus he himself gives clear warning that any such attempt to extract 'theses' will produce, not gold, but banality: 'If one tried to advance *theses* in philosophy, it would never be possible to debate them, because everyone would agree to them' (*PI* 128). An adequate interpretation of the

Investigations must rather strive to show how Wittgenstein uses his evocations of concrete examples of our practice of using language, not as a source of generalizations, but as a means to overcome the particular misunderstandings and false pictures that our urge to explain throws up, and to achieve a recognition that there is nothing that needs to be explained. Wittgenstein's philosophical aim is not to arrive at conclusions, but to bring about a gradual acceptance of the fact that our attempts at explanation are empty and that 'since everything lies open to view there is nothing to be explained' (*PI* 126). It is in the detailed workings of the dialectical process through which he brings this acceptance about that Wittgenstein's conception of philosophical method is revealed. We must, therefore, resist the attempt to sum up, or to state philosophically exciting conclusions, and allow instead for a series of clarifications to take place in which 'the philosophical problem ... completely disappears' (*PI* 133). In this way, we never lose sight of the fact that 'the work of the philosopher consists in assembling reminders *for a particular purpose*' (*PI* 127, my italics); the dialectical structure of the work – seen in the interaction of Wittgenstein's different voices – is thereby acknowledged as an essential part of his method, and is not seen as a mere stylistic device which obscures the general views that are being surreptitiously advanced, and which our exposition must somehow draw out.

Thus it is crucial to the nature of the fundamental change in our style of thought that this dialectical process is intended to bring about that we do not attempt to express its results in the form of positive doctrines. Wittgenstein is not merely putting forward a style of thought that goes in the opposite direction from the one we want to take, but this new style of thought is one that eschews the abstract theorizing which he believes lies at the root of philosophical confusion. His aim is to achieve the kind of understanding that comes from seeing the particular, concrete case in the right light. Such an approach does not issue in anything that could properly be called a theory, or even in anything that could be adequately set out in a series of positive claims. It is not merely that the examination of particular concrete cases 'gets its light, that is to say its purpose, from the philosophical problems', but the 'understanding which consists in "seeing connexions"' is fundamentally opposed to the formulation of general

29

philosophical doctrines. This again serves to bring out the way in which Wittgenstein's remarks are meant to work on the individual reader, and to explain the peculiar elusiveness of the text. Understanding the *Investigations* requires us to accept that it sets out to bring about a shift in our understanding which cannot be conveyed to a passive audience in the form of 'results' or 'conclusions'. This is not to say that the *Investigations* is in any way mystical; there is, for instance, no suggestion that the understanding that Wittgenstein offers to the individual reader cannot be communicated or shared. It is only that it cannot be communicated in the form of a statement of systematic doctrines or theories. This understanding must be conveyed to someone else in the way it is conveyed to an individual reader, through a process of guidance and persuasion, which responds to the inevitable temptations to misunderstand with an examination of particular cases which aims at getting him to see things differently. It is not that the other has to guess the vital thing, but that it is actually through coming to see the particular cases in a new way that we will achieve the change of vision which constitutes the shift in understanding. This understanding is expressed, not in doctrines, but in a change of attitude which is connected with the emergence of a concern with what lies open to view in the concrete details of our practice, and with the abandonment of the attempt to construct elucidations or speculative accounts.

On this interpretation, the *Investigations* is not viewed as a work that concerns itself with a large number of discrete topics – names, ostensive definition, meaning, rules, understanding, sensations, etc. – and provides a corrective to our thinking on each of them. There is, rather, an attempt to produce an overall shift in how we approach philosophical questions or the desire for understanding that they express. This means that there is not only a profound unity to the work, but there is a powerful cumulative effect that is properly achieved only if we read the book as a whole. We cannot locate the understanding that Wittgenstein offers us in the dismantling of specific false pictures, or in the description of one or two concrete cases that reveal how a bit of our language functions. Rather, Wittgenstein wants to work on us (or better, he wants us to work on ourselves) in such as way that a whole style of thought which we find natural – the theoretical attitude – is gradually replaced by a recognition that it is 'by arranging what we have always known' (*PI* 109) that we both overcome our philosophical illusions and achieve the understanding we seek. The aim is to bring about a change in our attitude, or in how we see things, that goes against the grain of our natural inclinations, and which can only be communicated or shared by means of an equally laborious process, aimed at working on the individual's style of thought, to the one Wittgenstein undertakes. This not only makes the *Investigations* difficult to understand, it makes it exceptionally difficult to write about.

References and further reading

Aidun, D., 'Wittgenstein's Philosophical Method and Aspect-Seeing', *Philosophical Investigations*, vol. 5, 1982.

Anscombe, G. E. M., 'On the Form of Wittgenstein's Writing', in R. Kiblansky, ed., *Contemporary Philosophy: A Survey*, vol. 3 (Florence: La Nuova Italia, 1969).

Baker, G., '*Philosophical Investigations* section 122: neglected aspects', in R. L. Arrington and H.-J. Glock, eds, *Wittgenstein's* Philosophical Investigations: *Text and Context* (London: Routledge, 1991).

Baker, G. and Hacker, P. M. S., *Wittgenstein: Understanding and Meaning* (Oxford: Blackwell, 1983).

Barnett, W., 'The Rhetoric of Grammar: Understanding Wittgenstein's Method', *Metaphilosophy*, vol. 21, 1990.

Binkley, T., *Wittgenstein's Language* (The Hague: Martinus Nijhoff, 1973).

Bouveresse, J., ' "The Darkness of this Time": Wittgenstein and the Modern World', in A. Phillips Griffiths, ed., *Wittgenstein Centenary Essays* (Cambridge: Cambridge University Press, 1992).

Cavell, S., 'The Availability of Wittgenstein's Later Philosophy', in G. Pitcher, ed., *Wittgenstein: The Philosophical Investigations* (New York: Doubleday, 1966).

—— 'Declining Decline: Wittgenstein as a Philosopher of Culture', *Inquiry*, vol. 31, 1988.

Fann, K. T., *Wittgenstein's Conception of Philosophy* (Oxford: Blackwell, 1969).

—— ed., *Ludwig Wittgenstein: The Man and His Philosophy* (Hassocks: Harvester Press 1978).

Gasking, D. A. T. and Jackson, A. C., 'Wittgenstein as Teacher', in K. T. Fann, ed., 1978.

Genova, J., *Wittgenstein: A Way of Seeing* (London: Routledge, 1995)

Grayling, A., *Wittgenstein* (Oxford: Oxford University Press, 1988).

Hacker, P. M. S., *Insight and Illusion* (Oxford: Oxford University Press, 1986).

Heal, J., 'Wittgenstein and Dialogue', in T. Smiley, ed., *Philosophical Dialogues: Plato, Hume, Wittgenstein*, Proceedings of the British Academy (Oxford: Oxford University Press, 1995).

Heller, E., 'Wittgenstein: Unphilosophical Notes', in K. T. Fann, ed., 1978.

Hilmy, S., *The Later Wittgenstein: The Emergence of a New Philosophical Method* (Oxford: Blackwell, 1987).

—— ' "Tormenting Questions" in *Philosophical Investigations* section 133', in R. L. Arrington and H.-J. Glock, eds, *Wittgenstein's Philosophical Investigations: Text and Context* (London: Routledge, 1991).

Hughes, J., 'Philosophy and Style: Wittgenstein and Russell', *Philosophy and Literature*, vol. 13 1989.

Janik, A. and Toulmin, S., *Wittgenstein's Vienna* (London: Weidenfeld and Nicolson, 1973).

Kenny, A., 'Wittgenstein on the Nature of Philosophy', in B. McGuiness, ed., *Wittgenstein and his Time* (Oxford: Blackwell, 1982).

Minar, E., 'Feeling at Home in the Language (what makes reading the *Philosophical Investigations* possible?), *Synthèse*, vol. 102, 1995.

Rowe, M. W., 'Goethe and Wittgenstein', *Philosophy*, vol. 66, 1991.

—— 'Wittgenstein's Romantic Inheritance', *Philosophy*, vol. 69, 1994.

Savickey, B., 'Voices in Wittgenstein's *Philosophical Investigations*', M.Phil. thesis, Cambridge University, 1990.

—— 'Wittgenstein's Method of Grammatical Investigation', D.Phil. thesis, University of York, 1995.

Chapter 2

Wittgenstein's critique of Augustine

Philosophical Investigations 1–38

Introduction

In the Preface to the *Investigations*, Wittgenstein remarks that he felt it would be useful to publish his first book, the *Tractatus Logico-Philosophicus*, and the *Investigations* together, on the ground 'that the latter could be seen in the right light only by contrast with and against the background of my old way of thinking' (*PI*, p. viii). The 'old way of thinking' that he refers to here may reasonably be taken to be the theoretical attitude which I characterized in the previous chapter, and which is clearly exemplified in the approach to language that Wittgenstein adopts in his early work. Thus one of the major projects of the *Tractatus* is to construct a theory of what language's ability to represent the world consists in. The central idea of the theory is the claim that propositions are a form of picture. A proposition consists of elements (names) placed in a determinate relation to one another. The

proposition represents a possible state of affairs insofar as the elements of the proposition (the names) stand for objects and the relation between the names within the proposition represents a possible arrangement of the objects for which the names stand. So the basic signifying unit of language is the name. Each name stands for an object. By putting names together to form propositions we construct *pictures* or *models* of possible states of affairs, where the latter are conceived as constructions out of the objects for which names stand.

This image of language as a system of propositions, each one of which is a picture of a possible state of affairs, was suggested in part by the striking developments in the techniques for constructing logically precise languages, governed by strict rules for the formation of sentences, that had been made by Frege and Russell during the course of their work on mathematical logic. However, Wittgenstein takes the analogy between language and a precise calculus, and between propositions and pictures, not 'as what it is, as . . . an object of comparison' that might be used to illuminate the way our language functions, but as an elucidation of the essence of language: 'as a preconceived idea to which reality *must* correspond' (*PI* 131). The theory of representation that Wittgenstein constructs in the *Tractatus* uses these analogies as the basis of an explanation of what language's ability to represent consists in. The appeal of the theory lies, not only in its apparent explanation of language's representational capacities, but in its providing a solution to a number of philosophical problems about the nature of the proposition that had been thrown up by the work of Russell and Frege. The theory is not based on observing how our everyday language actually functions, but arises out of Wittgenstein's explanatory ambitions and his literal application of the analogy between language and a calculus, and between propositions and pictures. It is Wittgenstein's sense of a need to solve a particular set of puzzles, together with his literal application of the above analogies, that determines his line of thought and blinds him to the contrast between what his theory of representation leads him to claim and the workings of our ordinary language.

The difference between Wittgenstein's early and later approaches to the philosophical problems concerning how language functions is clearly seen in the style of the two books. The writing in the *Tractatus*, by sharp contrast with the *Investigations*, is spare and abstract and the work is almost completely lacking both in familiar instances of our ordinary use of language and in representations of our everyday, lived world. The claim that language is a system of propositions that picture possible states of affairs leads Wittgenstein to focus on one narrow aspect of our language, and to ignore all the non-fact-stating uses that we make of it. It is the need to press home the analogy between propositions and pictures that leads him into holding that the world consists of simple objects arranged into facts and that propositions are composed of names of these simple objects, arranged in such a way as to represent a possible arrangement of the simple objects for which the names stand. This pairing off of names and simple objects, which Wittgenstein believes must exist in order for language to represent the world, is not apparent in the sentences of ordinary language, but must be revealed through analysis. Thus he is led to postulate an idealized system of propositions, constructed by means of the concatenation of logically proper names of simple objects, which he believes must lie behind the familiar sentences of our ordinary language. Likewise, he is committed to the existence of simple objects which constitute the meaning of logically proper names, and which form the basic, indestructible, constituents of the facts that fully analysed propositions model. It is the relation that holds between these two idealized systems – the system of elementary propositions and the system of possible atomic facts – that is held to underpin language's ability to represent the world. Thus Wittgenstein's urge to explain language's representational powers leads him into postulating an idealized machinery of fully analysed, elementary propositions, lying behind the surface of our ordinary language, which he insists must be there even though we do not yet perceive it.

The approach that Wittgenstein takes in the *Tractatus* to the problem of understanding how language functions does not merely exemplify the style of thought to which the *Investigations* is opposed, but also leads him to embrace many of the myths and misunderstandings about language that he later associates with the urge to explain. His remark in the Preface to the *Investigations*, quoted at the opening of this chapter, brings out the essential responsiveness of his later philosophical method to this style of thought and the false pictures that it generates. Yet insofar as this style of thought is one that we naturally adopt when we become reflective about how language functions, and insofar as the temptations to misunderstand are rooted in the forms of language itself, it would be a mistake to interpret Wittgenstein's remark in the Preface as suggesting that the *Investigations* is somehow addressed purely to views that he held in the *Tractatus*. It is rather that in the picture theory of the proposition, which he puts forward in the *Tractatus,* we see an example of the style of thought, and of the temptations associated with it, that are the real target of his remarks.

'Five red apples'

Both the responsiveness of the *Investigations* and the universality of its target are expressed in Wittgenstein's choice of the following quotation from Augustine's *Confessions* as the opening passage of the work:

> When they (my elders) named some object, and accordingly moved towards something, I saw this and I grasped that the thing was called by the sound they uttered when they meant to point it out. Their intention was shown by their bodily movements, as it were the natural language of all peoples: the expression of the face, the play of the eyes, the movement of other parts of the body, and the tone of voice which expresses our state of mind in seeking, having, rejecting, or avoiding something. Thus, as I heard words repeatedly used in their proper places in various sentences, I gradually learnt to understand what objects they signified; and after I had trained my mouth to form these signs, I used them to express my own desires.

> (*PI* 1)

It may seem puzzling that Wittgenstein should choose this quotation as his starting point, rather than one from Russell or Frege or from his own early work. In fact Wittgenstein's choice of a passage from Augustine serves to bring out some important aspects of his philosophical approach. First of all, by using a passage from Augustine's

Confessions, written in the fourth century AD, Wittgenstein brings out the universality of the temptations he is concerned with. There can be little doubt that these temptations are expressed in his own early work, and in the theories of Frege and Russell, or that they continue to exert an important influence on modern philosophy of language, but Wittgenstein doesn't want these temptations to be linked too closely with the work of any particular philosopher. These temptations are rooted in the forms of our language and Wittgenstein is interested in investigating them at their source, where they first arise and become the foundation for future philosophical enquiry. The beauty of the passage from Augustine is that it presents us with the first, primitive impulse to theorize about language, to try to explain or model how it functions. It therefore allows Wittgenstein to focus that much more clearly both on its origins in the forms of our language and on the contrast between this move towards abstraction and explanation and his own attempt to get us to look at language when it is functioning within the everyday, practical lives of speakers.

Wittgenstein's initial response to the passage from Augustine is to focus on a view of the essence of language which he finds expressed in it. In summarizing this view, Wittgenstein focuses on the picture of language as a system of signs that is given meaning through each sign's being correlated with an object for which it stands:

> These words, it seems to me, give us a particular picture of the essence of human language. It is this: the individual words in language name objects – sentences are combinations of such names. – In this picture of language we find the roots of the following idea: Every word has a meaning. The meaning is correlated with the word. It is the object for which the word stands.
>
> (*PI* 1)

However, it would be wrong to think that this picture of how language functions is the only theme in Augustine's thought about language that Wittgenstein is interested in and responds to. In fact, several further themes that can be found in Augustine's reflections are gradually woven in with the one that Wittgenstein has just identified.

The importance of Augustine's reflections as a source of themes to which Wittgenstein responds can be seen more clearly if we look at an earlier passage from the *Confessions*:

> Little by little I began to realize where I was and to want to make my wishes known to others, who might satisfy them. But this I could not do, because my wishes were inside me, while other people were outside, and they had no faculty which could penetrate my mind. So I would toss my arms and legs about and make noises, hoping that such few signs as I could make would show my meaning, though they were quite unlike what they were meant to mime.

> (St Augustine, 1961, p. 25)

Just prior to the passage that Wittgenstein quotes, Augustine again describes his frustration at not being able to convey his wishes, and he suggests that he uses his intelligence in realizing that other people used words to name objects, and in undertaking to learn which object each sound names.

In these passages from Augustine we can discern a number of major themes that Wittgenstein gradually takes up. Thus, we can see Augustine's tendency to think of the human subject in terms of a private essence or mind – in which there are wishes, thoughts, desires, etc. – and a physical interface with the outside world. The private essence is conceived as somehow already fully human, but as lacking the capacity to communicate with others. It already possesses its own internal articulations into particular thoughts and wishes, which cannot yet be expressed, in much the way that the physical world is seen as articulated into particular objects that the names of language unproblematically latch on to. The primary purpose of language is to communicate the thoughts and wishes that are initially locked within this private sphere. It is the private essence that makes the essential link between a word and the object which is its meaning, and understanding is conceived as the mind's making the appropriate connection between a sound and the object it signifies. As we cover the first forty paragraphs of the *Investigations*, we shall see each one of these ideas become a focus of Wittgenstein's grammatical enquiry, and some of them remain a central topic throughout the work.

Wittgenstein begins his commentary on the passage from the *Confessions* by observing that Augustine does not distinguish between different kinds of word, but takes one sort of word – ' "table", "chair", "bread", and people's names' – as a model, and derives his general picture of how language functions from this one sort of case. Wittgenstein clearly sees this tendency to take a central case and derive a general model from it as both an important element in the theoretical attitude and a major source of false pictures. Our general sense of a need 'to penetrate phenomena' predisposes us to neglect the wide horizon of human linguistic activity, and to focus on particular linguistic elements in isolation from both the field of language and the actual employment of this language by speakers. Our attitude towards these particular examples is one of studying them closely in order to discern their essence (e.g. the essence of naming). The tendency to take a narrow or over-simplified view of the phenomenon of language is thereby combined with a tendency to idealize or mythologize it, which arises in connection with our desire to provide a clear model that explains how it functions.

Against both of these inclinations, Wittgenstein directs us to imagine a concrete instance of people using a simple language in the course of their everyday lives:

> Now think of the following use of language: I send someone shopping. I give him a slip marked "five red apples". He takes the slip to the shopkeeper, who opens the drawer marked "apples"; then he looks up the word "red" in a table and finds a colour sample opposite it; then he says the series of cardinal numbers – I assume that he knows them by heart – up to the word "five" and for each number he takes an apple of the same colour as the sample out of the drawer.
>
> *(PI* 1)

Although this example presents a simple language, or a simple use of language, it does not involve the sort of oversimplification that we find in Augustine. First of all, although the example is simple it is, in an important sense, complete, insofar as it presents this simple language in its natural environment, when it is actually functioning, and not as a system of words or sentences abstracted from use.

Secondly, Wittgenstein does not use this particular concrete case as the basis for deriving any claim about the essence of language, but simply as a means to draw our attention to the natural embedding of language within the active lives of speakers, and to a richness and complexity in the phenomenon of language that Augustine overlooks, and which only becomes apparent when we see language functioning.

Augustine thinks of language as a medium for communicating thoughts and wishes which are first of all inside us. In the example Wittgenstein presents it is clear that no such thing is in question. Here we see language functioning as a tool within a particular practical activity – shopping – where the point of using language is not to convey our state of mind, but to bring about a certain sort of response in our interlocutor. When we see language functioning in this way, we do not feel the same inclination to ask what object is signified by the words 'red' or 'five'. For it is clear that what is in question is how the shopkeeper *operates* with these words, how he *acts*, rather than any correlation between these words and an object:

> But what is the meaning of the word 'five'? – No such thing was in question here, only how the word 'five' is used.
>
> (*PI* 1)

Thus, Wittgenstein's concrete example begins to work against Augustine's temptations both to think about language in abstraction from its use and to look for the essence of meaning. When language is functioning, it is clear that different expressions play quite different roles. Wittgenstein invents this example of a simple language, in which the individual words have clear, distinct techniques associated with them, in order to bring out, on the one hand, how language is interwoven with non-linguistic activity, and on the other, how it is in *use* that the different functions of expressions become apparent. In this way, a concrete example is made to work against our philosophical temptations, without itself being used as a source of philosophical doctrines.

'Block!', 'Pillar!', 'Slab!', 'Beam!'

Wittgenstein uses the example he presents in *PI* 1 to draw our attention to the variety of linguistic techniques that exist even in a simple language. In *PI* 2, he introduces a different kind of critical approach. Here he is not concerned to draw our attention to elements of language that falsify Augustine's over-simple description, but asks us 'to imagine a language for which the description given by Augustine is right' (*PI* 2). Thus we are asked to imagine a language consisting of the words 'block', 'pillar', 'slab' and 'beam', whose function, like that of 'table', 'chair', 'bread', etc., is to pick out a particular sort of object. We are to imagine this language as the whole language of a community of speakers, but again we are to imagine it functioning in its natural environment, as it is woven into the practical lives of those who use it. Wittgenstein now uses this example to explore the picture of language acquisition that Augustine presents us with, by asking us to imagine in detail how a child would be taught this language, and how we would judge that he had succeeded in mastering it.

We are to imagine that the 'block', 'pillar', 'slab', 'beam' language is the whole language of a tribe of builders. Children belonging to this tribe must be acculturated into it. Wittgenstein describes how this will involve them in learning both how to build and how to use and respond to language, as it is used within the context of this building activity:

> The children are brought to perform *these* actions, to use *these* words as they do so, and to react in *this* way to the words of others.
>
> (*PI* 6)

As part of this training process, children will be taught to make an association between a word and a certain shape of building stone. This is clearly part of the picture that Augustine presents. However, Augustine describes this process in such a way that the child is credited with an innate insight into the technique of assigning names to things; the child is described as already understanding what the adults are doing when they utter a sound while pointing to an object.

Wittgenstein insists, by contrast, that we should not call the process in which the teacher points 'to the objects, direct[s] the child's attention to them, and at the same time utter[s] a word; for instance, the word 'slab' as he points to that shape' (*PI* 6) 'ostensive definition'. By 'ostensive definition' Wittgenstein means an act of giving the meaning of a word by pointing to an exemplar. The teacher's initial acts of pointing at a shape and saying the appropriate sound cannot be taken as an ostensive definition of a word, since the child is not yet in a position to understand what the adult does as defining a name, for the child is not yet master of the technique of naming, he 'cannot as yet *ask* what the name is' (*PI* 6). Thus Wittgenstein calls the process we've just described 'the ostensive teaching of words' (*PI* 6).

Let us suppose that this ostensive teaching of words does eventually succeed in establishing an association between, e.g., the word 'slab' and a particular shape of building stone. What does such an association amount to? It is very likely, Wittgenstein suggests, that our first thought will be 'that a picture of the object comes before the child's mind when he hears the word' (*PI* 6). Some such picture is clearly suggested by Augustine's idea that he gradually learns which objects the words of his language signify. Wittgenstein does not deny that something like this may well happen, but he asks us to explore the connection between the pupil's getting an image of a slab-shaped piece of stone when he hears the word 'slab' and his coming to understand the call 'Slab!', as it is used in the context of the activity of building. Does the fact that the word 'slab' prompts the pupil to form an image of a slab mean that he has understood the word, or mastered the language? To answer this question, Wittgenstein suggests, we need to ask what the *purpose* of the word 'slab' is in the language of this tribe.

Again, we find that Wittgenstein's response to Augustine here is concessive rather than confrontational. He does not claim that it *couldn't* be the case that the purpose of a language is to evoke images in the mind of a hearer. Uttering a word in this language, he suggests, might be 'like striking a note on the keyboard of the imagination' (*PI* 6). However, this is *not* the purpose of the use of the language of the imaginary tribe of builders; it is not the purpose of their use of the words 'slab', 'block', 'pillar' and 'beam' to evoke images in the mind of their hearers. Wittgenstein concedes that forming such images might help a hearer attain the actual purpose of uttering these words, but the actual purpose was described in *PI* 2:

> A is building with building-stones; there are blocks, pillars, slabs and beams. B has to pass the stones, and that in the order in which A needs them. For this purpose they use a language consisting of the words "block", "pillar", "slab", "beam". A calls them out; – B brings the stone which he has learnt to bring at such-and-such a call.

Given that this is the purpose of the utterance of words in this language, would the fact that the child forms an image of a slab when it hears the word 'slab' be enough to effect an understanding of the word? Again, Wittgenstein does not say that it would not, but rather draws our attention to an aspect of the training with language that the Augustinian picture neglects. We have been thinking of what is accomplished by the ostensive teaching of words purely in terms of what goes on in the child's mind, and have neglected the way in which the training with the language is embedded in an overall training in the tribe's practice of building. When we focus on the embedding of linguistic training in the wider context of learning to build, we see how this neglected aspect of the process is actually paramount to our ordinary idea of what constitutes understanding: 'Don't you understand the call "Slab!" if you act upon it in such-and-such a way?' (*PI* 6). There is no doubt that the ostensive teaching of words plays a role in bringing this about, but the function of the words of this language is given only with its embedding in the activity of building, and it is only by mastering this function – i.e. by mastering the use of words within this activity – that the pupil fulfils our ordinary criteria for understanding the language.

In *PI* 7, Wittgenstein introduces the concept of a *language-game* in order to bring into prominence the fact that language functions within the active, practical lives of speakers, that its use is inextricably bound up with the non-linguistic behaviour which constitutes its natural environment. He introduces the concept in connection with three different sorts of activity:

1 One party calls out words, the other acts on them.
2 The pupil utters a word when the teacher points to a stone.
3 The pupil repeats the word after the teacher.

The latter two activities occur during the pupil's instruction in the language, and Wittgenstein remarks that while these activities 'resemble language', they are not language proper. These activities resemble language insofar as they employ words and link this employment with the activity of pointing at particular kinds of stone, but they represent preliminaries to the full-blown use of language within the activity of building. Wittgenstein uses the term 'language-game' in connection with *both* the activities by means of which we teach children language *and* the activity of using language within the context of purposive activity. In the *Brown Book* (dictated 1934–5) Wittgenstein uses the term principally in connection with the first idea, but by the time of the *Investigations* the second idea has assumed a far greater importance.

Wittgenstein's concept of a language-game is clearly to be set over and against the idea of language as a system of meaningful signs that can be considered in abstraction from its actual employment. Instead of approaching language as a system of signs with meaning, we are prompted to think about it *in situ*, embedded in the lives of those who speak it. The tendency to isolate language, or abstract it from the context in which it ordinarily lives, is connected with our adopting a theoretical attitude towards it, and with our urge to explain *how* these mere signs (mere marks) can acquire their extraordinary power to mean or represent something. Wittgenstein's aim is to show us that in this act of abstraction we turn our backs on everything that is essential to the actual functioning of language; it is our act of abstracting language from its employment within our ordinary lives that turns it into something dead, whose ability to represent now cries out for explanation. The sense of a need to explain how language (conceived as a system of symbols) has the magical power to represent the world is thus connected with our failure to look at it where it actually functions. Wittgenstein does not set out to satisfy our sense of a need for a theory of representation (a theory that explains how the dead sign acquires meaning), but to dispel this sense of a need through getting us to look at language where it is actually doing work, and where we can see its essence fully displayed. In directing us, through the concept of a language-game, to 'the spatial and temporal phenomenon of language, not [to] some non-spatial, non-temporal phantasm' (*PI* 108), Wittgenstein hopes gradually to bring us to see that 'nothing out of the ordinary is involved' (*PI* 94), that everything that we need to understand the essence of language 'already lies open to view' (*PI* 126).

Wittgenstein explores the processes involved in a child's becoming master of a language-game further by asking us to imagine an expansion of the 'slab', 'block' language of *PI* 2. The expanded language includes numerals, words for 'there' and 'this', which are used in connection with a pointing gesture, as well as a number of colour samples. He describes a possible exchange within this extended language as follows:

> A gives an order like: "d – slab – there". At the same time he shews the assistant a colour sample, and when he says "there" he points to a place on the building site. From the stock of slabs B takes one for each letter of the alphabet up to "d", of the same colour as the sample, and brings them to the place indicated by A.
>
> (*PI* 8)

This extended language clearly introduces words that function in a quite different way from 'slab' and 'block'. We've already seen, in *PI* 1, that the picture of meaning that Augustine presents simply doesn't apply to the words 'a', 'b', etc., and it is equally clear that it does not fit the words 'there' and 'this'. What Wittgenstein now explores is how well Augustine's emphasis on ostensive teaching describes the process whereby the child is trained in these additional linguistic techniques.

When a child learns this extended language, it will have to learn the series of numerals by heart and to say them always in the same order with none missed out. It will also have to learn how to use the numerals in giving and responding to orders, so that the use of the numerals becomes tied in the appropriate way with non-linguistic behaviour. Wittgenstein allows that there may be some role for

45

ostensive teaching to play here. For example, the teacher might point to slabs and count 'a, b, c slabs', and he might also teach the first six numerals, which describe groups that can be taken in at a glance, by simply pointing and saying 'b slabs', 'c slabs', and so on. But can the words 'there' and 'this' be taught ostensively? If the child takes 'there' and 'this' to describe the place or the thing pointed to, then it will not have understood the function of these words. The over-simplified picture of meaning that Augustine adopts invites the idea that ostensive teaching provides a model for the process of language acquisition. Yet once we become aware of the variety of linguistic techniques that exist even in this very simple language-game, then we begin to see that Augustine has taken one striking case as a model for all, and that in fact training with the language is as varied as the techniques that constitute it.

Wittgenstein now asks, 'What do the words of this language signify?' (*PI* 10). This is the sort of question that invites us to think of language in abstraction from its use and hence to form a false picture of how it functions. Wittgenstein responds, therefore, by putting the question in question: 'What is supposed to show what they signify, if not the kind of use they have? And we have already described that' (*PI* 10). When we ask the question 'What do the words of this language signify?', we have a particular idea of the form of answer that is required, one that is connected with the idea of pointing to what is signified by a word. But we have seen that it is the *use* of a word that shows its significance, and not an object that can be pointed to. Yet our urge for generalization may still prompt us to look for some canonical form for specifying the meaning of expressions; the canonical form, just by being generally applicable, may still seem to us to capture something essential about meaning. Wittgenstein goes on, therefore, to show how empty this idea of a canonical form is. He does not suggest that no such canonical form could be found, but assuming that we *could* construct a canonical form, along the lines of 'This word signifies *this*' or 'the word ... signifies ...', Wittgenstein shows how little is thereby accomplished.

Firstly, although the sentence ' "slab" signifies *this* object' may distinguish the shape of building block that 'slab', as opposed to 'block', refers to, it does not indicate anything about how the word 'slab' is actually used. The technique for using the word is simply presupposed in this canonical description. Thus, the canonical description does not bring us any closer to the essence of meaning, for the entire framework of employing names within a language-game is not described but presupposed. Secondly, although in a particular case of misunderstanding, the sentence ' "a", "b", "c" signify numbers' may tell us that these words don't function like 'slab' and 'block', the use of the canonical form does not serve to bring the meaning of these different types of expression any closer together. The function of these words is, as we've seen, completely different, and putting them into a common schema does nothing to establish a common feature that could be identified as the essence of meaning: 'assimilating the descriptions of the uses of words in this way cannot make the uses themselves more like one another. For, as we've seen, they are absolutely unlike' (*PI* 10). The construction of a canonical form for specifying the meaning of expressions accomplishes nothing at all; in fact, it only serves to make fundamentally different types of expression look more similar than they actually are.

Wittgenstein compares the different functions of expressions in a language to the different functions of tools in a tool-kit. The emphasis this places on the practical use of language, on its embedding in a wider activity, and on the idea of training and practical mastery of a technique is absolutely central to the vision of language that Wittgenstein gradually places before us. The comparison is one which brings out the everydayness of language, which focuses on the humdrum aspect of its practical role in our lives, and which thereby makes language look less 'gaseous'. The comparison also works against our urge to look for the representational essence of language, for we simply don't feel the same need to explain what makes a tool a tool, or to describe a common essence of tools. What makes a tool a tool is simply that it is *used* as a tool, each kind of tool in its own specific way. The aspects of language that are brought to the fore by the tool analogy are ones that escape our notice when we do philosophy precisely because of our tendency to think of words, not as they are applied and used, but as they are written or spoken, aside from their actual use or application. But apart from their application, all words seem just meaningful, and the temptation is to think that they must all be made meaningful in the very same way.

Concerning the extended language of *PI* 8, Wittgenstein also raises the question of whether the colour samples should be considered part of the language. Clearly, the idea that they should be so considered is at odds with Augustine's picture, in which the samples will be thought of as (showing) *what* the word 'red' means, and will therefore be put on the 'world' or 'meaning' side, rather than on the side of language. It is this idea that meaning consists in a connection between a word and an object, or the general idea of an opposition between words on the one hand and meanings on the other, that Wittgenstein's remarks have been working against. In looking at the simple language-games of *PI* 1, *PI* 2 and *PI* 8, we have begun to see language in terms of techniques that speakers employ within their active, everyday lives. Insofar as the colour samples constitute instruments of the language that are used by speakers in the course of giving instruction, it is appropriate, Wittgenstein suggests, to consider them as part of language: 'It is most natural, and causes least confusion, to reckon the samples among the instruments of language' (*PI* 16).

Wittgenstein's critique of Augustine may at this point seem to amount to no more than the claim that language contains, not merely names of objects, but a wide variety of types of expression, each of which functions in a different way. This would suggest that Wittgenstein thinks Augustine is wrong only in being partial, and not in his whole approach to understanding the structure and function of language. Wittgenstein's critique would, in that case, be seen as motivating a project of systematic classification of the different categories of expression of our language, and of the different techniques associated with them. In *PI* 17, Wittgenstein makes it clear that he rejects any such project. We might, he says, group words into kinds for some particular purpose, with some specific aim in mind, but, by implication, none of these classifications should be thought of as uncovering the intrinsic structure of language. There is, therefore, nothing in his critique of Augustine that can properly be taken to suggest that there is some correct classification of different sorts of expression. The distinctions between expressions that he has focused on, and which are clearly seen only when we look at the *use* of expressions, are introduced with a quite specific philosophical aim in mind, namely as a counter to our related tendencies to think about the function of language in abstraction from its use and to idealize and over-simplify its workings. Thus the examples Wittgenstein constructs are not to be regarded as a sketch for a burgeoning theory that might, within the spirit of his investigation, be worked up into something precise or systematic; his interest in these particular, concrete cases is exhausted by their role in overcoming specific philosophical confusions and in countering our urge to generalize.

Wittgenstein now moves on to make a number of important points that arise in connection with a comparison between the simple language-games he has described and our own. We might, he suggests, feel that the language-game of *PI* 2, and the extended version of it, cannot possibly be complete languages because they consist only of orders. Wittgenstein responds to this by asking whether our language is complete. Was it complete before the new, highly technical concepts of modern science were introduced? This clearly raises a number of important issues. First of all, there is the question whether the notion of a complete language makes sense. The theory of representation that Wittgenstein constructed in the *Tractatus* can be interpreted as entailing, not only that the question makes sense, but that every meaningful language must, of necessity, be complete: 'If all the true elementary propositions are given, the result is a complete description of the world' (*TLP* 4.26). He appears to be willing to accept, as a consequence of this, that all languages that describe the world must be translatable without remainder into one another: 'Any correct sign-language must be translatable into any other . . .; it is *this* that they all have in common' (*TLP* 3.343). These claims are all grounded in a theory of representation which requires a strict formal isomorphism between the system of elementary propositions and the totality of possible facts. But even leaving this particular theory of meaning aside, one may still recognize the appeal of the idea, for those who think that the essence of language consists in naming and describing, that all languages must contain a fact-describing core, for it is this that seems to constitute its essential link with the world it represents.

Wittgenstein has, of course, long ago abandoned both the *Tractatus* theory of representation and the theoretical style of thought that it exemplifies. He has offered us instead a picture of language as a set of instruments or techniques that are employed by speakers in the course of their everyday lives. This picture is not presented in the form of a new theory of representation, but as a way of looking at language – 'an object of comparison' (*PI* 131) – which counters our temptation to think of language in abstraction from its use. But insofar as he has moved from the idea that the essence of language resides in its modelling facts to a picture of it as a motley of different techniques, the very idea of completeness has ceased to make sense. There is no essential structure or function against which the notion of completeness can be defined; it makes no more sense to speak of a complete language than to speak of a complete tool-kit. The techniques that constitute a language take their point from what lies around them, in the lives of those who use the language, rather than from an abstract and idealized conception of what representation *must* consist in. New techniques arise and others fall away, not in response to any constraint imposed by the essence of language, but in response to the needs and purposes of those who employ them. Wittgenstein captures this idea of language as a shifting motley of techniques by comparing it with a city (*PI* 18), in which ancient streets are constantly added to and what is there is subject to continual modification; the idea of completeness simply doesn't apply.

Secondly, the idea that the simple language-games that Wittgenstein describes are incomplete shows how we are inclined to judge these language-games from the perspective of our own language. From the perspective of our language, these simple language-games certainly do look incomplete. Yet it would never strike us to claim that our own language is incomplete, even though its symbolism might develop in a number of ways. Nor did our language strike speakers as incomplete before the symbolism of modern chemistry and other sciences was introduced. It makes no sense to speak of language as either complete or incomplete, for language represents a form of limit to those who speak it; it represents the point from which we judge. Our language is not superior to the language-games Wittgenstein describes in the sense of being closer to some ideal, or complete, symbolism; it is simply richer and more complex. The concept of incompleteness, like the concept of completeness, belongs with the false idea of an absolutely correct or essential system of representation.

It is here that Wittgenstein introduces the notion of a form of life: '[T]o imagine a language means to imagine a form of life' (*PI* 19). The idea of language as a form of life, like the idea of a language-game, is to be set over against the idea of language as an abstract system of signs; it again serves to bring into prominence the fact that language is embedded within a horizon of significant, non-linguistic behaviour. Thus, just as the term 'language-game' is meant to evoke the idea of language in use within the non-linguistic activities of speakers, so the term 'form of life' is intended to evoke the idea that language and linguistic exchange are embedded in the significantly structured lives of groups of active human agents. The concept of life, as Wittgenstein uses it here, is not biological life, nor is it an ahistorical idea of the life of a particular species. The idea of a form of life applies rather to historical groups of individuals who are bound together into a community by a shared set of complex, language-involving practices. These practices are grounded in biological needs and capacities, but insofar as these are mediated and transformed by a set of intricate, historically-specific language-games, our human form of life is fundamentally *cultural* (rather than biological) in nature. Coming to share, or understand, the form of life of a group of individual human beings means mastering, or coming to understand, the intricate language-games that are essential to its characteristic practices. It is this vital connection between language and the complex system of practices and activities binding a community together that Wittgenstein intends to emphasize in the concept of a 'form of life'.

Within Augustine's account of how we come to acquire language, there is contained the idea of a completed, or structured, human consciousness inside the child, which exists prior to the child's acquisition of language. According to Augustine, the child acquires language in order to express the thoughts and wishes that are already there inside it. Wittgenstein's idea that the concept of language is internally linked with that of a form of life suggests, by contrast, that the adult human subject emerges slowly, as its life becomes structured through the acquisition of new and more complex language-games. In acquiring a language, the child comes to inhabit a social world of practices, the structure of which is grounded, not merely in concepts, but in ways of acting and responding that essentially involve the *use* of language. The human subject does not exist absolutely, either as consciousness or as body, but develops or evolves as it acquires a more and more intricate form of life, and as the phenomena that constitute its world become, thereby, ever richer and more complex. In the topic that Wittgenstein next takes up, the temptation to ignore the discernible structures of our form of life, and to appeal instead to hidden inner structures that are thought to explain how language functions, is explored further.

Meaning and use

The question Wittgenstein now raises is whether 'Slab!' in the language of *PI* 2 means the same as our *word* 'slab' or the same as our *elliptical sentence* 'Slab!' It cannot, he suggests, mean the same as our word 'slab', for 'Slab!' in the language of *PI* 2 is a complete call. But if 'Slab!' must be seen as a complete sentence, it surely, he suggests, can't be the equivalent of our elliptical sentence 'Slab!' For the latter is a *shortening* of our sentence 'Bring me a slab', and the language of *PI* 2 does not contain any equivalent of this longer sentence. The question arises, therefore, of what ground there could be for calling the 'Slab!' of *PI* 2 a shortening of the sentence 'Bring me a slab', when the latter sentence was never in question and does not exist within the language-game of which 'Slab!' is a part. Why shouldn't we, he asks, take 'Bring me a slab' as a *lengthening* of the sentence 'Slab!'?

Here the temptation to appeal to an intrinsic, inner structure – to the thought that is really expressed by 'Slab!' – is very strong. For we want to say that what the speaker of the language of *PI* 2 *really means* when he calls 'Slab!' is: 'Bring me a slab'. We feel that the thought, or meaning, or the intention that lies behind the speaker's utterance is one that is properly, or canonically, expressed only by the fuller sentence. It is this that makes us want to say that 'Slab!'

is elliptical for 'Bring me a slab', even though the longer sentence does not exist in the language of *PI* 2. The ellipsis of 'Slab!' is seen as *absolute*, because the meaning itself, as it exists in the mind of the speaker, has a complexity that is expressed only by the longer sentence. This thought certainly contains echoes of the *Tractatus*, where the logical form of a proposition is something that must be revealed through analysis, and where analysis is thought of as uncovering the intrinsic logical form of the proposition (thought) that a sentence expresses. But more generally, the thought above reveals a temptation to think of the mind as possessing an inner structure, which may be only loosely connected with the manifest forms of human behaviour, and which constitutes the essence of psychological states like meaning and intending.

Wittgenstein now sets out to put this idea of an absolute, internal structure lying behind behaviour in question. Thus, when the interlocutor claims that 'if you shout "Slab!" you really mean: "Bring me a slab" ', Wittgenstein asks: 'But how do you do this? How do you *mean that* while you *say* "Slab!"?' In what sense does 'Bring me a slab' reveal the real form of what is meant when a speaker says 'Slab!'? And how does the speaker manage to mean the more complex sentence when he says the simple one? How does the thought he has, or what he means when he says 'Slab!', come to have this additional complexity? Wittgenstein asks: 'Do you say the unshortened sentence to yourself?' The answer is clearly, no. Why, then, do we feel we must translate 'Slab!' into another sentence in order to say what someone means by it? Why isn't it equally correct to say that when someone says 'Bring me a slab', he really means 'Slab!'? The interlocutor responds: 'But when I call "Slab!", then what I want is, *that he should bring me a slab*!' Wittgenstein replies: 'Certainly, but does "wanting this" consist in thinking in some form or other a different sentence from the one you utter?' (*PI* 19).

Wittgenstein now raises the question of what makes the sentence 'Bring me a slab' more complex than the sentence 'Slab!' Couldn't one say the sentence 'Bring me a slab' and mean it as one long word? What makes it the case that this sentence consists of four words rather than one? He suggests that we mean the sentence as four words insofar as we use it *in contrast* with other possible sentences of our language, such as 'Bring *him* a slab', or 'Bring me *two* slabs', and so on. He then asks what it means to use this sentence 'in contrast' with these others. Surely these other sentences don't hover before my mind when I call 'Bring me a slab'. He goes on:

> No. Even if such an explanation rather tempts us, we need only think for a moment of what actually happens in order to see that we are going astray here. We say that we use the command in contrast with other sentences because *our language* contains the possibility of these other sentences.
>
> (*PI* 20)

It is not, therefore, the existence of structure *inside* the speaker's mind (or brain) that grounds our saying that he means the sentence as four words rather than one. What makes it the case that he means it as four words lies in the grammatical possibilities of the language of which he is a master. Wittgenstein goes on:

> For what goes on in you when you give such an order? Are you conscious of its consisting of four words *while* you are uttering it? Of course you have a *mastery* of this language – which contains these other sentences as well – but is this having a mastery something that *happens* while you are uttering the sentence?
>
> (*PI* 20)

This question touches on our temptation to picture psychological phenomena (such as understanding or mastery) in terms of a determinate, inner state that exists, as it were complete, inside the subject's mind (or brain). Thus we imagine the linguistic mastery that grounds my meaning 'Bring me a slab' as four words in terms of an inner structure that lies behind my utterance of this sentence. For it must, we feel, be the case that my meaning the sentence as four words rather than one consists in something that obtains *at the time* of my saying these words. This picture of the mind as an internal mechanism, whose inner structure underlies and explains the structure of outward behaviour, is immensely compelling, but it stands in fundamental opposition to the idea that everything we need to understand psychological phenomena 'already lies open to view' (*PI* 92). It is this picture of the mind as an internal mechanism, or repository of psychological states, that forms one of the major targets of the *Investigations*, and Wittgenstein introduces his opposition to it as follows:

> I have admitted that the foreigner [who thinks that 'Bring me a slab' is one word rather than four] will probably pronounce a sentence differently if he conceives it differently; but what we call his wrong conception *need* not lie in anything that accompanies the utterance of the command.
>
> (*PI* 20)

Wittgenstein is here directing us to look for what grounds the structure of an utterance of the sentence 'Bring me a slab', not in what *accompanies* the saying of the sentence, but in what, as it were, *surrounds* it. Thus he introduces the idea that it is nothing that occurs *at the time*, or in the speaker's mind, that determines that he means it as four words rather than one. We can imagine, for example, that exactly the same thing goes on in the mind of the foreigner who means the sentence as one word and the native speaker who means it as four. To understand the difference between the native speaker and the foreigner we should look at the background to the utterance of these words, that is, at something which does not accompany their utterance, but rather forms its context or horizon. The mastery that grounds the native speaker's meaning the sentence as four words does not consist in facts that obtain at the time of utterance, but in an indeterminate horizon of actual and potential use of language that surrounds it; it is this surrounding use of language that lends his current utterance of the sentence whatever structure it possesses. So the structure of the state of meaning or understanding 'Bring me a slab' as four words derives, not from something intrinsic to the internal workings of the mind of the subject, but from the structure of the language-game that he is participating in, and which is revealed by the wider context of his linguistic and non-linguistic behaviour. It is this characteristic feature of psychological concepts – i.e. the way in which their ascription essentially depends upon what lies around them, not physically, but in the sense of what happens before and after – that reveals a fundamental distinction between psychological phenomena and physical phenomena. The structure and complexity of psychological states does not lie in the structure and complexity of some inner mechanism (mental or physical), but in the complex (temporally extended) form of life that is apparent in an individual's behaviour and accessible from a third-person point of view. We are not yet in a position to understand fully the nature of Wittgenstein's opposition to what clearly remains a dominant picture of mental phenomena, to judge whether he provides a serious alternative to it, or to decide whether in opposing the dominant picture he is espousing a version of logical behaviourism. All these questions will be given a fuller treatment in the chapters on Wittgenstein's philosophy of psychology.

Wittgenstein now takes up the question of ellipsis again. What is it that makes us say that 'Slab!' is elliptical for 'Bring me a slab'? It is not, he suggests, because it is a shortened form of the thought that accompanies the utterance of 'Slab!', but because *in our language* 'Bring me a slab' represents a kind of paradigm. The interlocutor then raises the following question: ' "You grant that the shortened and unshortened sentence have the same sense. – What is this sense then? Isn't there a verbal expression for this sense?" ' (*PI* 20). Wittgenstein responds by directing us away from a concern with an ideal expression of this sense towards the shared use that forms the background to a particular utterance of each of these sentences. Thus it is the fact that these sentences share a use, or play the same role, within a wider language-game that constitutes their having the same sense. Instead of looking for an idealized expression of this sense, we are directed towards the function that these sentences have within the practice of using language which forms the framework for the use of these sentences on particular occasions.

In *PI* 21, Wittgenstein further explores the role of the background – of what happens before and after a particular utterance – in determining what is meant, by considering the question of what makes it the case that someone who utters the words 'Five slabs' means it as an order rather than a report. Again, he suggests that it is nothing that accompanies the utterance of these words, nor anything intrinsic to the way these words are said (though this may well be different in each case), that makes it the case that the words are meant one way rather than another. We could imagine that both the order and the report are given in exactly the same tone of voice, but that 'the application' of each should still be different. The notion of 'the application' of an utterance of these words is intended to invoke the whole context of behaviour in which the utterance of 'Five slabs' is embedded, and it is presented by Wittgenstein in contrast to anything that happens at the time the words are spoken. The idea that the difference between meaning 'Five slabs' as an order and as a report depends upon the application thus serves to bring out that it is not something in the mind of the speaker that accompanies the utterance of these words, but what surrounds it (in the sense of what happens before and afterwards), that determines how the words are meant. It is the distinctive form of what lies on the surface – in the pattern of activity within which the use of language is embedded – that grounds the distinction between an order and a report, and not a hidden internal state of the speaker.

The idea that it is the part that uttering a sentence plays in the language-game that determines whether its utterance constitutes an order or a report clearly goes against the idea, associated with the picture of language as a calculus, that the distinction between orders and reports is grounded in the formal properties of the sentence as such. The emphasis on formal, grammatical differences between sentences that our way of thinking creates has led philosophers to suppose that there are three basic types of sentence – assertions, questions, commands – corresponding to the three distinct grammatical forms. Wittgenstein's contrasting emphasis on the role that utterances play in the language-game prompts us to look at the different ways in which we actually use sentences, as the ground upon which distinctions are to be drawn. When we look at how sentences are used – at the distinct language-games we play with the sentences of our language – then we are faced not with three types, but with a countless number:

> There are *countless* kinds [of sentence]: countless different kinds of use of what we call "symbols", "words", "sentences". And this multiplicity is not something fixed, given once and for all;

but new types of language, new language-games, as we may say, come into existence, and others become obsolete and get forgotten.

(*PI* 23)

Wittgenstein underlines the reorientation away from thinking of language as a calculus, or system of sentences, towards thinking of it as essentially connected with the notion of application as follows:

Here the term 'language-game' is meant to bring into prominence the fact that *speaking* a language is part of an activity, or of a form of life.

(*PI* 23)

Language is essentially embedded in structured activities that constitute a 'form of life'. Almost all of the activities that human beings engage in are ones that are intrinsically connected with, or somehow grounded in, our use of language; our form of life is everywhere shaped by the use of language, and it is this that I tried to capture earlier by saying that our form of life is fundamentally cultural in nature. Learning our language, or coming to participate in our form of life, is essentially connected with acquiring mastery of countless kinds of language-game. In *PI* 23, Wittgenstein offers the following long, and clearly incomplete, list of some of the characteristic language-games that constitute our form of life:

Giving orders, and obeying them –
Describing the appearance of an object, or giving its measurements –
Constructing an object from a description (a drawing) –
Reporting an event –
Speculating about an event –
Forming and testing a hypothesis –
Presenting the results of an experiment in tables and diagrams –
Making up a story; and reading it –
Play-acting –
Singing catches –

Guessing riddles –
Making a joke; telling it –
Solving a problem in practical arithmetic –
Translating from one language to another –
Asking, thanking, cursing, greeting, praying.

Thus, learning our language means becoming acculturated, that is, coming to participate in a vast network of structured activities that essentially employ language. This rich conception of what is involved in the acquisition of language contrasts sharply with Augustine's impoverished idea of learning language, which his conception of language as a system of meaningful signs makes almost inevitable. Approaching language in abstraction from its use leads us to neglect, or misunderstand, the rich diversity of language-games that we come to participate in as we acquire a mastery of our language. This diversity in how we use language is regarded by the philosopher as something incidental to its essence; there is no acknowledgement that the structure and function of language are inextricably linked with the structure and function of the complex activities in which its use is embedded. Wittgenstein's idea that the structure and function of language are revealed only *in situ*, when it is embedded in the active lives of those who speak it, acknowledges that these diverse uses of language are an essential part of it. For it is the structures and distinctions that are revealed in our actual use of language, and not those that remain when language is abstracted from its application, that show us how our language functions, or what sort of phenomenon it is.

In *PI* 24, Wittgenstein explicitly warns us against the dangers of taking too narrow a view of language and neglecting the enormous cultural landscape that it represents. It is, he suggests, by neglecting the rich diversity in our language-games that we are led to ask questions like 'What is a question?' We are led into looking for the essence of questions as a single, identifiable linguistic form whose essence we can attempt to model. But now think of all the different language-games that involve questioning:

Testing a schoolboy on his knowledge of history.
Playing twenty questions.

Questioning a murder suspect.
Saying 'How are you?' to an acquaintance.
Asking someone to marry you.
Asking for a pay rise.
The probing of a psycho-analyst.
The questions in a marriage service.

What we have here is a range of profoundly different practices or language-games, each one of which invokes a complex cultural setting. It is the distinctions that exist between these culturally complex phenomena that Wittgenstein wants to draw our attention to, for it is in these distinctions that the true complexity of the phenomenon of human language is revealed. The fact that each of the above language-games uses the same particular surface grammatical structure does nothing to bring these profoundly different practices closer together, but by focusing on this one, superficial similarity we become blind to the differences that actually reveal the nature of the phenomenon of language. Instead of observing the differences that lie open to view in our distinct practices of using language, we go in search of a chimera: the essence of the question. The differences that Wittgenstein wants us to focus on are not incidental to language, for our understanding of our language is essentially connected with an ability to understand and participate in all these complex language-games. It is only if we have already taken the step of abstracting language from its use that we will be tempted to ignore the differences in our practice and go in search of the essence of assertions, questions, names, and so on; for when we address ourselves to the spatial and temporal phenomenon of language, then we see that the distinctions between language-games that we observe make no connection with the abstract categories that we've constructed. The philosopher's concern with the construction of an account of the essence of meaning, of assertion, of questions, etc. does not only 'send us in pursuit of chimeras' (*PI* 94), but it ignores the real distinctions and complexities that are revealed only when we look at language when it is functioning, within our day-to-day practice of using it.

Ostensive definition

Wittgenstein now takes up again the earlier, Augustinian theme that learning language is essentially learning to give names to objects. The investigation that we have just been engaged in has gradually worked to lead us away from thinking of naming as a mental act that takes place within the mind of a speaker, and towards thinking of naming in terms of a linguistic technique that is employed within a language-game: 'To repeat – naming is something like attaching a label to a thing. One can say that this is preparatory to the use of a word. But *what* is it preparation *for*?' (*PI* 26). This question clearly focuses more closely on the specific linguistic technique of employing a name, of applying it in a language-game, and on the relation between the application of this technique and the initial act of naming (or applying a label to a thing). In the discussion that follows, Wittgenstein tries to show, not only how over-simplified our picture of naming is, but also that our idea of it as essentially an intellectual or mental act is mistaken.

In *PI* 27, Wittgenstein writes: ' "We name things and then we can talk about them: can refer to them in talk." ' This sentence expresses our inclination to think of naming in very simple, unproblematic terms. It's easy: we just name things, and then we can use the name to talk about them. The role of the technique of using the name is pictured as having been made clear by the simple act of pointing and repeating the name. But is the role of the name, the technique of using it, given in the act of naming? If we think of defining the words 'NN', 'three', 'table', 'red', 'square', and so on, by pointing to an appropriate object and repeating the name, then it is clear that what counts as 'going on to talk about' these things – the technique of using the name – will be very different in each case. In one case the name is used only for one particular object; in another it can be used in connection with any kind of object provided it belongs to a group with a certain number of members; in another it is used in connection with a kind of object; in another it is used in connection with a particular quality of an object that can be possessed by objects of different kinds; and so on. How does an initial act of ostensively defining a name connect with these quite different linguistic techniques? In picturing naming as like applying a label to a thing we are focusing on one central case – the case of naming people or things – and overlooking the complexity that is inherent in our language-games; it is only when we turn our attention to language in use that we begin to see our original picture as a misleading over-simplification.

Wittgenstein does not dispute that we can ostensively define 'a proper name, the name of a colour, the name of a material, a numeral, the name of a point of the compass, and so on' (*PI* 28), but given the clear differences between the linguistic techniques – the application – involved in each case, a question arises over the connection between the ostensive definition (which takes the form of pointing and saying a word in all cases) and the technique of using the word defined. It is not that Wittgenstein is suggesting that ostensive definitions are in some way out of order – 'The definition of the number two, "That is called 'two'" – pointing to two nuts – is perfectly exact' (*PI* 28) – but, as a means to countering our tendency to form a false or over-simplified picture of naming, he wants us to look more carefully at what is actually involved in defining the number two in this way:

> But how can two be defined like that? The person one gives the definition to doesn't know what one wants to call "two"; he will suppose that "two" is the name given to *this* group of nuts! – He *may* suppose this; but perhaps he does not. He might make the opposite mistake; when I want to assign a name to this group of nuts, he might understand it as a numeral. And he might equally well take the name of a person, of which I give an ostensive definition, as that of a colour, of a race, or even of a point of the compass.
>
> (*PI* 28)

The act of pointing and saying a word leaves the technique of using the word open. There are lots of different techniques that constitute going on to talk about the thing named, and the act of ostensive definition leaves it open *which* of these language-games is in question. 'That is to say: an ostensive definition can be variously interpreted in *every* case' (*PI* 28). We might object here that the role of the word we are ostensively defining can be made clear by our saying, e.g., 'This *number* is called "two"', 'This *colour* is called "sepia"', and so on. The words 'number' and 'colour' can serve to show 'what place in language, in grammar, we assign to the word' (*PI* 29); that is, it makes the role of the word we are defining clear: it is used as the name of a number, or as the name of a colour, and so on. However, this doesn't settle our original question of the connection between the act of naming and the language-game in which we go on to apply the word defined. For our current response depends upon our having already mastered other linguistic techniques, and the same question arises concerning the connection between the definition of these words and the application that is made of them. How did we define these words? And couldn't these definitions be variously interpreted?

It is gradually becoming clear that we have no very clear idea of what is involved in teaching someone something's name. The fact that ostensive definitions frequently succeed in defining a word, and the fact that where misunderstandings arise, they can always be ruled out by using a word that makes the intended role of the word defined clear, only serves to make the whole process look much simpler than it is. But how do we know whether an ostensive definition has succeeded or not? How do we know whether it is enough to say, 'This is called "two"', pointing to two nuts, or whether we need to say, 'This *number* is called "two"'? It depends, Wittgenstein suggests, 'on whether without it the other person takes the definition otherwise than I wish. And that will depend on the circumstances under which it is given, and on the person I give it to' (*PI* 29). But how do I know whether someone has taken a definition 'as I wish'? Wittgenstein goes on: 'And how he "takes" the definition is seen in the use that he makes of the word defined' (*PI* 29). It is not what happens when he hears the definition, but what happens afterwards – the use that he goes on to make of the word defined – that shows how the pupil takes the definition. How someone means, or understands, a definition is not a matter of what goes on in his mind when he gives, or hears, it, but is fixed by the way the act of definition embeds in the structure of his wider linguistic performance.

However, this still leaves open the question of what has to be the case in order for someone to understand a definition. Supposing we accept that an ostensive definition can succeed in indicating the use of a word when 'the overall role of the word in the language is clear' (*PI* 30). There is still a question about what is involved in the role of a word's 'being clear'. We still have no very clear idea of what is involved in knowing the role of a word: 'One has already to know (or be able to do) something in order to be capable of asking a thing's name. But what does one have to know?' (*PI* 30). To help us answer this question, Wittgenstein looks at what might put someone in a position to understand the definition 'This is the king', as it is given in connection with learning to play the game of chess. He presents two sorts of example in which the background necessary to understand the definition is present. In the first case, someone has had the rules and the purpose of the game explained to him, perhaps with the help of diagrams. He has mastered these rules and is now taught which shaped piece is, or plays the role of, the king. In the second case, someone has learnt the rules of chess simply by watching and by practising, without ever having learnt the rules explicitly. If he is now presented with a set of chessmen of an unusual shape, he too might understand the definition 'This is the king'. In both cases, the ostensive definition succeeds because the pupil possesses a practical mastery of the rules of chess, so that 'the place' of the king in the overall practice of playing the game is already mastered or understood.

This clearly offers an analogy with the case of ostensively defining the words of a language. 'The shapes of the chessmen correspond here to the sound or shape of a word' (*PI* 31). It is, in other words, when someone is already master of the practice of employing the techniques that constitute our language-games that he is in a position to understand an ostensive definition, or equally, to ask for something's name. 'What colour is this?', 'What number comes after eleven?', 'Who is that?', and so on, all presuppose a mastery of the technique of naming colours, of counting, and of giving people proper names, respectively. The same practical mastery is presupposed in understanding 'This (colour) is called "red"', 'This (number) is called "two"', or 'This (man) is Ludwig Wittgenstein'. Given this practical mastery of linguistic techniques, we might go into a foreign country and learn the language of its inhabitants by means of ostensive definitions. We could use the practical mastery of our own language in understanding, or sometimes in guessing, the meaning of words that the native speakers ostensively define. Sometimes these guesses will be right, and sometimes they will be wrong, and what shows this is whether we actually go on to *use* the words defined in accordance with their role in the language-game of the native speakers.

Wittgenstein suggests that Augustine describes the child's learning its first language as if it was a foreigner coming into a strange country. It does not yet understand the language of the inhabitants of this strange country, but it is already master of the linguistic techniques that comprise the practical ability to use language: 'as if it already had a language, only not this one. Or again, as if the child could already *think* only not yet speak. And "think" would mean something like "talk to itself"' (*PI* 32). Any sense that the account of language acquisition that Augustine presents somehow *explains* how we learn language is thus shown to be an illusion. For the picture actually presupposes what it purports to explain, by assuming that the child possesses a mastery of the techniques that provide the necessary background to its understanding what is meant when an adult points and utters a sound. Augustine presents a picture of the phenomenon of language-acquisition that appeals to us only because the practical skills involved in using language are so familiar that we simply take them for granted in our overall account. What we don't see is that it is the very skills which our account takes for granted that are really in need of an attentive, careful description; we come to understand how our language functions, not by means of a speculative model of language acquisition, but by paying attention to what is actually involved in a speaker's acquiring a mastery of the practical ability to use language.

Suppose someone objects here that the child does not need to be a master of linguistic techniques in order to understand an ostensive definition, but simply needs to *guess* what the person giving the definition is pointing to. If the child guesses what the person giving the definition is pointing to, then this will fix what it is 'to go on and talk about' the thing that the name picks out; that is, it will fix the role of the name in the language-game. Wittgenstein tries to show, however, that we are tempted to say this only because we have an over-simple picture of what is involved in pointing to something. We don't see, for example, the complexity involved in the distinction between pointing to an object, pointing to its shape, pointing to its colour, and so on. Wittgenstein asks: 'And what does "pointing to the shape", "pointing to the colour" consist in? Point to a piece of paper. – And now point to its shape – now its colour – now its number (that sounds queer). – How did you do it?' (*PI* 33). Here, as before, we are tempted to answer this question by appeal to something that goes on in our minds while we point; we naturally think that it is what accompanies the act of pointing to the piece of paper that determines whether I am pointing to its shape, or to its colour, or to its number, and so on: 'You will say that you "meant" a different thing each time you pointed. And if I ask how that is done, you will say that you concentrated your attention on the colour, the shape, etc.' (*PI* 33). We have provided here a picture that satisfies us, that seems to answer the question that Wittgenstein has raised, but he goes on: 'But I ask again: how is *that* done?' (*PI* 33). How do I concentrate my attention on the colour rather than on the shape?

Wittgenstein does not dispute that there is such a thing as concentrating on the colour rather than on the shape of an object. Someone might, for example, point to a vase and say, ' "Look at that marvellous blue – the shape isn't the point." ' (*PI* 33). Equally, someone might say, ' "Look at that marvellous shape – the colour doesn't matter." ' (*PI* 33). And no doubt we will do something different in response to each of these instructions. However, does what we do in each case constitute what it *is* to concentrate on (or point to, or mean) the colour rather than the shape? Wittgenstein asks us to imagine a number of different cases in which we direct our attention to the colour of an object:

> Comparing two patches of blue to see if they are the same.
> Drawing someone's attention to the fact that the sky is beginning to show patches of blue.
> Asking someone to bring you the blue book from the table.
> Telling someone what a blue signal light means.
> Asking what a particular shade of blue is called.

Looking at the different effects that two shades of blue have in a particular context.

In all these cases we do something that is properly called attending to the colour, but *what* we do may be different in each case. In one case we might put up our hands to keep the outline from view, or we might simply glance in the direction indicated, or we might hold one patch of colour up against another, or we might stare at the colour and wonder where we had seen it before, or we might simply say something to ourselves, and so on. Any of these things might happen *while* we direct our attention to the colour, 'but', Wittgenstein suggests, 'it isn't these things themselves that make us say someone is attending to the shape, the colour, and so on' (*PI* 33). But then what is it that will make us say this?

Here Wittgenstein introduces an analogy with chess. We don't make a move in chess simply by moving a piece in such-and-such a way on the board. No more do we make a move simply because we have certain thoughts and feelings as we move the piece. Rather, moving a piece on a board constitutes a move in chess only 'in the circumstances that we call "playing a game of chess", "solving a problem in chess", and so on' (*PI* 33). Again, Wittgenstein is directing our attention away from what accompanies the move to the context or circumstances in which the act occurs; it is what happens before and afterwards, rather than anything that accompanies my act, that constitutes what I do as a move in chess. By analogy, it is what happens before and afterwards, rather than what happens while I attend to the colour of an object, that constitutes what I do as attending to (pointing at, meaning) the colour rather than the shape.

Suppose that it is the case that someone does always do and feel the very same thing when he points to the shape of an object. 'And suppose [he] give[s] someone else the ostensive definition "That is called a 'circle'"', pointing to a circular object and having all these experiences' (*PI* 34). And suppose the person to whom he gives the definition sees what he does and shares the feelings. Does it follow from this that he has understood the definition as it was meant? Can't we imagine that all this is true, and that he still interprets the definition differently, 'even though he sees the other's eyes following the outline, and even though he feels what the other feels' (*PI* 34). For how the person hearing the definition interprets it is shown by *the application* that he makes of it, by the language-game within which he goes on to use the word defined, and not by the feelings or experiences that accompany his hearing of the definition. How the hearer interprets the definition is shown by what he goes on to do when asked, for example, to 'point to a circle'; it is the role that he gives to the word that shows how he interprets or understands it:

> For neither the expression "to intend the definition in such-and-such a way" nor the expression "to interpret the definition in such-and-such a way" stands for a process which accompanies the giving and the hearing of the definition.

> (*PI* 34)

There are, of course, characteristic experiences associated with pointing to the shape, or pointing to the colour, but these experiences do not occur in all cases in which I mean the shape, or mean the colour. Moreover, even if these characteristic experiences did occur in all cases, they would still not be what makes something a case of pointing to the shape, or pointing to the colour. It is the *circumstances* or *context* – e.g. the fact that we are doing geometry, or that we are learning about the use of colour in painting, or that we are learning to fit the right piece into different shaped holes, etc. – that determines whether someone is pointing to the shape, or pointing to the colour. We learn the language-game 'Point to a chair', 'Point to a table', etc. by learning to respond to these orders by *behaving* in a particular way. But how do we learn to point to the shape, or to point to the colour, of an object? Do we get the child to attend to the experiences and feelings that it has while it is pointing? If we are inclined to think we do, then we should ask ourselves whether we get the child to attend to the characteristic experiences of 'pointing to a piece in a game *as a piece in a game*'? Yet one can say: ' "I mean this *piece* is called the 'king', not this particular bit of wood I am pointing to." ' (*PI* 35). We only get out of the muddle when we look at the act of pointing within its context. Then we can see that the significance of a particular act of pointing is fixed, not by what accompanies it, but by what surrounds it, by the form of the activity of which it is a part.

Wittgenstein diagnoses the temptation to look for an explanation of the difference between these different acts of pointing in some internal difference hidden within the mind of the speaker as follows:

> And we do here what we do in a host of similar cases: because we cannot specify any *one* bodily action which we call pointing to the shape (as opposed, for example, to the colour), we say that a *spiritual* (mental, intellectual) activity corresponds to these words. Where our language suggests a body and there is none: there, we should like to say, is a spirit.
>
> (*PI* 36)

When we cannot point to something in the public world of behaviour that distinguishes these two different acts of pointing to the shape or pointing to the colour, then we naturally form a picture of something internal that accompanies behaviour and constitutes it as one act or the other. When the difference doesn't lie in what the physical body does, it must lie in what the internal or mental 'body' does, that is, in the state of an internal mechanism. What Wittgenstein has tried to show us is, on the one hand, that there is nothing corresponding to this picture of distinct internal states for each of the distinct possibilities that our language-game presents (pointing to the shape, pointing to the colour, pointing to a piece in a game as a piece in a game, pointing to an official as an official, to a make of car as a make of car, and so on). And on the other, that even supposing we could find characteristic mental accompaniments for each of these possibilities, these could not ground the distinctions we're interested in. Against this temptation to hypothesize an internal ground for these distinctions, therefore, he points to the structure that is revealed when we view the physical act of pointing within the field of behaviour that surrounds it. The distinctions of structure that were absent in the physical act of pointing emerge clearly when we see the act in its context; the act together with the context of behaviour already possesses all the structure we need to distinguish pointing to the shape and pointing to the colour. The empty picture of a distinct internal something accompanying these acts proves to be superfluous. Reminding ourselves of how we actually use the expressions 'pointing to the shape', 'pointing to the colour', etc. reveals the real nature of the phenomenon: The essence of the distinction lies in a structure that can be discerned in what a speaker does over time, and not in anything that happens while he points.

Everything lies open to view

Wittgenstein has now explored a wide range of different examples as a means of presenting a critique of Augustine's picture of language. It is clear that this critique goes much deeper than a simple questioning of specific claims that Augustine makes. It touches, rather, the whole style of thinking about language that Augustine adopts. What is fundamentally at issue is the question of how we approach the problem of understanding the structure and function of language. Augustine approaches language as a system of signs whose capacity to represent requires elucidation in a theory that tells us what meaning consists in. It is not merely that Wittgenstein believes that the theories which Augustine presents are wrong in their details, but that in the very first step of abstracting language from its application Augustine situates himself towards it in a way that makes it impossible for him to achieve the understanding he seeks. In thinking about language as a system of signs, abstracted from its use within the ordinary lives of speakers, Augustine turns away from 'the spatial and temporal phenomenon of language' (*PI* 108) and towards an abstract phantasm. In this act of turning away from the practice of using language, Augustine inevitably loses sight of the way language actually functions, and is led into picturing language's ability to represent as 'some remarkable act of mind' (*PI* 38). Thus we are led to look for explanations of the phenomena of understanding, meaning, meaning one thing rather than another, and so on in the realm of the mind, or in what accompanies the actual use of words. The particular examples that Wittgenstein uses to counter these temptations to peel language off from our form of life, and to connect it with what is occurring in the mind of speakers, are not intended to form the basis of an alternative account of what meaning (or naming, or understanding) is. Rather, these examples are used as a means to recognizing, on the one hand, how false the pictures of language that we've constructed are, and on the other, that the concepts of language and linguistic mastery are not to be explicated by reference to hidden accompaniments to the use of words, but are essentially tied up with the idea of a distinctive pattern of behaviour or form of life.

It is essential to Wittgenstein's aim of resisting what he sees as the false abstraction and the mistaken explanatory ambitions of Augustine's approach that we do not attempt to present his objections to Augustine in the form of a theory about what constitutes the essence of language. Any attempt to derive theoretical elucidations from Wittgenstein's remarks is clearly at odds with the central idea that the value of the particular cases he describes lies in their ability to persuade us that 'everything lies open to view' (*PI* 126), and to overcome our sense that there is something which needs to be explained. Attention to the details of particular instances of language in use allows us to see that it is by seeing what lies on the surface in the right way that we achieve the understanding of what puzzles us. The whole point of Wittgenstein's opposition to Augustine's approach to language lies in his using particular cases to show that there is no need to speculate about the hidden accompaniments to the use of language in order to understand how language functions; we have simply to look and see how it functions. Thus, in all the topics we've covered, Wittgenstein shows that it is through achieving a clear view of the manifest workings of a particular concrete case, or range of concrete cases, that we arrive at the understanding we are seeking. To achieve his aim of overcoming, not merely particular doctrines, but Augustine's whole style of thought, Wittgenstein tries to show how the discernible structures of our practice of using language already reveal everything that we need to resolve the questions that puzzle us. This accounts both for the piecemeal nature of his critique and for his repeated refusal to be drawn into using his examples and analogies as the basis for constructing a general theory. The lesson of the individual investigations he has undertaken lies in our seeing that it is in the details of the concrete phenomenon of language-use that the structure and function of a particular piece of our language is revealed, and not in anything that lies hidden within the minds of those who speak it. In the next chapter we will see how this same underlying theme of reorientation, away from explanatory models or elucidations, towards a concern with what lies open to view is continued in Wittgenstein's discussion of rules and rule-following.

References and further reading

St Augustine, *Confessions* (Harmondsworth: Penguin, 1961).

Baker, G., *Wittgenstein, Frege and the Vienna Circle* (Oxford: Blackwell, 1988).

Baker, G. and Hacker, P. M. S., *Wittgenstein: Understanding and Meaning* (Oxford: Blackwell, 1983).

Birsch, D. and Dorbolo, J., 'Working with Wittgenstein's Builders', *Philosophical Investigations*, vol. 13, 1990.

Cavell, S., 'The Availability of Wittgenstein's Later Philosophy', in G. Pitcher, ed., *Wittgenstein: The* Philosophical Investigations (New York: Doubleday, 1966).

—— *Philosophical Passages* (Oxford: Blackwell, 1995).

Fogelin, R., *Wittgenstein* (London: Routledge, 1987).

Gaita, R., 'Language and Conversation: Wittgenstein's Builders', in A. Phillips Griffiths, ed., *Wittgenstein Centenary Essays* (Cambridge: Cambridge University Press, 1992).

Goldfarb, W. D., 'I Want You To Bring Me A Slab: Remarks on the Opening Sections of the *Philosophical Investigations*', *Synthèse*, vol. 26, 1983.

Hertzberg, L., 'Language, Philosophy and Natural History', in L. Hertzberg, *The Limits of Experience*, *Acta Philosophica Fennica*, vol. 56, 1994.

Kenny, A., *Wittgenstein* (Harmondsworth: Penguin, 1973).

—— *The Legacy of Wittgenstein* (Oxford: Blackwell, 1984).

Malcolm, N., *Nothing is Hidden: Wittgenstein's Criticism of his Early Thought* (Oxford: Blackwell, 1986).

—— 'Language Game (2)', in D. Z. Phillips and P. Winch, eds, *Wittgenstein: Attention to Particulars* (London: Macmillan, 1989).

Pears, D. F., *The False Prison*, vol. 2 (Oxford: Oxford University Press, 1987).

Rhees, R., 'Wittgenstein's Builders', in K. T. Fann, ed., *Ludwig Wittgenstein: The Man and his Philosophy* (Hassocks: Harvester Press, 1978).

Staten, H., *Wittgenstein and Derrida* (London: University of Nebraska Press, 1986).

Thompkins, E. F., 'The Money and the Cow', *Philosophy*, vol. 67, 1992.

Walker, M., 'Augustine's Pretence: Another Reading of Wittgenstein's *Philosophical Investigations*', *Philosophical Investigations*, vol. 13, 1990.

Chapter 3

Rules and
rule-following
Philosophical
Investigations
138–242

Introduction

After a number of detailed criticisms of the *Tractatus*, focusing on his early view of names and the determinacy of sense (*PI* 37–88), and the remarks on his philosophical method (*PI* 89–133), Wittgenstein takes up again the question of the connection between a name and its application, which we began to look at in the section on 'Ostensive definition' in the previous chapter. In *PI* 138, Wittgenstein asks us in what sense the meaning of a word (what is grasped in coming to understand it, or in hearing it and understanding it) can 'fit' the use that a speaker subsequently makes of the word. We sometimes speak of the meaning of a word being grasped 'in a flash', or of understanding a word *when* we hear it. This might naturally lead us to picture meaning as something that can be grasped by the mind in an instant. The use that a speaker makes of a word is, by contrast, something extended in time,

something that happens *after* he has heard the word and understood it. Yet, as we saw earlier, how someone goes on to use a word is a criterion of what he means by it; it reveals, for example, whether he means a word he ostensively defines as the name of the shape, the colour, the number, etc. of the object he points to. How does this criterion connect with the idea that meaning is something that can be grasped in an instant, or in a flash? For 'what we grasp [in a flash] is surely something different from the "use" which is extended in time!' (*PI* 138).

This question marks the beginning of a discussion that circles and loops around the topics of meaning, rules and understanding, more or less without a break, until *PI* 242. The discussion here is as complex and elusive as any in the *Investigations*, and there is an enormous temptation to suppose that Wittgenstein's remarks do not as they stand clearly reveal his thoughts on these topics, but offer us merely rough sketches that are in need of systematic arrangement into clearly stated theses and arguments in support of them. The attempt to rewrite these sections of the *Investigations* was undertaken by Saul Kripke in *Wittgenstein on Rules and Private Language* (1982). Kripke's book offers an inspired reading of Wittgenstein's elusive remarks, which in its power and clarity still provides a uniquely accessible route to engaging with Wittgenstein's text. Kripke himself expresses doubts as to whether his bold, clearly formulated arguments and claims would be approved by Wittgenstein, and as to whether they don't in some way falsify Wittgenstein's philosophical purpose. He presents his book, therefore, not as an exposition of Wittgenstein's argument, but of 'Wittgenstein's argument as it struck Kripke, as it presented a problem for him' (p. 5).

The power and importance of Kripke's book lies, in part, in the fact that he detects something extremely radical in Wittgenstein's remarks about meaning, rules and understanding. He sees Wittgenstein as posing a fundamental challenge to some of our most cherished philosophical ideas on these topics. In presenting this alleged challenge in a clear and compelling way, Kripke helped establish the importance of Wittgenstein's text for contemporary philosophy of language. He describes the challenge as 'a new form of scepticism' (p. 60). Behind Wittgenstein's wide-ranging and elusive remarks on meaning, understanding and rules, Kripke detects an entirely novel form of sceptical argument that allegedly establishes that there is no fact, either in my mind or in my external behaviour, that constitutes my meaning something by the words I utter, or that fixes what will count as a correct application of a rule that I grasp. The conclusion of this sceptical argument – that no one can ever mean anything by their words, or be following a rule that fixes what counts as a correct or an incorrect application of it – is clearly deeply paradoxical, and it is impossible that anyone should rest content with it. Kripke suggests that Wittgenstein's response to it is to present a *sceptical solution* – i.e. one that accepts the truth of the sceptical conclusion – to the problem that it poses about meaning and rule-following.

Kripke on Wittgenstein and rule-following

Let us begin by presenting the sceptical argument that Kripke finds in Wittgenstein. It is very natural to suppose that in learning to add I grasped the rule for addition in such a way that my intention to follow this rule in the future will determine a unique answer to subsequent addition problems in indefinitely many new cases. In particular, it is natural to suppose that when I respond '125' to the question '68 + 57 = ?', I am acting in conformity with my previous intention to use '+' in accordance with the rule for addition. My previous intention to mean addition by '+' determines '125' as the *correct* answer, as the answer I *should* give, even though I have never explicitly considered this particular case before, and even though I have never before added any number greater than 56.

The question that now arises is just what it is about my previous intention concerning the sign '+' that constitutes it as the intention to use this sign in accordance with the rule for addition. What, in other words, makes it the case that I meant addition by '+'? Or to put the same question another way, what is there about my previous intention that rules out the possibility that I actually intended to use '+' in such a way that the correct answer to '68 + 57 = ?' is actually '5', so that in answering '125' I have actually changed what I mean by '+'? It is, after all, agreed that I never explicitly gave myself any instruction concerning this particular sum, and that the sum involves numbers that are higher than any that I have previously added. At best, I intended to go on using '+' in the same way, or to apply the same function in each new case, but the question is what counts as the same here. For the sceptic can point out that I have only ever given myself a finite number of examples manifesting this function, which have all involved numbers less than 57, and that this finite number of examples is compatible with my meaning any one of an infinite number of functions by '+'. There is, for example, nothing to rule out that I intended to use 'plus' and '+' to denote a function which Kripke calls 'quus' and symbolizes by '⊕', and which is defined as follows:

$$x \oplus y = \quad x + y, \text{ if } x, y < 57$$
$$= \quad 5 \text{ otherwise}$$

If the sceptic is right, then there is no fact about my past intention, or about my past performance, that establishes, or constitutes, my meaning one function rather than another by '+'. Kripke's next step is to show that, this much established, the sceptic's argument must now inevitably become more general. For if there is no fact about my past intention or behaviour that determines which function I meant by '+', then there is equally no fact about my present intention or my present behaviour that establishes which function I now mean by '+'. The sceptical problem that finally emerges, therefore, is that one cannot give any content whatever to the notion of meaning one function or another by '+', either now or in the past. The concept of meaning or intending one function rather than another has been shown to make no sense. There is, therefore, nothing that makes it the case that I should answer '125', rather than '5', to the question '68 + 57 = ?', and nothing that justifies me in answering one way rather than the other. Every possible answer is compatible with some possible function, and thus the idea of any answer being the correct answer becomes completely idle or empty.

Kripke quickly scotches any idea that we can escape this sceptical problem by constructing an instruction that specifies, in terms of other rules, how the rule for addition is to be applied in new cases, e.g. by using the rule for counting to give an algorithm for addition. The problem is that whatever further rule I employ in giving myself an instruction about the rule for addition, there will always be a question as to how this further rule is itself to be applied. There will, Kripke suggests, always be a way of interpreting the additional rule that will bring its application into conformity with any possible interpretation of the original rule. Rules for interpreting rules don't get us any further. Nor is this problem restricted to the mathematical case. For any word in my language, we can come up with alternative interpretations of what I mean by it that are compatible with both my past usage and any explicit instruction that I might have given myself. Kripke sums up the sceptical argument as follows:

> This, then, is the sceptical paradox. When I respond in one way rather than another to such a problem as '68 + 57', I can have no justification for one response rather than another. Since the sceptic who supposes that I meant quus cannot be answered, there is no fact about me that distinguishes between my meaning plus and my meaning quus. Indeed, there is no fact about me that distinguishes between my meaning a definite function by 'plus' (which determines my responses in new cases) and my meaning nothing at all.

> (1982, p. 21)

Kripke calls what he believes to be Wittgenstein's way out of this paradox a 'sceptical solution' to it, and his point in so calling it is that he believes that Wittgenstein's account of rule-following begins by conceding to the sceptic that there is no fact about me that constitutes my meaning addition by 'plus', and which determines in advance what I should do to accord with this meaning. The intolerable paradox that this appears to create arises, Kripke suggests, only because we mistakenly insist upon construing the meaning of 'I mean addition by "+" ' on the model of a *truth-conditions* conception of meaning, i.e. one that assumes that the meaning of a sentence is given by a condition that specifies what must be the case in order for it to be *true*. For if we assume that the meaning of a sentence is given by its truth-conditions, then it would follow from the sceptic's discovery that there is no fact about me which distinguishes my meaning something specific by a word from my meaning nothing at all, and that any sentence of the form 'A means ... by "−"' is at best false, and at worst meaningless. Wittgenstein's claim, according to Kripke, is that we can avoid this paradox, while accepting the sceptic's conclusion that there is no fact, inside or out, that constitutes my meaning something by a word, provided we adopt an *assertability-condition* model of meaning, i.e. one that assumes that the meaning of a sentence is given by the conditions under which it can be *asserted*.

Thus Kripke sees Wittgenstein's response to the sceptical paradox as turning upon his moving from a truth-conditions account of meaning (such as he held in the *Tractatus*) to an account of meaning based on assertability conditions. In the *Investigations*, Kripke claims, Wittgenstein holds that there are two aspects to a sentence's meaning. First of all, there must be conditions under which the sentence is appropriately asserted (or denied); secondly, this practice of asserting (and denying) the sentence must play a significant role in our everyday lives. The first part of this account is familiar, for example, from the verificationist account of meaning put forward by the logical positivists. Kripke believes that it is the second part of the account – the emphasis on the role that the assertion of the sentence plays in our lives – that is original and distinctive to Wittgenstein. What is needed, on this account, to give meaning to assertions of the form 'I mean addition by "+"', 'Jones means addition by "+"', etc. is that 'there be roughly specifiable circumstances under which they are legitimately assertable, and that the game of asserting them under such conditions has a role in our lives' (Kripke, 1982, p. 78). The paradoxical, self-defeating consequences of the sceptic's discovery are avoided, on this account of meaning, insofar as 'no supposition that "facts correspond" to those assertions is needed' (p. 78).

The account of our language-game that Kripke now finds in the *Investigations* involves an asymmetry between first-person and third-person attributions of meaning. According to Kripke, Wittgenstein holds that it is part of our language-game that a speaker may, without any justification, follow his own confident inclination to respond in one way rather than another to each new occasion of applying a rule for the use of a word. If we confine ourselves to looking at one person in isolation, then the lesson of the sceptical argument is that this is all there is to be said. There is no fact about an individual considered in isolation that makes his brute responses as to how the rule is to be applied in each new case correct or incorrect. 'All we can say, if we consider a single person in isolation, is that our ordinary practice licenses him to apply the rule in the way it strikes him' (Kripke, 1982, p. 88).

The normative element – i.e. the distinction between a correct and incorrect use of a word or application of a rule – that is an essential part of our ordinary concept of meaning or rule-following only enters in when we consider the individual in relation to the wider community of speakers. The assertability condition for my asserting that *another* speaker means addition by '+' turns on whether the other's responses to particular addition problems agree with those that I am inclined to give, or, if our responses occasionally disagree, if I can interpret the other as at least following the proper procedure. In circumstances in which the other's responses diverge inexplicably from my own, I will deny that he has mastered the rule for addition, or that he means addition by '+'. If the responses of individual speakers generally diverged, then there would, Kripke allows, be little point to this practice of attributing meaning to others. However, the brute fact is that human beings are (roughly) in harmony when it comes to working out the answer to new addition problems, and this background of agreement in responses gives our language-game its point. Any individual speaker will be deemed to have mastered the concept of addition, or to mean addition by '+', whenever his responses to particular addition problems agree with those of the members of a wider community in a sufficient number of cases. An individual who passes this test will be admitted as a member of the community and trusted to participate in the countless everyday activities that involve the application of this mathematical technique.

Kripke is very careful to emphasize that the account of our language-game that he finds in Wittgenstein is not to be interpreted as yielding a definition of what following a rule correctly consists in. He writes:

> that Wittgenstein's theory is one of assertability conditions deserves emphasis. Wittgenstein's theory should not be confused with a theory that, for any *m* and *n*, the value of the function we mean by 'plus', *is* (by definition) the value that (nearly) all

the linguistic community would give as an answer. Such a theory would be a theory of the *truth* conditions of such assertions as 'By "plus" we mean such-and-such a function' or 'By "plus" we mean a function, which, when applied to 68 and 57 as arguments, yields 125 as value.'

(1982, p. 111)

It is essential to Kripke's idea that Wittgenstein *accepts* the sceptical paradox that he should not be taken as providing an account of what constitutes a particular response's being correct. Wittgenstein is seen as describing our language-game and the role that it plays in our lives, and as acknowledging that the point of our playing this game rests upon the brute, contingent fact of widespread agreement. All that we can say is that in our community we *call* '125' the correct answer to '68 + 57 = ?'; the idea that it *is* the correct answer has been shown to be empty.

Kripke's interpretation of Wittgenstein's remarks on rule-following has been subject to a vast and wide-ranging critical response. Whether there is a sceptical argument to be found in Wittgenstein's remarks, whether it is addressed to the concept of meaning as such rather than to some philosophical theory of meaning (e.g. to the view, sometimes known as Platonism, that meanings are abstract entities that determine or show how a word is to be applied), whether Wittgenstein offers a sceptical solution to the paradox, and whether the account of meaning and rule-following that he puts forward turns on the idea of agreement with a community of language users have all been topics of lively debate. Many commentators are agreed in finding the sceptical solution of the paradox that Kripke attributes to Wittgenstein to be in itself deeply unsatisfactory as an account of concepts of 'meaning' or 'following a rule'. Yet much of this critical commentary on Kripke shares his general sense that we must look behind Wittgenstein's piecemeal and unsystematic remarks for a unified account of what meaning or rule-following consist in. Thus, the temptation to read *PI* 138–242 as offering a theory of meaning and rule-following has provided a framework for a great deal of the discussion that followed on from Kripke's interpretation of these paragraphs.

Some commentators, however, have taken a more radical line against Kripke, by raising the question whether he is warranted in transforming Wittgenstein's wide-ranging remarks into a more or less systematic account of how meaning, or (on Kripke's interpretation) talk about meaning, is possible. John McDowell notes, for example, the tension between this style of interpretation and Wittgenstein's avowed philosophical aims:

> If one reads Wittgenstein as offering a constructive philosophical account of how meaning and understanding are possible, appealing to human interactions conceived as describable in terms that do not presuppose meaning and understanding, one flies in the face of his explicit view that philosophy embodies no doctrine, no substantive claims.
>
> (McDowell, 1992, p. 51)

Gordon Baker has also identified the need to read Wittgenstein's remarks as achieving a resolution of the tangle of philosophical problems that surround the concepts of meaning, rules and understanding by doing something *other* than provide a *theory* of what meaning or rule-following consist in:

> Wittgenstein thought that all of [his] observations are uncontroversial descriptions of familiar aspects of our practice of explaining and using the expressions 'a rule' and 'to follow a rule'. Together they were meant to give an *Übersicht* (overview) of what it is to follow a rule. To the extent that this attempt succeeds, it is an achievement as positive as the construction of any theory of rule following. By eliminating the illusion that anything stands in need of theoretical explanation, it pre-empts the place occupied by any possible theory of rule-following.
>
> (pp. 57–8)

The interpretation of *PI* 138–242 that follows is very much in sympathy with this more radical rejection of Kripke's approach. Although Kripke's interpretation provides an inspired reading of Wittgenstein's text, I believe that his intuition that his clear formulation of a sceptical argument, and his construction of a philosophical analysis of the concept of rule-following, are in some way at odds with Wittgenstein's philosophical aims is more or less correct. In transforming Wittgenstein's remarks into the articulation of a clear philosophical problem and its solution, Kripke inevitably erases all trace of the idea of a grammatical investigation, which I have suggested is the key to how to read Wittgenstein's work. By ignoring Wittgenstein's conception of the techniques and aims of his philosophical method, and by imposing an alien structure on Wittgenstein's remarks, Kripke loses contact with the real nature of Wittgenstein's response to what are essentially *philosophical* preconceptions about language, rules, meaning and understanding.

The connection between meaning and use

On Kripke's interpretation of him, Wittgenstein's investigation of rule-following begins in a philosophical argument that runs counter to our everyday experience of language. Faced with a sceptical argument of his own devising, Wittgenstein is seen as seeking to preserve our ordinary practice from the impact of this argument, by showing that our practice can exist *despite* the truth of what the sceptic discovers. Wittgenstein is held to achieve this aim by adopting a theory of meaning with a verificationist core, which directs us to abandon the futile search for truth-conditions and look instead for conditions under which sentences attributing meaning are asserted. Kripke then commits Wittgenstein to offering, on the basis of this general theory of meaning, an analysis of what we actually mean by 'I mean addition by "+"', 'Jones means addition by "+"', etc. that shows that we are in fact asserting nothing that the sceptic denies. The end of Wittgenstein's investigation, therefore, is a philosophical account of ordinary practice that enables us to see how it is possible, even though there is nothing that constitutes the meaning of our words. It is not merely that Kripke commits Wittgenstein to an account that seems to deny something vital to our ordinary conception of our language, but the structure of the argument he constructs is fundamentally at odds with Wittgenstein's conception of philosophical method and of how his philosophy stands in relation to our ordinary practice.

Let us return, then, to the issue that Wittgenstein raises in *PI* 138: what is the connection between the act of grasping the meaning of a word (of hearing a word and understanding it) and the use that is subsequently made of it? How can what I grasp in an instant connect with a use that is extended in time? Is it that the whole use somehow comes before my mind in an instant, when I hear a word and understand it in this way? But how can the whole use of a word come before my mind? Is it that what comes before my mind *fits* a particular use? These questions are clearly similar in form to those that Wittgenstein raised earlier on a wide range of topics. For example, how does someone say 'Slab!' and mean 'Bring me a slab'? How does someone mean 'Five slabs' as a report rather than an order? How do we give something a name? How do we teach someone a name? How do we point to the shape rather than the colour of an object? And so on. All these questions were intended to counter a philosophical tendency to misrepresent, or over-simplify, or take for granted some aspect of the way our language functions. These questions mark the beginning of a careful examina-tion of what is actually involved in these aspects of our practice, which aims, by focusing on the details of individual concrete cases, both to free us from our misrepresentations and achieve the under-standing we seek. In the same way, the question that Wittgenstein raises in *PI* 138 marks the beginning of a grammatical investigation designed to counter a temptation to misunderstand the relation between understanding and use and to achieve a clear idea of what is actually involved in 'grasping the meaning of a word', or in 'hearing a word and understanding it'.

Wittgenstein begins the investigation of the phenomenon of understanding by asking us to imagine the particular case of hearing and understanding the word 'cube' when someone says it to us. He asks us to reflect on what does actually come before my mind when I hear and understand the word 'cube' in this way. Perhaps, he suggests, what comes before my mind is a schematic drawing of a cube. Now the question is how does the schematic drawing that comes before my mind connect with the use that I go on to make of the word 'cube'. The interlocutor replies: ' "It's quite simple; – if that picture occurs to me and I point to a triangular prism for instance, and say it is a cube, then this use doesn't fit the picture"' (*PI* 139). Wittgenstein responds: 'Doesn't it fit? I have purposely so chosen the example that it is quite easy to imagine a *method of projection* according to which the picture does fit after all' (*PI* 139).

On Kripke's interpretation, we should view this as an instance of Wittgenstein's alleged sceptical argument. Yet it is striking how different the form of Wittgenstein's remark is from an argument to a general sceptical conclusion. He points out, for example, that he has 'purposely . . . chosen the example' so that we can quite easily imagine a way of projecting it that is different from the one that first strikes us. There is an implicit suggestion, therefore, that whatever temptation to misunderstand he is interested in, it is one that can be illuminated by looking carefully at *this particular case*. There is, on the other hand, no suggestion that he wishes to use the example as the basis for making a novel and *general* claim that whatever comes before my mind when I hear a word and understand it can always be interpreted in different ways. No general conclusion is at issue, for the example is being used in a quite different way. When I ask myself the question about the connection between what comes before my mind and the use that I go on to make of a word, there is a great temptation to misunderstand or misrepresent the nature of this link. Thus I am inclined to think that the picture of a schematic cube that comes before my mind when I hear and understand the word 'cube' is such that it *cannot* be applied to anything but a cube. Wittgenstein has purposely chosen the example, so that when we look carefully at this particular case we can quite easily see that this initial sense that the picture itself somehow imposes a particular use on us is quite empty. For when I reflect on matters, I see that it is quite easy to imagine another method of projecting the picture, e.g. one by which it fits a triangular prism.

Thus what the example of the word 'cube' shows us is that although 'the picture of the cube did indeed *suggest* a certain use to us . . . it was possible for me to use it differently' (*PI* 139). But then what picture of the connection between the picture and the use did I have that made me overlook this possibility of an alternative application? Was it a picture, Wittgenstein asks, that 'we should express by saying: I should have thought the picture *forced* a particular use on me' (*PI* 140, my italics)? But what exactly does this picture amount to: 'Is there such a thing as a picture, or something like a picture, that *forces* a particular application on us?' (*PI* 140, my italics). The point of the example is that we initially think that the picture of a cube is such a picture. When we recognize that there is something else that we would be prepared to call 'applying the picture of a cube', we see that all our idea that a particular use is forced on us amounts to is: 'only the one case and no other occurred to us' (*PI* 140). What is at issue here is not a sceptical argument about whether there is anything that constitutes the meaning of my words, but whether a particular picture I am tempted to form of the connection between what comes before my mind and the use I make of a word – the picture of what comes before my mind 'forcing' a particular use on me – has any real content.

At the end of *PI* 140, Wittgenstein draws the following conclusion:

> What is essential is to see that the same thing can come before our minds when we hear the word and the application still be different. Has it the *same* meaning both times? I think we shall say not.

This is not to be read as the sceptical claim that there is no such fact as the fact that I now mean cube by 'cube'; Wittgenstein is not here presenting us with a sceptical argument. His remark is rather to be read as drawing our attention to an ordinary, or familiar, possibility that we have overlooked, and which reveals the oddness of the picture we are tempted to form of the link between the picture that comes before my mind when I hear and understand the word 'cube' and the application that I go on to make of it. It is by examining the details of this particular case that Wittgenstein tries to counter our temptation to form a mythological picture of the nature of this link. For now we see that the same picture might come before our minds and the application still be different: the picture doesn't, after all, *force* a particular use on us. In the case where the applications are different, it is the use that is made of the word that shows what a speaker means by it, and not what comes before his mind when he hears the word and understands it.

Wittgenstein's interlocutor does not, however, immediately abandon the idea of a picture that forces a particular use on us. Couldn't it be the case, he asks, that, not merely the picture of the cube, but also the method of projecting it comes before my mind when I hear the word and understand it? For example, couldn't a picture come before my mind that shows two cubes connected by lines of projection? If we feel content with this suggestion, isn't it, Wittgenstein suggests, because only one application of this new picture occurs to us? Yet surely someone could describe an application of this picture that is different from the one that I naturally make, just as Wittgenstein did for the original drawing of a cube. So again we find that our sense of a picture's *forcing* a use on us is really no more than an expression of our own inclination to apply the picture in one particular way. We might describe this by saying that *an application of the picture comes before my mind*, but, Wittgenstein warns us, we need 'to get clearer about our application of *this* expression' (*PI* 141). What is it for an application of the picture to come before my mind? What is it for me to mean the picture to be applied in one way rather than another?

To explore this question, Wittgenstein now switches to a different form of grammatical investigation. Instead of looking carefully at what actually goes on in a particular case of hearing a word and understanding it, he asks us to think of how we would explain various methods of projection to someone, and how we would judge whether the projection that we intend comes before his mind. He accepts that we have two different criteria for this: 'on the one hand the picture (of whatever kind) that at some time or other comes before his mind; on the other, the application which – in the course of time – he makes of what he imagines' (*PI* 141). He now asks: 'can there be a collision between a picture and application?' (*PI* 141). Clearly there can. But this is not because the picture *forces* a particular application on us; not because it *cannot* be applied differently from the way we apply it. The possibility of a collision arises simply insofar as 'the picture makes us expect a different use, because people in general apply *this* picture like *this*' (*PI* 141). Wittgenstein goes on: 'I want to say: we have here a *normal* case, and abnormal cases.'

There is clearly no sense of a sceptical climax in the final sentences of *PI* 141. There is no suggestion either that the picture of a cube is unusable or that there is no sense to the notion of a clash between this picture and an application of it. There is rather a recognition that the picture *has* a use – 'people in general apply *this* picture like *this*' – and that it is in virtue of this use of the picture that we can speak of a clash between it and a particular application. On Kripke's interpretation, the dialectic of *PI* 138–41 is between a sceptic about meaning and the voice of untutored common sense. On the current reading, it is between a voice that expresses the temptation to form a mythological picture of the connection between a picture and an application which is made of it and Wittgenstein's therapeutic voice. Wittgenstein's therapeutic voice guides us over the details of a particular, concrete case in such a way that we *both* recognize the oddness – and the emptiness – of our idea of a picture that forces a use on us *and* see that actually 'nothing out of the ordinary is involved'. The connection between a picture and its application, which gives the idea of a clash between picture and application its content, is grounded in the practice of using the picture, in the fact of its having a use, and not in a mysterious power of the picture to *force* a particular use on us.

The dialectic of these paragraphs repeats, therefore, the pattern we saw in the remarks discussed in the previous chapter. As before, Wittgenstein uses the grammatical investigation of a particular concrete case in order to resist a false picture of meaning or understanding that the forms of our language – e.g. 'I grasp the meaning *in a flash*' – tempt us to adopt. He is neither providing an analysis of our ordinary sentences, nor putting forward a theory of meaning that explains how our ordinary language functions. The central idea of his grammatical conception of philosophical method is that the cure for the temptations to misunderstand lies in a careful attention to the detailed structure of our practice of using language. The temptations to misunderstand arise because we are too hasty in constructing what initially seems to us to be a clear picture of how a part of our language functions. What Wittgenstein shows us is that when we come to try to apply our picture to a particular concrete example, it proves unusable. In coming, through a grammatical investigation of particular cases, to a clearer perception of what is actually involved, we begin to recognize, not only the emptiness of our initial idea, but also that everything that we need to understand how this part of our language functions is already there in front of our eyes, observable in the surface structure of our ordinary practice. By comparing our philosophical picture with reality, we begin to see that our urge to *explain* the link between the act of grasping the meaning of a word and the use that is made of it has produced only an empty construction.

Meaning and understanding

The false picture of the connection between what occurs in a speaker's mind when he hears and understands a word and the use that he subsequently makes of it is linked with the following idea: that a speaker's understanding of his language is a form of *mental state* which is the *source* of his ability to go on and use the words of his language correctly. The thought that what comes before a speaker's mind when he hears and understands a word must somehow force a particular application on him is clearly linked with – is one way of giving expression to – this picture of what the state of understanding must consist in. Even if this particular picture of meaning has proved empty, we may still feel that the concept of understanding requires that something like this *must* be the case. To deny it would, it seems, be to claim that our infinite ability to use language cannot be explained in terms of a finite, generative base; it would be to suppose that the difference, between someone who understands a language and someone who does not, does not lie in the presence or absence, respectively, of a finite internal state which is the source of the infinite capacity. In *PI* 138–41 we have seen the beginning of Wittgenstein's attempt to persuade us that this picture of a super-strong connection between what is in the mind when I understand a word and the use that I go on to make of it is nothing more than a mythology that arises in a temptation to misunderstand the forms of our language. The mythological nature of the picture of the link between understanding and use that we construct – as well as the way the concept of understanding actually functions – are only fully revealed, however, through the extended grammatical investigation of this region of our language. This grammatical investigation shows that the concept of understanding functions quite differently from the way our philosophical picture of what understanding must consist in suggests.

What is it, then, that tempts us to picture understanding as a mental state that is the source of correct use? Suppose we are teaching a pupil how to construct different series of numbers according to particular formation rules. When will we say that he has mastered a particular series, say, the series of natural numbers? Clearly, he must be able to produce this series correctly: 'that is, as we do it' (*PI* 145). Wittgenstein points here to a certain vagueness in our criteria for judging that he has mastered the system, in respect of both how often he must get it right and how far he must develop it. This vagueness is something that Wittgenstein sees as a distinctive characteristic of our psychological language-game, one that distinguishes it from the language-game in which we describe mechanical systems. Part of the aim of his grammatical investigation of the differences between psychological language and other regions of our language-game is to get us to accept this vagueness as part of its essence, and not to see it as a sign of the indirectness of our knowledge of another's mental states. We shall explore this point in more detail in Chapter 5. For the moment, Wittgenstein's immediate concern is with the specific temptation to picture understanding as a determinate state lying *behind* the correct use that constitutes a criterion by which we judge a pupil to have mastered the system of natural numbers:

> Perhaps you will say here: to have got the system (or, again, to understand it) can't consist in continuing the series up to *this* or *that* number: *that* is only applying one's understanding. The understanding itself is a state which is the *source* of the correct use.

> (*PI* 146)

Wittgenstein asks us what we are thinking of here. Aren't we thinking once again of the act of understanding as the grasp of something that compels us to apply a word (develop a series) in a particular way? 'But this is where we were before' (*PI* 146). We have already seen that we can give no content to this idea of 'logical compulsion'.

When we tried to apply this picture to a particular concrete case (the picture of the schematic drawing of a cube), we found that it made no connection with anything: the idea that the picture forces a particular use on us was found to be empty. Instead, we found that the possibility of a clash, between the picture and a use that is made of it, depends upon a connection between the picture and a given application that is grounded in the fact that there is a practice of using the picture in a particular way. Insofar as the idea that understanding is 'the *source* of the correct use' is just another expression of the temptation to believe that something comes before the speaker's mind and compels him to use a word in a particular way, it is as empty as our earlier sense that the drawing of a cube forces a particular use on us. The picture of the link between understanding and use is just the same empty notion that Wittgenstein has already shown to have nothing corresponding to it. It may well be that, for example, a formula's coming to mind is a criterion of a pupil's having understood a series, but only because this formula is *used* in a particular way, and not because it is somehow 'the source' of a given series. We have only to reflect that it is quite possible for the appropriate formula to come before a pupil's mind and yet for him still not to understand the series to see once again that our picture of 'logical compulsion' is empty.

The interlocutor now switches to a different source of his sense of a need to picture understanding as a mental state that is the source of correct use:

> When *I* say I understand the rule of a series, I am surely not saying so because I have *found out* that up to now I have applied the algebraic formula in such-and-such a way! In my own case at all events I surely know that I mean such-and-such a series; it doesn't matter how far I have actually developed it.
>
> (*PI* 147)

I don't have to watch what I do in order to know what I mean by a word, or to know which series I am developing. This again suggests that I must grasp something which already anticipates the use that I go on to make of a word. How, if this weren't the case, *could* I know what I mean by a word *before* I actually apply it? Clearly, we do want to say that we know what we mean by a word independently of watching ourselves use it, but the question is, What is the *grammar* of the concept of 'the state of knowing the meaning'? Before undertaking Wittgenstein's grammatical enquiry, we are tempted to connect this concept with the idea of a state that somehow already anticipates my future use of a word, but our reflections on the case of the schematic cube have begun to show that the idea is problematic, that there is nothing corresponding to it. But if this idea is empty, how can I know in my own case that I have understood a word or grasped a rule? We once again seem forced back on the picture of a state that is the source of correct use.

The question of the grammar of the concept of the state of knowing/understanding the meaning of a word brings us to the heart of Wittgenstein's grammatical investigation of this region of our language. The chief purpose of this investigation is that we should become clear about how this particular part of our language functions. It is crucial, therefore, that we pay very careful attention to what Wittgenstein says in these paragraphs (*PI* 148–55). Central to these passages is an attempt to loosen the grip of the picture of understanding as an internal, mental state, by revealing the grammatical differences – i.e. the differences in use – first, between the concept of understanding and the concept of a conscious mental state, and second, between the concept of understanding and the concept of an internal mechanism. An important part of Wittgenstein's idea of a grammatical investigation is that it should make us alive to the distinctive grammatical features that characterize our concepts. Some of the temptations to misunderstand how language functions that he is out to overcome arise in our failure to observe these grammatical differences among our concepts. This failure leads us into drawing misleading analogies, into asking inappropriate questions, making false comparisons, drawing false inferences, and so on. The confusions that arise in the wake of these temptations are overcome, Wittgenstein believes, by observing the differences in grammar and accepting them as revealing a distinction in the kind of phenomena our concepts describe. Thus it is by drawing our attention to grammatical differences between concepts that describe conscious mental states, concepts that describe mechanical systems and the concept of understanding that he tries to reveal to us the distinctive grammar of the latter. This clarified view of the grammar of the concept of understanding will, he believes, release us from confusions that spring, at least in part, from a false sense of analogy between these different regions of our language.

It is part of the distinctive grammar of concepts that describe conscious mental states – e.g. the concept of being in pain, of being depressed, of hearing a buzzing sound, etc. – that temporal concepts like duration, interruption and continuity, as well as concepts of intensity or degree, all make clear sense when applied to them. The concept of understanding, by contrast, is not linked with the idea of anything's 'occurring in our minds', but introduces an idea of a disposition or ability. We do not talk about the intensity or degree of understanding in the same sense in which we talk about the intensity or degree of pain, but more in the sense of capacity or breadth. And while we may, in special circumstances, be able to date the onset of the ability to understand, or to speak of its being interrupted, the concept of understanding does not relate to concepts of duration in the same way as concepts of occurrent conscious states do. Even supposing that the weak links between temporal concepts and the concept of understanding make it appropriate to speak of understanding as a state, it is clearly a (grammatically) different kind of state from being in pain or being depressed, and we need to get a good deal clearer about its distinctive grammar. What *sort* of state is the state of understanding? The danger in calling it a *mental* state is that, instead of trying to describe its grammar by observing how the concept actually functions, we just form a vague picture of understanding as like a conscious mental state *only unconscious*. This does not make the grammar of the state of understanding any clearer (in fact, it could be said to obscure it), but at the same time it allows us to neglect the real work involved in making the grammar clear. Hence:

> Nothing would be more confusing here than to use the words "conscious" and "unconscious" for the contrast between states of consciousness and dispositions. For this pair of terms covers up a grammatical difference.

> (*PI* 149)

In the absence of a clear view of the grammar of the concept of understanding, there is also a temptation to picture it in terms of the internal structure of a mental apparatus (the brain, say) which explains a speaker's ability to use the language. Again, Wittgenstein suggests that this picture does not fit the grammar of the concept, for our use of the concept shows that we are not describing the determinate state of an internal mechanism. Thus there is, for example, no criterion for a speaker's understanding a word, or knowing how to add, that invokes 'a knowledge of the apparatus, quite apart from what it does' (*PI* 149). Rather, our use of the concept of understanding is linked in complex ways with a speaker's participation in a characteristic form of life. It misrepresents Wittgenstein's thought here to say that the criteria for understanding are purely behavioural. This rendering of his thought does not capture the particular form of complexity that he detects in the way our concept of understanding functions. He does not claim that the sense of the concept of understanding consists in the behavioural criteria for its application. It is rather that the field within which this concepts gets its sense (that is to say, its use) is the complex form of life that is revealed in the way speakers live and act, both in their past history and in their current and their future ways of acting and responding. The tempting idea that the concept of understanding describes the state of an internal mechanism simply misses the way the concept connects, not with anything that happens at the time of its being attributed, but with an ongoing pattern of performance. Instead of recognizing the concept's dependence upon a horizon of past training, manifest abilities and forms of responsiveness, we form a simple mechanical picture that expresses little more than the fact that this 'is a form of account which is very convincing to us' (*PI* 158).

Wittgenstein brings out the grammatical connection between the concept of understanding and the pattern of past performance by means of the following example. 'A writes series of numbers down; B watches him and tries to find a law for the sequence of numbers. If he succeeds he exclaims: "Now I can go on"' (*PI* 151). It is, clearly, just the sort of case in which we feel tempted to think of understanding as a state that makes its appearance in a moment, and which explains B's ability to go on with the series correctly.

Wittgenstein now goes on to imagine what might actually happen when A writes down, for example, the numbers 1, 5, 11, 19, 29 and B suddenly knows how to go on. He suggests that any number of things might happen here. B might come up with the formula $a_n = n^2 + n - 1$; or he might see that the pattern of differences is 4, 6, 8, 10 . . . ; or he might say to himself 'Yes, I know *that* series' and continue it just as we would the series 1, 3, 5, 7, 9 . . .; or he might say nothing at all to himself, but just take the chalk and continue the series, perhaps with 'what may be called the sensation "That's easy"' (*PI* 151). Now, he asks, do any of the processes described actually constitute the state of understanding? The problem in identifying the state of understanding with any of these processes is that we can easily imagine cases in which what is described occurs and the speaker would nevertheless still not understand. Even if the right formula occurs to a speaker, we may still imagine that he cannot go on to develop the series correctly when asked to do so.

This fact may, of course, tempt us to the following thought: ' "He understands" must have more in it than: the formula occurs to him. And equally, more than any of these more or less characteristic *accompaniments* or manifestations of understanding' (*PI* 152). Having failed to find the state of understanding in anything that occurs when B suddenly understands, we are tempted into creating a chimera: 'the mental process of understanding which seems to be hidden behind these coarse and therefore more visible accompaniments' (*PI* 153). But what idea do we have of this hidden process of understanding? And how, if the process is hidden, does B know that it has occurred when he says 'Now I understand'? '[I]f I say [the process] is hidden – then how do I know what I am to look for? I am in a muddle' (*PI* 153). At this point, Wittgenstein directs us to what we have so far neglected, namely, the field within which the words 'Now I understand', 'The formula . . . occurs to me', etc. are used. The muddle that we create by inventing the chimerical idea of a mental process occurring behind those that are observed is resolved when we look at how our language-game actually functions, at how our use of the concept of understanding connects with the distinctive background of a characteristic form of life.

How, then, are the sentences 'Now I understand', 'Now I see the principle', and so on actually used? They are not, as we've just seen, used to describe any process that constitutes the state of understanding; the very idea of such a process has proved impossible to pin down. But in that case, how can I know that I am in a position to utter these words? What justifies me, on a particular occasion, in saying that I can go on? Wittgenstein writes:

> If there has to be anything 'behind the utterance of the formula' it is *particular circumstances*, which justify me in saying I can go on – when the formula occurs to me.
>
> (*PI* 154)

Thus I use the words 'Now I understand' with a particular background or history: I have, for example, been trained in the use of algebraic formulae; or I have a proved knack for seeing numerical patterns; or I have been trained to recognize numerical series, including this one. My use of the words does not connect with my observing a process, or with my hypothesizing a process I do not see, but with the structure of the life into which I have been acculturated, and which is revealed in the form or pattern of my past performance. It is this background or history which gives my words the significance they have, which motivates my use of them on a particular occasion, and which grounds the response that other speakers have to them. The grammar of the concept of understanding does not send us further inwards towards a determinate state of a mechanism, but spreads over the surface of our practice and connects it with the complex and involved patterns of our characteristic form of life.

Wittgenstein's directive – 'Try not to think of understanding as a mental process at all' (*PI* 154) – is not, therefore, to be understood as an assertion of an uncompromising behaviourism, or as an expression of anti-realism concerning mental states. It is rather to be construed as a remark about the grammar of the concept of understanding. Wittgenstein intends his directive to warn us against adopting an over-simplified and inappropriate picture of the grammar of this concept, and to get us to open our eyes to the way in which this concept reverberates with the characteristic structures of our form of life. It is part of the grammar of the concept of understanding that it doesn't describe something whose nature is constituted by what is happening 'at the time'; the concept of understanding connects rather with a distinctive pattern in the life of speakers, which serves to give the words 'Now I understand' their significance on any particular occasion. There may be characteristic experiences associated with suddenly coming to understand a word or the principle of a series, but these characteristic experiences are not the understanding. The grammar of this concept, the employment of the words 'Now I understand' in ordinary linguistic intercourse, is not linked with a mental accompaniment to the saying of these words, but to the circumstances in which they are said.

These points may still seem to leave a difficulty for our understanding of the first-person case. If the formula's occurring to me does not *on its own* justify my saying 'Now I can go on', then how can I know that I use these words correctly? Do I have to rely on my knowing that a connection has been established between a formula's coming to my mind, in just these circumstances, and my actually continuing the series correctly? And do I have to be claiming that such an empirical connection exists when I say, in particular circumstances, 'Now I can go on', on the basis of a formula's occurring to me? All this clearly gives a wrong picture of how the characteristic patterns of our form of life provide 'the scene of our language-game' (*PI* 179). The words 'Now I can go on' are correctly used when the formula occurs to me, given that I already share in the form of life that forms the essential background to our use of these words. My words do not, however, implicitly *refer* to the circumstance of my sharing a form of life, rather our form of life – e.g. our shared practice of using and teaching mathematics – forms an indeterminate and unspoken horizon within which our language-game functions. Teaching a child to use the words 'Now I understand' will not turn on drawing his attention either to anything 'occurring in his mind' or to an empirical connection between his thinking of a formula and his going on correctly. Rather, the teacher responds with encouragement to the emerging patterns in the child's behaviour that signify increasing mastery. The child responds in turn with a growing sense of confidence and facility that prompts him to take the vital step of continuing independently. The use of the words 'Now I understand',

'Now I can go on', and so on are learnt in the context of the development of autonomous, confident responses that are in harmony with a particular practice, and not in connection with either the introspection of internal mental states or the hypothesizing of empirical regularities.

Wittgenstein's description of the first-person use of the words 'Now I can go on' is not, as Kripke suggests, given in response to a sceptical problem about meaning, the problem, namely, that there is no *fact* that constitutes my understanding of a word. Wittgenstein is concerned with a grammatical investigation of our ordinary language-game that is aimed at drawing our attention to the kind of concept (the kind of fact) that the concept (the fact) of understanding is; his remarks are purely descriptive of how our words are used, how they are taught, and so on. The whole purpose of his description, like the purpose of his grammatical enquiries in general, is to reveal that the picture we're inclined to construct in response to the question 'What is understanding?' is empty, and that everything that we need to remove our puzzlement lies already open to view in our practice of using language. Thus the idea of an inner state, either conscious or unconscious, plays no role in the language-game that is played with the words 'Now I understand'. The grip of this tempting picture of understanding is loosened by our coming to see that it makes no connection with the way the concept of understanding actually functions:

> The criteria which we accept for ... 'understanding', are much more complicated than might appear at first sight. That is, the game with these words, their employment in the linguistic intercourse that is carried on by their means, is more involved – the role of these words in our language other – than we are tempted to think.
>
> (*PI* 182)

What we gradually come to see is that we have formed a picture that attributes a certain form (or grammar) to the phenomenon of understanding – namely the form of an inner state – but the actual form of this phenomenon, as revealed by the grammar of the concept, is much more complex and entirely different. Our picture appeals to us only because we command no clear view of the grammar of the psychological concepts involved, and are therefore free to imagine them in terms of a simple, quasi-mechanical model. One of the major aims of Wittgenstein's grammatical investigations is to show, not only the emptiness of this crude picture, but that the distinctive grammar of these concepts already reveals the true nature of the phenomena with which we are concerned.

The connection between a rule and its application

Achieving a clearer view of the use of the words 'Now I understand' may help us to resist the idea that these words describe an internal mental state. However, clearing up this particular bit of our grammar is not on its own enough to free us from the mythology of internal states completely, for there are other aspects of our language that seem to impose this picture on us. There are other points at which we will be tempted to say that it *must* be the case that understanding is a state which a speaker acquires 'in a flash', and which compels him to apply a word (develop a series) in a particular way. It is only by working through these other sources of temptation that we can hope to work free of the picture entirely. In *PI* 185, Wittgenstein constructs an example which he uses to bring out more clearly what is involved in other aspects of our language-game that we are tempted to misrepresent in terms of the myth of understanding as a state which is the source of correct use.

This example goes back to the case of teaching a pupil to continue series of numbers which a teacher writes down. Wittgenstein describes the case he now wants us to consider as follows:

> Now – judged by the usual criteria – the pupil has mastered the series of natural numbers. Next we teach him to write down other series of cardinal numbers and get him to the point of writing down series of the form
>
> 0, n, 2n, 3n, etc.
>
> at an order of the form " + n"; so at the order "+ 1" he writes down the series of natural numbers. – Let us suppose we have

done exercises and given him tests up to 1000. Now we get
the pupil to continue a series (say + 2) beyond 1000 – and he
writes 1000, 1004, 1008, 1012.

We say to him: "Look what you've done!" – He doesn't
understand. We say: "You were meant to add *two*: look
how you began the series!" – He answers: "Yes isn't it right?
I thought that was how I was *meant* to do it." – Or suppose
he pointed to the series and said: "But I went on in the same
way."

(*PI* 185)

Wittgenstein describes this case as one in which the pupil's natural
reaction to the training he has received is different from our own:
'It comes naturally to this person to understand our order with our
explanations as *we* should understand the order: "Add 2 up to 1000,
4 up to 2000, 6 up to 3000, and so on"' (*PI* 185). And he compares it
with a case of someone's reacting to the gesture of pointing by looking in the direction of the line from finger-tip to wrist, rather than vice
versa. The example presents us, therefore, with what Wittgenstein earlier described as an 'abnormal case' (*PI* 141). There is nothing in the
training or in the instructions that we receive that (in some mysterious
way) *compels* a particular application of the rule, but we all normally
respond to this training and these instructions by going on to use the
rule in one particular way. The same training and the same instructions
strike the pupil that Wittgenstein describes in *PI* 185 in a quite different way. The issue here is not, as Kripke suggests, scepticism about
meaning. Rather, Wittgenstein is using the abnormal case as an object
of comparison, in order to throw light on aspects of the normal case
that we are tempted to misunderstand. In particular, the abnormal
case is used to shed light on what is involved in my meaning or understanding the order '+ 2' in one way rather than another (e.g. normally
rather than abnormally), and on what makes one, rather than another,
response to the order the one that is *correct*. In both cases we are
involved in a grammatical investigation, and not in providing a philosophical gloss on, or a justification of, our ordinary practice.

What makes it the case, then, that '1000, 1002, 1004, 1006
. . .' is the *correct* response to the order 'Add 2'? 'How is it decided

what is the right step to take at any particular stage?' (*PI* 186). The interlocutor suggests that ' "[t]he right step is the one that accords with the order – as it was *meant*" ' (*PI* 186). The question is, however, What does meaning in this sense amount to? We certainly didn't explicitly think of the steps 1000, 1002, 1004, 1006 when we gave the order; or if we did, there are clearly other steps that we didn't think of. And here we are pushed back on to the temptation to think of meaning or understanding as a state that already anticipates *all* the applications that can be made of a word. For we want to say: ' "[W]hat I meant was, that he should write the next but one number after *every* number that he wrote; and from this all those propositions follow in turn" ' (*PI* 186). It is, it seems, only by appeal to some such picture of an infinite number of propositions having already been determined that we can make sense of the idea that '1000, 1002, 1004, 1006 ...' is the correct, and '1000, 1004, 1008, 1012 ...' an incorrect, response to the order 'Add 2'.

In the very next paragraph, Wittgenstein makes it clear that what is at issue here is not the facts, but, as it were, the form of the facts (the grammar of our concepts):

> "But I already knew, at the time when I gave the order, that he ought to write 1002 after 1000." – *Certainly; and you can also say you meant it then*; only you should not let yourself be misled by the grammar of the words "know" and "mean".
>
> (*PI* 187, my italics)

We want to picture this knowing or meaning as an act in which 'the order [has] in its own way already traversed all these steps: [so] that when you meant it your mind as it were flew ahead and took all the steps before you physically arrived at this or that one' (*PI* 188). It seems to us that the very notion of one response's being correct *requires* that the answers are 'in some *unique* way predetermined, anticipated' (*PI* 188). But we still 'have no model of this superlative fact' (*PI* 192); no idea corresponds to what we want to express with the words 'the order (as it is meant) already completely determines every step from one number to the next'. Or, if any idea does attach to these words, then, Wittgenstein suggests, it is the perfectly *ordinary* idea of there existing a regular practice of employing a rule in which everyone takes the same step at the same point, or of there being rules that determine a unique value for every argument (e.g., like 'y = 2x', and unlike 'y > x'). When we want to appeal to the entirely mysterious idea that the steps are determined in some *unique* way – in the way that 'only the act of meaning can anticipate reality' (*PI* 188) – then we are not describing anything that actually happens, but, rather, there is something about our language-game that makes this picture very natural to us.

Wittgenstein begins to release us from this strange picture by offering us the following, mundane comparison:

> When you said "I already knew at the time ..." that meant something like: "If I had then been asked what number should be written after 1000, I should have replied '1002'." And that I don't doubt. This assumption is rather of the same kind as: "If he had fallen in to the water then, I should have jumped in after him." – Now, what was wrong with your idea?
>
> (*PI* 187)

Here Wittgenstein refers us back to our own way of responding to the rule. We can say 'I already knew at the time ...', but these words connect, not with an act of meaning that mysteriously anticipates the future, but with our practice of using a rule and our trained responses to it. Thus my training in the practice of using the rule has brought it about that I now act, without hesitation, at each new point. The sense of a clash between the response that was meant and the one that the abnormal pupil actually gives does not arise in a conflict between his reaction and the rule itself, but between his reaction and the one I have. 'I already knew at the time ...' does not mean that all my responses must in some mysterious way be already present or anticipated. Rather, these words receive their significance from the form of life that constitutes 'the scene of the language-game'; it is not what accompanies the saying of these words that gives them their sense, but the practice of using language in which their use is embedded; it is my practice that is invoked by these words, and not a mysterious mental act.

However, this may still leave obscure what it is that makes the response '1000, 1002, 1004, 1006 ...' *correct*. Hasn't it been agreed that the reaction of the abnormal pupil would, on some interpretation, count as an application of the rule 'Add 2'? In that case, aren't we in a position of having to accept that whatever a speaker does is, on some interpretation of it, in accord with the rule? My response may clash with that of the abnormal pupil's, but how does it achieve the distinction of being the correct response, the one that should be made? Again, we may feel that we must appeal to the idea that use is in some special way predetermined, if we are to be able to make sense of the contrast between a correct and an incorrect response. Wittgenstein responds to this rekindling of the temptation to mythologize the concept of meaning by pointing to the way in which the distinction between correct and incorrect is actually grounded in the different ways in which the normal and the abnormal reaction connect with the surrounding practice. We don't find the basis for this distinction where we're inclined to look for it – in the rule itself, or in something that accompanies the saying of the rule – but in the field that surrounds the giving of the order and the response that is made to it. Wittgenstein sums up these points as follows:

> Let me ask this: what has the expression of a rule – say a sign-post – got to do with my actions? What sort of connexion is there here? – Well, perhaps this one: I have been trained to react to this sign in a particular way, and now I do so react.
>
> But that is only to give a causal connexion; to tell how it came about that we now go by the sign-post; not what this going-by-the-sign really consists in. On the contrary; I have further indicated that a person goes by a sign-post only insofar as there exists a regular use of sign-posts, a custom.

(*PI* 198)

It is clearly tempting to construe these remarks as a theory of rule-following, or as an analysis of the concept of a rule. However, Wittgenstein himself explicitly characterizes his observations as 'grammatical', as 'a note on the grammar of the expression "to obey a rule"' (*PI* 199). Thus the connection between a rule and a practice that Wittgenstein makes is not put forward as a philosophical analysis of the concept of 'a rule', but is intended to describe what is observable in the structure of our language-game, in how our concepts actually function. By comparing the normal and the abnormal case, Wittgenstein enables us on the one hand to overcome our temptation to say that the rule itself (how the rule is meant) must somehow compel a particular application of it, and on the other to recognize that the clash between a rule and an application that is made of it lies in the fact what we apply *this* rule like *this*. No sceptical crisis is generated in connection with the concept of a rule. There is instead an attempt to show that 'in our failure to understand the use of a word we take it as the expression of a queer *process*' (*PI* 196). The struggle is to get us to see that in inventing the idea of a 'queer process' – the act of meaning that anticipates the future – we have constructed a chimera, and that in fact 'nothing out of the ordinary is involved' (*PI* 194). When we look at what is actually involved in the language-game of following rules and teaching others to follow rules, we find that there is nothing corresponding to the idea of a process in which the future is mysteriously anticipated in the present; the connection between a rule and its application is seen to lie in our practice of using it.

In *PI* 201, Wittgenstein writes:

> This was our paradox: no course of action could be determined by a rule, because every course of action can be made out to accord with the rule. The answer was: if everything can be made out to accord with the rule, then it can also be made out to conflict with it. And so there would be neither accord nor conflict here.

The paradox that Wittgenstein here describes is not to be understood as a sceptical crisis that he has generated for the concept of a rule as such. Rather, the paradox refers to our initial sense of perplexity at the discovery that the idea of 'logical compulsion', which we want to use to describe the connection between a rule and its application, cannot be given any content. The exploration of abnormal cases has revealed to us that there are other things that we would be willing to call 'an application of the rule'. Our initial reaction to this revelation is to feel that it shows that *anything* that a speaker does can, on some interpretation, be shown to be correct. Wittgenstein helps us to see that this sense of a threat to the order of our linguistic practice is empty, by pointing out that it would mean the end to the very notion of a rule's being applied correctly or incorrectly. We can see we have gone wrong simply because our reflections lead to the conclusion that one of the most familiar aspects of our human form of life is actually impossible. Far from constituting the paradox, the sense of a sceptical undermining of our ordinary concepts of rules and rule-following is used as a means to free us from our sudden feeling that, in the absence of a workable concept of 'logical compulsion', speakers could start applying our rules in any way they pleased. If our reflections lead us into the extraordinary position of saying, against our ordinary experience, that there can be neither accord nor conflict with a rule, then we know that we are deep in misunderstanding.

In the second paragraph of *PI* 201, Wittgenstein goes on to identify our misunderstanding:

> It can be seen that there is a misunderstanding here from the mere fact that in the course of our argument we give one interpretation after another; as if each one contented us at least for a moment, until we thought of yet another standing behind it.

The misunderstanding that is expressed in the fear of impending chaos with which *PI* 201 opens (quoted above) is the thought that, if the rule itself does not compel an application, then our use of the rule must be completely unconstrained. We can see that this is a misunderstanding simply by observing that in the course of our discussion we have continually come up with pictures and rules that *do* seem to us to require or compel a particular use, i.e. which seem to us to meet our demand for a 'superlative link' between rule and application. It is only when someone points out to us that we would be prepared to acknowledge a different use as an application of the rule or picture that we become aware of the possibility of using it differently. Normally, the possibility of these other applications doesn't even occur to us; we simply apply the picture or rule in the way we have been trained – in the way that accords with our practice of using it – and nothing occurs to worry us.

Thus we can see that ordinary practice does not depend upon the spurious idea of a mysterious link between a rule and its use, simply by observing the fact that our ordinary experience of the rules of our language involves a sense of how the rule must be applied that is completely independent of this notion. The discovery that the idea of logical compulsion, which we construct in the course of philosophical reflection on the concepts of a rule and understanding a rule, is a chimera leaves the actual ground of our practice of rule-following completely untouched. Our everyday experience of the 'Add 2' rule is that we *must* say '1000, 1002, 1004, 1006 . . .' The emptiness of the idea that there is something in the rule itself that compels this application shows only that our practice of following rules is not dependent on this altogether mysterious idea. What our practice of teaching and following rules reveals is 'that there is a way of grasping a rule which is *not* an *interpretation*' (*PI* 201), that is, which does not depend upon the formulation and selection of hypotheses about how the rule is to be applied. This way of grasping the rule consists simply in our *responding* to the rule in the way we have been trained, in accordance with the practice of using it. This unreflective, practical grasp of a rule 'is exhibited in what we call "obeying the rule" and "going against it" in actual cases' (*PI* 201), that is, in the ways of acting or responding to the rule that fall within our practice.

In *PI* 202, Wittgenstein strikingly links these grammatical observations concerning the concept of a rule with the question of whether there can be a private rule, or whether it is possible 'to obey a rule "privately"':

> And hence also 'obeying a rule' is a practice. And to *think* one is obeying a rule is not to obey a rule. Hence it is not possible to obey a rule 'privately': otherwise thinking one was obeying a rule would be the same thing as obeying it.

The remark is clearly very brief, and interpretation of it must inevitably depend upon the interpretation of the remarks that lead up to it. In the light of what has gone before, therefore, I want to read *PI* 202 as a further note on the grammar of rules. We have seen that the link between a picture, or a rule, and its application lies in the fact that there is a practice of using it. The grammar of the concept of a rule links it, therefore, with a characteristic pattern of activity, or form of life, and not with anything that occurs 'in the minds' of those who use the rule. Thus the concept of a rule is essentially linked with the idea of participating in a practice of using it, and not with the characteristic psychological accompaniments to following, or being in the grip of, a rule. It is not the psychological accompaniments to following a rule (thinking one is obeying a rule) that constitute one's act as an act of obeying a rule or going against it, but what surrounds one's act. Without this surrounding the concept of obeying a rule or going against it is completely empty; for it is nothing that occurs at the time, or 'in the mind', that gives the concept of a rule its content, but the existence of a particular form of practice. Yet to make sense of the notion of a private rule (of a rule that is not linked with a practice of using it), we would have only the psychological accompaniments to rule-following to appeal to, and these do not connect with the grammar of the concept of a rule. Reduced to the psychological accompaniments to rule-following, we cannot make the distinction between thinking you are obeying a rule and actually obeying it, for this distinction is grounded in the practice of using the rule. The idea of a rule in a purely private domain, cut off from the realm of practice, simply makes no sense, for the concept of a rule is, in the end, the concept of a certain form of practice. (I shall argue in the next chapter that Wittgenstein's discussion of the idea of a private language, in *PI* 243ff., raises a different question from the one raised here: namely, the question of whether a psychological concept can be defined on the basis of introspection.)

The logical 'must'

Wittgenstein sums up his treatment of the idea of 'logical compulsion' in *PI* 218–21. He begins by asking, 'Whence comes the idea that the beginning of a series is a visible section of rails invisibly laid to infinity?' (*PI* 218). The image of rails is clearly one way of expressing our sense that all the steps have already been taken before we physically arrive at this or that point. Thus, 'infinitely long rails correspond to the unlimited application of a rule' (*PI* 218). Wittgenstein now suggests that what we mean to express with this picture of infinitely long rails, or with the words 'All the steps are already taken', is the following:

I no longer have any choice. The rule, once stamped with a particular meaning, traces the line along which it is to be followed through the whole of space.

(PI 219)

He asks:

But if something of this sort really were the case, how would it help?

(PI 219)

Let us suppose that there really are rails laid down in a Platonic heaven corresponding to all the future applications of a rule. What difference would this make? Could we, for instance, consult these rails in order to determine how the rule is to be applied in a new case? Clearly not. These objectively existing rails can make no contact with our human practice of following rules, or of judging, in particular cases, whether a rule has been applied correctly. The Platonic heaven which we are tempted to think is vital to the stability of our practice could not, even if it existed, provide our practice with any foundation, for there is no independent criterion for our practice's having engaged with these Platonic rails.

Wittgenstein now goes on:

No; my description only made sense if it was understood symbolically. – I should have said: *This is how it strikes me.*

When I obey a rule, I do not choose.

I obey it *blindly.*

(PI 219)

But what is the purpose of that symbolical proposition? It was supposed to bring into prominence the difference between being causally determined and being logically determined.

(PI 220)

My symbolical expression was really a mythological description of the use of a rule.

(PI 221)

Thus I use the picture of rails invisibly laid to infinity in order to give expression to my own sense that I no longer have a choice in how a word that I understand, or a rule that I've mastered, is to be applied in a new case. My response to the training that I have received is such that at each new step, e.g. in the development of a series, no doubt arises; I simply react without hesitation, in accordance with the practice of employing the rule, and no other way of responding presents itself as a possibility. It is this characteristic experience of rule-following – this characteristic sense of inexorability in how the rule is to be applied – that we express 'symbolically' (i.e. metaphorically) in the picture of infinitely long rails. The picture thus captures something characteristic about our ordinary experience of grasping a rule. Problems arise, however, when we're tempted to interpret this picture, not as a metaphor, but literally, so that the image of Platonic (i.e. real but non-material) rails stretching to infinity, marking out all the correct applications of a rule, comes to represent the essential difference between being causally determined and being logically determined. Having interpreted the picture literally, I must now give content to the idea that there really is something which 'traces the lines along which it is to be followed through the whole of space'. When I find that there is nothing corresponding to this picture, I am left feeling that 'every course of action can be made out to accord with [a] rule' (*PI* 201). Wittgenstein responds to the muddle, by pointing out that no such thing was ever in question. For the fact is 'the rule can only seem to me to produce all its consequences in advance if I draw them as a *matter of course*' (*PI* 238). What makes this a case of 'logical', rather than causal, compulsion (i.e. a case of following a rule) lies, not in the *way* in which I'm compelled – not in the rule itself somehow compelling me – but in the fact that my response to the rule is part of a particular language-game (or practice) of rule-following. The idea that there really are Platonic rails laid to infinity proves to be no more than a philosophical illusion, thrown up by a combination of our ignorance of the grammar of the concept of 'a rule' and a temptation to put a false construction on the things that someone in the grip of a rule is inclined to say.

Wittgenstein expresses the same thought in *PI* 206 as follows: 'Following a rule is analogous to obeying an order. We are trained to do so; we react to an order in a particular way.' And here he raises the question: 'But what if one person reacts in one way and another in another to the order and the training? Which one is right?' In order to show us what is wrong with the idea that it makes sense, in these circumstances, to speak of one person being right, he asks us to imagine that we go as explorers to an unknown country in which the inhabitants speak a language that is completely foreign to us. 'In what circumstances would you say that the people there gave orders, understood them, obeyed them, rebelled against them, and so on?' (*PI* 206). It is clearly only by discerning a certain structure in their activity of using sounds, that is, by uncovering the characteristic form of life that realizes or constitutes rule-following. What we are concerned with is the detecting of a certain form or pattern in the practice of this community that identifies what they are doing as a practice of giving orders, obeying them, rebelling against them, and so on. Wittgenstein's remark that it is 'the common behaviour of mankind [that] is the system of reference by means of which we interpret an unknown language' is to be interpreted, therefore, as drawing our attention to the fact that it is in the forms and patterns of a shared practice, or way of using signs, that we discover the rules for the employment of the linguistic techniques of a radically foreign language, and not in anything that is hidden in the minds of its speakers.

Wittgenstein further underlines this point by imagining that when we actually undertake the task of discerning a structure in their practice of using words, we find that we cannot succeed. '[W]hen we try to learn their language we find it impossible to do so. For there is no regular connection between what they say, the sounds they make, and their actions' (*PI* 207). Even if we imagine that the effect of gagging these people is that they can no longer act coherently, so that 'without sounds their actions fall into confusion' (*PI* 207), still, Wittgenstein suggests, 'there is not enough regularity for us to call it "language"' (*PI* 207). Giving orders, making reports, describing a scene, telling a story, etc. represent particular forms of life; when we cannot discern this form, then we cannot say that people are using a language.

Wittgenstein's idea that a certain characteristic order or structure in our ways of acting – the 'common behaviour of mankind' – is essential to language is not, on this interpretation, to be understood as a theory about the conditions for the possibility of language. Like all the other points that he makes, this point about regularity or order is to be construed as a grammatical observation concerning the grammar of our concept of a language, or the concept of a rule. Our concept of a language describes, not an abstract system of signs with meaning, but a particular form of life, namely, one that displays the characteristic regularities or patterns that constitute the following of rules. Central to the idea of the form of life that our concept of language picks out is that there exists a pattern or structure in the activity of using words which fixes what counts as applying the words of the language correctly or incorrectly. If we cannot discern this structure in an activity involving the use of sounds, then it is not merely that we don't have enough evidence to call it language, but the criteria that would *identify* the activity as one of using language are not met. The agreement or harmony that Wittgenstein suggests is essential to our concept of language is the agreement that constitutes the characteristic form of life that speaking a language (giving orders, making reports, and the rest) consists in. He characterizes this harmony or agreement as follows: 'It is what human beings *say* that is true or false; and they agree in the *language* they use. That is not agreement in opinions but in form of life' (*PI* 241). He makes the same point about a harmony in our ways of acting being essential to the concept of a language in *PI* 242: 'If language is to be a means of communication there must be agreement not only in definitions but also (queer as this may sound) in judgements'; that is to say, in our *use* of words.

This brings us to the end of the interpretation of Wittgenstein's remarks on meaning and rule-following. It is, I hope, clear that it would be a mistake to suppose that the force of these remarks is to be summarized by means of the following claims: Meaning is use. Speaking a language is a practice. Understanding is not a mental state that is the source of correct use. And so on. The philosophical signif- icance of Wittgenstein's remarks does not lie in these 'conclusions', which are on their own thin and obscure, and which are clearly not intended to serve as the basis for the construction of a more elabo- rate theoretical machinery. The real purpose of the journey that has been made lies, on the one hand, in the overcoming of certain deep- seated philosophical myths and inclinations, and on the other, in the reorientation of our style of thought towards what lies open to view in our practice of using language. The above generalizations altogether fail to capture this more profound shift in how we approach the task of understanding how language functions. Thus the Augustinian impulse to abstract language from its natural setting in our form of life, and think of it as a system of meaningful signs, has been repeatedly shown to produce over-simplification, idealization, spurious explanation, empty concepts and pictures which either make no contact with anything that actually happens, or which simply cannot be applied. Against this urge to move in a direction that produces only confusion and misunderstanding, Wittgenstein has continually worked to redirect our attention towards the concrete, spatial and temporal phenomenon of language-in-use. In this way he has sought to correct our misconceptions, to enrich our vision of language by revealing its essential connection with our complex practice of employing it, and to bring about a state of intellectual peace in which we no longer feel ' "But *this* isn't how it is!" . . . "Yet *this* is how it has to *be*!" ' (*PI* 109). It is this reorientation of our thought away from abstractions and generalizations towards a careful attention to what lies before our eyes, in the forms of our concrete practice of using language, that is the real lesson of Wittgenstein's remarks, and this is something that cannot be expressed in a generalization.

References and further reading

Anscombe, G. E. M., 'Wittgenstein: Whose Philosopher?', in A. Phillips Griffiths, ed., *Wittgenstein Centenary Essays* (Cambridge: Cambridge University Press, 1992).

Baker, G., 'Following a Rule: The Basic Themes', in S. H. Holtzman and C. M. Leich, eds, 1981.

—— *Wittgenstein: Rules, Grammar and Necessity* (Oxford: Blackwell, 1985).

Baker, G. and Hacker, P. M. S., *Scepticism, Rules and Language* (Oxford: Blackwell, 1984).

Boghossian, P. A., 'The Rule Following Considerations', *Mind*, vol. 98, 1989.

Budd, M., 'Wittgenstein on Meaning, Interpretation and Rules', *Synthèse*, vol. 58, 1984.

—— *Wittgenstein's Philosophy of Psychology* (London: Routledge, 1989).

Cavell, S., 'The Availability of Wittgenstein's Later Philosophy', in G. Pitcher, ed., *Wittgenstein: The* Philosophical Investigations (New York: Doubleday, 1966).

—— *The Claim of Reason: Wittgenstein, Skepticism, Morality and Tragedy* (Oxford: Oxford University Press, 1979).

—— *Conditions Handsome and Unhandsome* (London: University of Chicago Press, 1990).

Fogelin, R., *Wittgenstein* (London: Routledge, 1987).

Goldfarb, W. D., 'Wittgenstein, Mind and Scientism', *Journal of Philosophy*, vol. 86, 1989.

—— 'Wittgenstein on Understanding', in P. A. French, T. E. Uehling and H. K. Wettstein, eds, *The Wittgenstein Legacy*, *Midwest Studies in Philosophy*, vol. XVII (Notre Dame, Indiana: University of Notre Dame Press, 1992).

Holtzman, S. H. and Leich, C. M., eds, *To Follow a Rule* (London: Routledge, 1981).

Kripke, S. A., *Wittgenstein on Rules and Private Language* (Oxford: Blackwell, 1982).

McCulloch, G., *The Mind and Its World* (London: Routledge, 1995).

McDowell, J. H., 'Wittgenstein on Following a Rule', *Synthèse*, vol. 58, 1984.

—— 'Meaning and Intentionality in Wittgenstein's Later Philosophy', in P. A. French, T. E. Uehling and H. K. Wettstein, eds, 1992.

McGinn, C., *Wittgenstein on Meaning* (Oxford: Blackwell, 1984).

Pears, D. F., *The False Prison*, vol. 2 (Oxford: Oxford University Press, 1987).

Savigny, E. Von, 'Common behaviour of many a kind: *Philosophical Investigations* section 206', in R. L. Arrington and H.-J. Glock, eds, *Wittgenstein's* Philosophical Investigations: *Text and Context* (London: Routledge, 1991).

Staten, H., *Wittgenstein and Derrida* (London: University of Nebraska Press, 1986).

Chapter 4

Privacy and private language
Philosophical Investigations 243–275

Introduction

In this chapter we shall begin to look at how Wittgenstein applies the philosophical approach we've seen him adopt in the philosophy of language to the philosophy of psychology. It is, as we've seen, characteristic of Wittgenstein's philosophical method to focus on the original source of philosophical confusions, which he believes to lie in the forms of our language. He does not address the familiar doctrines of traditional philosophy directly, but goes back to their roots in the first temptation to form false pictures of language or psychological phenomena, which the grammar of our concepts presents. Thus he wants us to step back from our concern with the construction of theoretical accounts of the nature of consciousness, or of the relation between consciousness and the brain, and examine the steps by which we are led to approach the problem of understanding the nature of psychological processes in the way that we do. Why do we

113

go on trying to explain the relationship between consciousness and brain-processes? Why do we feel a need to prove that other people have minds? How do we come to feel these problems as problems, when these things do not normally come into consideration within our ordinary lives? It is not the philosophical accounts we construct which interest Wittgenstein, but the 'logical sleight-of-hand' (*PI* 412) by which we come to approach the task of understanding mental processes as one of constructing a theory of the mind. His technique, once again, is to press us to examine the foundations of our traditional enquiry and to reveal the mythologies which lie at its root. Alongside this critique of our traditional ways of thinking, Wittgenstein continually works to show that the understanding which we mistakenly seek through a theoretical elucidation of mental phenomena is achieved by means of a proper attention to the distinctive grammar of our psychological language-game.

We have already seen this technique at work in the investigation of the concept of understanding. The underlying force of Wittgenstein's investigation of this concept is to direct us away from a concern with speculating about what is occurring, as it were, inside the subject (either in his mind or in his brain) towards a concern with what the grammar of the concept (how the concept functions) reveals about the nature of the state it describes. When we looked carefully at the grammar of this concept – at how we use the words 'I understand', 'He understands', and so on – we find that it simply doesn't function in the way we are inclined to suppose, namely as a name of a process occurring inside the speaker when he hears a word and understands it. Our fruitless attempt to say what this inner state consists in is remedied, not by the construction of a still more subtle account, but by a recognition that the state of understanding is quite other than the picture of an inner state suggests. When we look at it functioning, we see that the concept of understanding does not describe a determinate state of an internal mechanism, but depends for its sense upon the background of the distinctive form of life within which it is used. Thus, the use of the words 'Now I understand', or 'He understands correctly', does not connect with an inner process that occurs inside the speaker, but with the structure of the life into which the speaker has been acculturated and which gives his current actions their particular significance. Wittgenstein's grammatical investigation works, on the one hand, to expose the emptiness of the picture of understanding as a mental state whose nature requires elucidation in an account of what this state consists in. On the other hand, it shows how a grasp of how the concept of understanding actually functions gives us the satisfaction which eluded us as long as we were caught in the trap of trying to specify the mental state which is the source of our ability to use language.

At *PI* 243, this concern with countering our false pictures of the nature of psychological phenomena through a grammatical investigation of how our psychological concepts actually function becomes the dominant theme of Wittgenstein's remarks. The task he has set himself is to make us aware of the distinctive and complex grammar of the wide range of psychological concepts that constitutes our immensely rich psychological language. As always, he wants to use this new awareness both to counteract the false pictures that we are tempted to construct and to show that it is by paying attention to the distinctive grammar of our concepts that we come to understand the nature of the phenomena that these concepts describe. For ease of exposition, I have broken my discussion of these remarks into two parts. In the current chapter, I will concentrate on Wittgenstein's remarks on privacy and private language, which occur between *PI* 243 and *PI* 275. In the next chapter, on the inner and the outer, I will focus much more widely on Wittgenstein's extended discussion of the relation between psychological concepts and behaviour. This division is, at least to some extent, artificial, for Wittgenstein's remarks represent a continuous discussion of the grammar of our psychological language-game and the temptations to misunderstand that it presents. The central theme of this discussion is a concern to overcome what Wittgenstein sees as our tendency to misapply the picture of the distinction between psychological processes and behaviour as a distinction between the inner and the outer. The division I have made separates out, I hope not too misleadingly, the way in which the misapplication of this picture leads us, on the one hand, to overestimate the role of introspection in defining psychological concepts, and on the other, to misrepresent the relation between psychological concepts and forms of human and animal behaviour.

The idea of a private language

Wittgenstein's discussion of philosophical psychology begins with the remarks on the idea of a private language that have become familiar as 'Wittgenstein's private language argument'. This is without doubt the most referred-to aspect of Wittgenstein's later philosophy and it could be argued that it represents Wittgenstein's most significant contribution to the philosophy of mind. Those who are inclined to accept the argument as valid see it as providing a decisive refutation of the philosophy of Descartes, classical empiricism, phenomenalism and sense-data theories of perception. Those who reject it have argued, on the one hand, that it represents nothing more than a verificationist theory of meaning used in defence of a version of logical behaviourism, and on the other, that it goes counter to our commonsense intuition that psychological concepts (e.g. of desire and belief) describe internal states that play a causal role in explaining a subject's behaviour. It is beyond the scope of this book even to begin to describe the vast debate to which Wittgenstein's remarks on private language have given rise. The central concern of the current chapter is to achieve an accurate reading of these remarks and to show how they function within Wittgenstein's philosophy of psychology as a whole. The interpretation of the remarks on private language which follows does not present them as providing the foundation of Wittgenstein's philosophy of psychology, but as one small element in an overall attempt to get us to see how our psychological language-game functions. The view of our ordinary language-game which emerges, far from endorsing logical behaviourism, aims to reveal that our intuition of a distinction between the inner and the outer is grounded in the grammatical differences between concepts belonging to different regions of our language.

The first thing we need to get clear about in interpreting Wittgenstein's remarks on private language is just what he has in mind when he speaks of a 'private language'. He defines such a language, at *PI* 243, as one in which 'the individual words ... are to refer to what can only be known to the person speaking; to his immediate private sensations. So another person cannot understand the language.' The idea of a private language is introduced in explicit contrast to our ordinary psychological language, and the question Wittgenstein raises concerning it is whether we can *imagine* such a language. But what might make us think that we could imagine such a language? To help us answer this question, and thus to focus on the issue raised by Wittgenstein's remarks, I want to look at a discussion of psychological language that occurs in William James's book *The Principles of Psychology*, a text with which Wittgenstein was well acquainted and to which he often refers.

In the context of a discussion of sources of error in psychology, William James introduces the idea of an *ideal* psychological language that would constitute 'a special vocabulary for subjective facts'. James imagines this pure or ideal psychological language as one which would have no link with the objective world, but which would simply record or name the distinct subjective states that are revealed to a subject by means of pure acts of introspection. This idea of an ideal or pure language of subjectivity is connected in James, not with a commitment to Cartesian dualism, but with what he takes to be the undeniable sense of 'the bare phenomenal fact' of consciousness, and thus with the thought that introspection is the method by which we discover the essence of the states and processes to which our psychological expressions refer. Thus, he believes that 'introspective observation is what we have to rely on first and foremost and always' in psychology, because it is by means of introspection that we 'discover states of consciousness' (1981, p. 185). It is because James thinks that the essence of psychological states is known through introspection that he believes that a pure psychological language would be one which is completely free of any objective reference, one in which words are linked directly with what the subject's acts of introspection discover.

As I remarked just now, James's discussion of an ideal psychological language, based purely on acts of introspection, occurs in the context of his exploration of some of the main sources of error in scientific psychology. He complains that our ordinary psychological language 'was originally made by men who were not psychologists, and most men today employ almost exclusively the vocabulary of outward things.' In the case of sensation language, for example, he makes the following observation:

> The elementary qualities of sensation, bright, loud, red, blue, hot, cold, are, it is true, susceptible to being used in both an objective and a subjective sense. They stand for outer qualities and for the feelings which these arouse. But the objective sense is the original sense; and still today we have to describe a large number of sensations by the name of the object from which they are most commonly got. An orange colour, an odour of violets, a cheesy taste, a thunderous sound, a fiery smart, etc., will recall what I mean.

> (1981, p. 193)

The problem is that the objectivity of our ordinary psychological language may lead us to incorporate into the essence of a given mental state more than the bare introspection of that state could possibly warrant. Thus we may be prompted by the objectivity of the language in which we describe mental states to introduce elements that are necessarily absent from the mental state itself, which 'is aware of itself only from within' (pp. 193–4). James warns us that we must not be misled by our language into 'counting [a mental state's] outward, and so to speak physical, relations with other facts of the world, in among the objects of which we set it down as aware' (p. 196). Similarly, he expresses the worry that our ordinary psychological language leads us to overlook psychological phenomena for which it has no name, and that our language imposes an order and structure on these phenomena that they do not actually possess. A pure language of subjectivity that ensured us a psychology free from these errors would, James suggests, be a completely disembodied language, lacking any connection with the objective world, whose terms are defined entirely on the basis of introspection.

James does not explicitly raise the question whether the pure language of subjectivity, whose absence he laments, would be one that could be understood only by the person speaking. However, I believe that we can still use James's discussion to focus on the central issue which is raised by Wittgenstein's remarks on private language. What prompts James to postulate this ideal psychological language is his sense that it is through *introspection* that we grasp the essence of particular psychological states. This sense that we grasp what a sensation, a thought, an image, etc. is on the basis of an introspective knowledge of our own case is a central theme of Wittgenstein's remarks on the philosophy of psychology, and his remarks on private language can be seen as the beginning of his exploration of the way this picture influences our idea of how psychological concepts are defined. The thought that introspection is essential to our understanding of psychological concepts is a highly intuitive one. If the essence of psychological phenomena – what distinguishes them from physical phenomena – lies in their possessing a *subjective* or *phenomenological* aspect, then it is surely by introspection alone that we discover the essence of these phenomena. To reject the idea that introspection is essential to a grasp of what, for example, a sensation is seems like a rejection of the distinctively subjective nature of sensations, and a consequent blurring of the distinction between the psychological and the physical. It is not dualism as such, but simply the thought that, as Nagel puts it, '[for] an organism [to have] conscious experience *at all* means ... that there is something it is like to *be* that organism' (1979, p. 166), which underlies our sense that it is through introspection, or looking inwards, that we achieve an understanding of what our psychological concepts refer to or describe.

Wittgenstein himself acknowledges the appeal of the idea that we discover what a given psychological state consists in by observing what goes on in us when we are in that particular state. Thus:

> What is pain? One is tempted to take present pain as a specimen.

> Surely what puzzles us isn't a word but the nature of a phenomenon. To investigate the nature of a phenomenon is to *look closer*.

> (*WLPP*, p. 3 and p. 5)

Yet he also believes that our intuition here is a mistaken one; introspection, or looking inwards, does not provide a means by which we

119

can grasp the nature of a given psychological state. Thus, '[i]t shews a fundamental misunderstanding, if I am inclined to study the headache I have now in order to get clear about the philosophical problem of sensation' (*PI* 314). The act of turning my attention inwards to what is going on inside me, for example, when I feel pain, or when I suddenly understand a word, does not tell me what a sensation is, or what understanding consists in. It is not that Wittgenstein wishes to deny that introspection is possible, or that its results may be of interest to us, but only to show that introspection is not a means by which we discover what sensations, thoughts, images, and so on are; it is not a means to defining a psychological term: 'Introspection can never lead to a definition. It can only lead to a psychological statement about the introspector' (*RPP* 1, 212).

Wittgenstein's own idea that we achieve clarity concerning the nature of sensations or thought by describing the use of the words 'pain' or 'to think', clearly goes counter to the intuition that it is only through introspection that we discover the essence of these phenomena. Thus the idea that the question 'What is a sensation?' is answered by reminding ourselves of 'the kind of statement we make about phenomena' (*PI* 90) stands in direct opposition to the thought that we get clear about what a sensation is, or define the concept of 'sensation', by concentrating our attention on what is occurring subjectively when, for example, I am in pain. It is essential to Wittgenstein's philosophical purpose, therefore, that he shows us that our natural inclination to picture introspection as essential to our understanding of the essence of psychological states is fundamentally mistaken. And just as James uses the image of an ideal psychological language, whose terms are defined ostensively, as a means of expressing his commitment to the central role of introspection in psychology, so Wittgenstein explores the idea of such a language in order to show that the idea that introspection can lead to a definition of a psychological term is an illusion.

Our ordinary sensation language

It is a striking feature of Wittgenstein's discussion of the idea of a private language that, having introduced it in *PI* 243, he immediately drops it and takes up a grammatical investigation of our ordinary sensation language. In *PI* 244, our initially vague and over-simplified picture of what is involved in giving names to sensations – 'There doesn't seem to be any problem here: don't we talk about sensations every day, and give them names?' – is replaced by a realistic account of how we use contexts in which the child has hurt himself to teach him, first of all, exclamations, and later, words, with which to express his pain: 'A child has hurt himself and he cries; and then adults talk to him and teach him exclamations and, later, sentences. They teach the child new pain-behaviour.' In looking at how we teach a child the word 'pain', Wittgenstein is already drawing our attention to the fact that we teach the use of the word without ever attempting to direct the child's attention inwards. Rather, we train the child in the use of a linguistic technique which enables him to express what he feels, not merely in cries and exclamations, but in articulate language. Thus we are already beginning to see that introspection plays no part in the training we receive with sensation words; learning what pain is – what the word 'pain' means – does not depend upon a process of 'looking inwards' or 'concentrating my attention on what is occurring inside me'. The remarks on private language continue this investigation of the role of introspection in defining psychological terms, but before he takes up this theme, Wittgenstein explores the grammar of our ordinary sensation language a little further.

At the end of *PI* 244, his interlocutor attempts to gloss Wittgenstein's observations on how we might teach a child the word 'pain' as follows: ' "So you are saying that the word 'pain' really means crying?" ' If the word 'pain' is not introduced by means of an inner ostensive definition, then surely what the child feels is not part of its meaning. The meaning of the word 'pain' is connected purely with the outward behaviour. Wittgenstein responds to this thought as follows: 'On the contrary: the verbal expression of pain replaces crying and does not describe it.' This is to be understood as a remark about the grammar of the word 'pain', i.e. as a description of the sort of technique that the use of the words 'I'm in pain' represents. The way that these words connect with what the child feels is through his learning to use them as a technique for giving expression to how he feels. No act of inner ostensive definition is required for the words

'I'm in pain' to connect with what is felt; the connection is secured by the grammar of the concept, by virtue of the fact that it is used as a new means to express what is felt. The connection between 'pain' and what a subject feels is achieved, not by where the child looks when he learns the word, but by the grammar of the concept that he is being taught. Thus, offset against Wittgenstein's attempt to wean us from the intuition that psychological phenomena are known through introspection is an attempt to show us that it is the distinctive grammar of psychological concepts that reveals the nature of the phenomena they describe.

This theme is continued in the remarks immediately following *PI* 244. In *PI* 246, Wittgenstein raises the question of the privacy of sensations directly: 'In what sense are my sensations *private*?' Now clearly there is a sense in which we want to say that pain *is* private. We want, for example, to draw a distinction between pain and crying; we want to say that pain is private in a way that crying is not. Wittgenstein clearly accepts the distinction that we want to make here, but he thinks that we are tempted to interpret it in the wrong way. We are inclined to construe the relative privacy of pain in terms of a picture of an object that only the subject who feels the pain has access to: another person can see the crying, but only the person who has the pain can see the pain. Thus: 'only I can know whether I'm in pain, another person can only surmise it.' Wittgenstein objects to this way of expressing the distinction on the grounds that it is completely at odds with our ordinary use of the words 'know' and 'pain'. If we reflect on our ordinary use of these words, then we shall see that I am never said to *know* of my pain – I just *have* pain – and that people very often *do know* of another's pain. The attempt to do justice to the distinction between pain and crying in terms of a subject's unique access to his sensations leads to our saying something which, at any other time, we would regard as nonsense. The distinction is undoubtedly a real one, but this is clearly not the way to make it.

The distinction that we have just tried to understand as a qualitative difference between kinds of object – private (accessible only to the subject) versus public (accessible to everyone) – Wittgenstein now presents as a grammatical difference between two kinds of concept. The distinction that we want to make when we say that the pain is private is one which is to be understood in terms of the grammatical differences between the concept pain and, for example, the concept crying. One important element in this grammatical difference lies in a distinctive asymmetry that characterizes the use of the former concept. Thus the first-person use of the concept pain diverges from the third-person use of the concept in a variety of ways. For example, the words 'I'm in pain' give expression to pain, whereas the words 'She's in pain' do not; I cannot be said to learn of my pain, whereas others can; other people may doubt whether I'm really in pain or only pretending, whereas it makes no sense for me to doubt it; and so on. One of Wittgenstein's aims is to bring us to accept that this complexity in the grammar of our sensation concepts is not something which needs to be explained – e.g. by reference to the fact that pain is something which we know directly (through introspection) in our own case and indirectly in the case of others – but is something which *in itself* reveals the fundamental distinction between sensations and behaviour. The distinction that we attempt to mark with the words 'pain is private' is not a perceived, qualitative difference between kinds of object, but a grammatical difference between sensation concepts and concepts of behaviour, which itself reveals that we have to do with two quite distinct kinds of thing. It is through the grammatical differences between kinds of concept that we distinguish the kinds of thing that our concepts describe: '*Essence* is expressed by grammar' (*PI* 371).

The words 'Sensations are private', or 'Only you can know if you had that intention', are, therefore, to be understood as grammatical remarks: 'The proposition "Sensations are private" is comparable to "One plays patience by oneself" ' (*PI* 248). We might find ourselves saying these things when we're explaining the meaning of the words 'pain' or 'intention' to someone, as a means of removing certain confusions. In that case, our words are an attempt to say something about how the words 'pain' and 'intention' are used, or about how their use is distinguished from the use of, say, the words 'crying' or 'dancing': 'You don't say of toothache *that it is internal*. You *compare* moaning and toothache with "external" and "internal" ' (LSDPE, p. 347). The expressions 'private', 'inner', 'hidden' are all attempts to capture this distinctive grammar, and might therefore be regarded as marking a boundary between our psychological language-game and the language-game of physical description. Wittgenstein does not wish to deny the aptness of these pictures, but his overall aim is to get us to recognize that the distinction which they are intended to capture is, at bottom, a grammatical one. Thus:

> [The] asymmetry of the [psychological language-]game is brought out by saying that the inner is hidden from someone else. Evidently there is an aspect of the *language-game* which suggests the idea of being private or hidden.

> What I want to say is surely that the inner differs from the outer in its *logic*. And that logic does indeed explain the expression "the inner", makes it understandable.

> (*LWPP* 2, p. 36e and p. 62e)

There is, however, a temptation to resist Wittgenstein's attempt to make us content with grammar, as the ground of the distinction between, for example, sensation and behaviour, and to look for a deeper explanation of the grammatical difference in the intrinsic nature of the things themselves. It is this sense that the grammar of the concept of pain reflects the fact that pain is a private object that is expressed by the interlocutor at the opening of *PI* 253: ' "Another person can't have my pains." ' The interlocutor here presents a picture of pain as something that is owned and accessible only to the person who has it, as something that he identifies or knows simply by turning his attention inwards to what only he can perceive. Wittgenstein responds to this picture with a question: 'Which are *my* pains? What counts as a criterion of identity here?' How does the interlocutor know which are *his* pains? Can he know it purely on the basis of concentrating very hard on what he feels? But this doesn't fix a criterion of identity; it doesn't determine what it is that the act of looking inwards is supposed to identify. Our grasp of a criterion of identity for pain depends upon our mastery of the use of the concept of pain, and in particular, of the use of the expression 'same pain'. But our ordinary use of these words does not make provision for the kind of distinction between 'my pain' and 'his pain' that the interlocutor's words attempt to make. 'Another person can't have my pains' tries to draw a distinction between pains that are qualitatively similar (my pains are *like* his) but numerically distinct (my pains are distinct from his pains); in this way, it treats the grammar of the word 'pain' as on a par with the grammar of the word 'chair', for which we do understand the distinction between 'a similar chair' and 'the same chair'. When we look at how these concepts are actually used, however, we see that they function grammatically in quite different ways, for while we talk of people feeling pain, and of their feeling the same (i.e. similar) pains, we don't identify or count pains in the way that we identify and count chairs. We talk about pain, about my having the same pain today as I had yesterday and about my having the same pain as you, but all of this talk depends for its sense upon a language-game which serves to fix the grammar of the word 'pain'; and this grammar simply lacks the structure that is needed for the interlocutor's words – ' "Another can't have my pains" ' – to make sense. There is nothing independent of this language-game – nothing that is fixed simply by looking inwards – that can determine a criterion of identity for pains. It is by making ourselves aware of how we use the words 'pain', 'my pain', 'his pain', 'same pain', and so on, that we articulate the criterion of identity for pain, and not by looking inwards and saying 'THIS'.

The remarks immediately following *PI* 243 thus serve to bring out that it is the grammar of the concept of pain which gives us our grasp of what pain is, which grounds the distinction between pain and crying, and which fixes the kind of thing that the concept of pain describes. Our inclination to interpret the boundary between the psychological and the physical in terms of a distinction between what is only accessible to introspection and what can be seen and known by all has repeatedly been shown to produce merely nonsense. The boundary itself is not, however, threatened by this failure, for it is one that is there in the grammar of our concepts. Our sense that there is an essential difference between pain and crying shows that we are conversant with this grammatical distinction, but we need to be reminded of it. The inclination, which our grasp of the distinction gives us, to over-emphasize the role of introspection in understanding psychological concepts leads us over and over again to neglect the grammatical distinction, or to suppose that it can be explained by something independent. Wittgenstein's grammatical enquiry provides a counter to the temptation to interpret the privacy of sensation in a way that links it essentially with introspection, by taking us back to an appreciation of the grammatical differences that are the real foundation of our intuition of a distinction between pain and crying. These paragraphs can be seen, therefore, as setting up a fundamental opposition between introspection and grammar as a source of our grasp of what pain is, or of what distinguishes pain from pain-behaviour. The discussion of the idea of a private language, which Wittgenstein takes up again in *PI* 256, can now be read as putting the idea that it is introspection, rather than grammar, that tells us what a sensation is under still further pressure.

The private language argument

Wittgenstein reintroduces the idea of a private language as follows:

> Now, what about the language which describes my inner experiences and which only I myself can understand? *How* do I use words to stand for my sensations? – As we ordinarily do? Then are my words tied up with my natural expressions of sensation? In that case my language is not a 'private' one. Someone else might understand it as well as I. – But suppose I didn't have any natural expression for the sensation, but only had the sensation? And now I simply *associate* names with sensations and use these names in descriptions.

> (*PI* 256)

At first sight there doesn't seem to be anything problematic in this idea: 'I simply *associate* names with sensations and use these names in descriptions.' But what are we thinking of here? Aren't we thinking that the grammar of the name – how the name is to be used – can somehow be fixed by this simple act of 'association', so that when I introduce the name by 'associating' it with the sensation it is already clear *what it is* that I intend the name to name. What is expressed here is not merely the over-simplified picture of what is involved in giving something a name, which Wittgenstein discussed in the opening paragraphs of the *Investigations*, but also the quite specific idea that I can derive a knowledge of what a sensation is – define a psychological expression – simply by looking inwards and attaching a label to what I find there. The issue that the remarks on private language focus on, therefore, is whether it makes sense to suppose that a psychological term could be defined like this, on the basis of introspection alone.

At the beginning of *PI* 257, Wittgenstein puts both a question – ' "What would it be like if human beings showed no outward sign of pain (did not groan, grimace, etc.)?" ' – and the answer to it: ' "Then it would be impossible to teach a child the use of the word 'toothache' " '. This suggests that we should take neither the question nor the answer that is given to it to express Wittgenstein's therapeutic voice. Rather, we should take these words to express the interlocutor's sense that, deprived of our ordinary technique for talking about pain, which is tied up with the natural *expression* of pain, the concept of toothache is not deprived of sense, it merely becomes impossible to *teach* it to someone. If we think we can derive our idea of what pain is independently of our grasp of our ordinary technique for talking about pain, simply on the basis of introspection, then the fact that we can't teach someone the use of these words is incidental to his ability to define them. He simply has to look inwards and 'associate' the word with the appropriate sensation. Thus, we might suppose that 'the child is a genius and itself invents a name for this sensation' (*PI* 257).

When Wittgenstein takes up the question, 'But what does it mean to say that [the child] has "named his pain"?', he identifies what is problematic in this idea with the absence of a grammar which could serve to fix what it is that the child has named. We think that the genius child has merely to turn his mental attention to what he feels and repeat to himself the words 'I'll call this "toothache" ', but how does this act of turning his attention inwards serve to fix a criterion of identity? Thus:

> How has [the child] done this naming of pain?! And whatever he did, what was its purpose? – When one says "He gave a name to his sensation" one forgets that a great deal of stage-setting

in the language is presupposed if the mere act of naming is to make sense. And when we speak of someone's having given a name to pain, what is presupposed is the existence of the grammar of the word "pain"; it shews the post where the new word is stationed.

(*PI* 257)

What the idea of a private language forces us to focus on, therefore, is the implication of the following two facts for our idea that we grasp what a sensation is on the basis of introspection. First, the act of naming presupposes a grammar, or technique of employing a word within a language-game; and second, the mere act of looking inwards does not supply this grammar, or specify a technique of employment.

In *PI* 258, Wittgenstein introduces an example in which I associate a certain sensation with a sign 'S', with a view to keeping a diary about its recurrence. Again, he imagines that I introduce 'S' simply by 'speak[ing], or writ[ing] the sign down, and at the same time ... concentrate my attention on the sensation – and so, as it were, point to it inwardly'. And now he asks what this ceremony of looking inwards and repeating the sign is for. How does it serve to establish a meaning for 'S'? He goes on:

> Well, that is done precisely by the concentrating of my attention; for in this way I impress on myself the connexion between the sign and the sensation. But "I impress it on myself" can only mean: this process brings it about that I remember the connexion *right* in the future. But in the present case I have no criterion of correctness. One would like to say: whatever is going to seem right to me is right. And that only means that here we can't talk about 'right'.

This paragraph is generally taken to be the crux of the private language argument. Here we get the proof that the user of the private language – let's call him 'the private linguist' – fails to give a meaning to 'S'. On one standard interpretation, the argument of *PI* 258 is rendered as follows: The private linguist introduces 'S' by associating it with a sensation, but given that the original sensation is no longer available when he comes to use 'S' in the future, there is nothing that can serve as a sample by reference to which this future use of 'S' can be justified. All that the private linguist has to go on in the future is his *memory* of the sample sensation, but since this memory of the sample can serve as a criterion only if it is itself a correct memory of the sample, there is no non-circular means of justifying a future use of 'S'. Thus, 'I have no criterion of correctness' is to be glossed as 'I have no non-circular, usable criterion of correctness', and that is why 'whatever is going to seem right to me is right', and why, therefore, 'it makes no sense to talk about "right"'. On this interpretation of *PI* 258, 'S' has no meaning because there is no way of fixing that a future use of 'S' is correct. The only remedy for this state of affairs is to provide some form of independent check on the use of 'S', by linking its use with *public* criteria of application. It is not that the first-person use of 'S' must itself be guided by these public criteria, but there must be public criteria against which the subject's application of 'S' in a new case can be checked for correctness.

On this interpretation, the point of Wittgenstein's remarks on private language is to prove that the meaningfulness of a psychological concept depends upon its possessing public criteria of application. Thus, in his review of the *Investigations*, Norman Malcolm writes: 'Once you admit the untenability of "private ostensive definition" you will see that there must be a *behavioural* manifestation of [e.g.] the feeling of confidence. There must be behaviour against which his words "I feel confident . . ." can be checked' (Malcolm, 1963, p. 113). The same theme can be discerned in the following quotes:

> What Wittgenstein aimed to show is not that sensation language, like the rest of language, is essentially shared, but that it is essentially shareable.
>
> (Hacker, 1990, p. 21)

> It follows [from the private language argument] that any genuine (rule-governed) language must refer only to things and properties whose presence can be publicly verified: in particular, there must be public criteria for the presence of sensations if meaningful sensation words are to be possible.
>
> (McGinn, 1984, pp. 48–9)

> [T]he self ascription of an 'inner process' [is] criterionless; and without outward criteria a sign that supposedly stands for the 'inner process' will not be rule-governed.
>
> (Budd, 1989, p. 61)

> [Wittgenstein shows] that both 'private' experience and the language we use to speak of it are in fact neither of them *private*; there are and have to be *public criteria* for the application of expressions about pains, moods, and the rest, in order for there to be such expressions at all.
>
> (Grayling, 1988, pp. 86–7)

It is the emphasis that this interpretation places on proving that psychological concepts must possess public criteria that has led critics of the private language argument to argue that it is no more than a verificationist defence of logical behaviourism, that is, of the view that the meaning of a psychological concept consists in the public criteria that warrant its ascription. For it seems that the whole point of the argument is to force us to accept that the meaning of psychological concepts consists in their possessing public criteria of application against which a first-person use of the concept can be checked, and without which the first-person use is simply meaningless. Defenders of Wittgenstein have certainly not accepted this criticism, but rather than enter into the details of this debate, I want to suggest that Wittgenstein's remarks can be read in a different way. Rather than see these remarks as a proof that psychological concepts require behavioural criteria of application, I shall read them as an attempt to show that we cannot derive an idea of what a given psychological state is simply through introspection. The moral of the argument, on this reading, is not that our psychological concepts *must* possess public criteria, but that it is only by reminding ourselves of the grammar of our ordinary psychological concepts that we can grasp the essence, or nature, of a given kind of psychological state. Such a reading avoids any suggestion that Wittgenstein uses the remarks on private language to put forward a behaviourist theory of how psychological concepts must function; the remarks provide a critique of the idea that a psychological concept can be defined on the basis of introspection alone; they are not intended to serve as a proof of what must be the case. The relationship between our psychological concepts and behaviour is something Wittgenstein reveals through a grammatical investigation of how our concepts actually function (as we'll see in the next chapter); it is not something that he presents as the conclusion of an argument intended to establish what must be the case.

Let us return, then, to *PI* 258. The opening of the paragraph – 'Let us imagine the following case' – suggests that *PI* 258 is a comment on *PI* 257, where, as we've already seen, Wittgenstein points out that what is problematic in the idea that the child 'invents a name for the sensation' is that there is nothing that determines the grammar of the name he introduces (i.e. there is nothing that determines *what it is* that he has named). This suggests that 'in the present case I have no criterion of correctness' should be read as follows: When 'I speak, or write the sign down, and at the same time concentrate my attention on the sensation', I do not thereby determine a linguistic technique for using (i.e. a grammar for) 'S'. There is nothing that can count as a correct use of 'S' in the future because there is no linguistic technique of using 'S' fixed by my act of looking inwards and concentrating my attention on what I feel. The problem here is not that 'S' refers to something that is (can be) introspected, but that the private linguist tries to determine what 'S' refers to by a bare act of introspection, i.e. by 'concentrat[ing] my attention on the sensation – and so, as it were, point[ing] to it inwardly' (*PI* 258). The emphasis, as in *PI* 257, is on the impossibility of giving a name to a sensation – determining what a sensation is – simply by looking inwards and saying a word; directing attention inwards and saying 'S' is not a way of giving a definition. On this interpretation of it, there is quite clearly nothing in *PI* 258 that implies that language cannot connect with the inner; the whole force of the remark is that it cannot connect with it on the basis of acts of introspection: 'Introspection can never lead to a definition' (*RPP* 1, 212).

This reading of *PI* 258 receives considerable support from *PI* 260–2. These paragraphs reinforce the point that there is nothing that fixes the grammar of 'S', or determines the nature of the linguistic technique that the private linguist is attempting to introduce. It is the lack of a grammar for 'S', rather than the lack of an independent check on its future use, that is underlined in the paragraphs following *PI* 258. Thus, in *PI* 260, 'a note has a function, and this "S" so far has none' emphasizes the fact that 'S' lacks a use; that is to say, there is nothing that fixes what it is that the private linguist makes a note of when he writes down 'S' in his diary. 'S' has not been connected with any linguistic technique which 'shows the post where the new word is stationed', and which could therefore serve to determine a meaning for 'S'. The same point is repeated in *PI* 262:

> It might be said: if you have given yourself a private definition of a word, then you must inwardly *undertake* to use the word in such-and-such a way. And how do you undertake that? Is it assumed that you invent the technique of using the word; or that you found it ready made?

The idea that the remarks on private language are focusing on an opposition between the grammar of our linguistic techniques and bare introspection, as a source of a grasp of what psychological expressions mean or refer to, is also reinforced by *PI* 261. Here Wittgenstein asks us what reason we have for calling 'S' the sign for a sensation. He goes on:

> For "sensation" is a word of our common language, not of one intelligible to me alone. So the use of this word stands in need of a justification which everybody understands.

It is tempting to read this as insisting that describing 'S' as the name of a sensation requires that a particular use of 'S' can be justified by reference to public criteria ('a justification which everybody understands'). However, the context makes it clear that what is at issue in *PI* 261 is not the justification of a particular application of 'S', but our justification for calling 'S' the *sign for a sensation*. The concept of sensation is defined by our ordinary technique for talking about sensations, and, if we are to be justified in calling 'S' a concept of sensation, it needs to be shown that 'S' constitutes a technique of this kind. It is not enough that the private linguist assures us, on the basis of his act of introspection, that he is naming a sensation, for being a name of a sensation means being a concept of a certain kind, i.e. having a particular use or grammar. It is only by showing that

'S' has the characteristic use of a sensation concept that we could justify calling 'S' the name of a sensation. But given that the private linguist sets up the connection between name and object simply by turning his attention inwards and saying 'S', there can be no question of justifying the claim that 'S' names a sensation by reference to its possessing the distinctive use that characterizes our concepts of sensation. For it is part of the description of the example that 'S' does not connect with our established techniques for talking about sensations. In fact, given that 'S' is introduced purely on the basis of looking inwards and saying a word, there is no justification for *any* description of 'S' which identifies its function with that of one of our ordinary linguistic techniques, all of which have a distinctive use to which 'S', by definition, fails to conform. Thus, if we set out to say what *kind* of thing 'S' refers to, we 'get to the point where [we] would like just to emit an inarticulate sound' (*PI* 261). But if this sound does not connect with some specific linguistic technique, then it accomplishes nothing more than the original act of looking inwards: we still have no idea of what it is that 'S' is supposed to name.

Those who read Wittgenstein's remarks on private language as a proof that psychological concepts must possess public criteria of application are inclined to regard the whole of *PI* 243–315 as a more or less continuous discussion of the issue of private versus public language. If we take the overall purpose of Wittgenstein's remarks to be an investigation of the grammar of our ordinary language-game, and see the remarks on private language as focusing purely on the question of the possible role of pure acts of introspection in defining psychological terms, then it is more natural to take *PI* 262 as the end of Wittgenstein's discussion of the topic of private language. *PI* 263 is, in that case, to be read as introducing a change of topic. Rather than considering the question of whether we can define a sensation word (grasp what a sensation is) purely on the basis of introspection, *PI* 263 raises the more general issue of the role that an introspected sample sensation, or private ostensive definition, plays in defining our ordinary sensation words.

Thus the fact that Wittgenstein uses the example of 'pain', rather than 'S', in *PI* 263 shows that his discussion is no longer focused purely on the question whether we can imagine a private language of sensation, but has widened out to consider the issue of the role of private ostensive definition in our acquiring mastery of our ordinary sensation language. The discussion of the idea of a private language has already begun to expose the weaknesses in the idea that we define sensation words on the basis of introspection, Wittgenstein now extends his critique by showing that introspection – looking inwards and concentrating on what you feel – has no role to play, even in a case where the grammar of the concept makes it clear that what is referred to, for example by the word 'pain', is a sensation. In this way, *PI* 256–62 are to be regarded as something of an aside in a wider discussion aimed at achieving clarity regarding the role of introspection in our coming to understand our ordinary psychological concepts; the remarks on private language provide a vivid illustration of the fact that an expression cannot be defined by an act of introspection alone. This suggests that the remarks on private language should not be regarded as the foundation of Wittgenstein's philosophy of psychology, but simply as one element in a critique of introspection which, in accordance with Wittgenstein's general philosophical approach, is principally grounded in a grammatical investigation of our ordinary language-game.

The role of private ostensive definition in our ordinary sensation language

In *PI* 263, Wittgenstein writes:

> "But I can (inwardly) undertake to call THIS 'pain' in the future." – "But is it certain that you have undertaken it? Are you sure that it was enough for this purpose to concentrate your attention on your feeling?" – A queer question.

The use of quotation marks suggests that we should read this paragraph as involving three different voices: two distinct interlocutors and Wittgenstein's therapeutic voice. The fact that the two questions occur in quotation marks makes it clear that they both involve some sort of misunderstanding. But why does Wittgenstein call the question raised by the second interlocutor a 'queer question'? Is it because the questions, like the assertion which precedes them, fail to question what might be meant, in this context, by the words 'concentrating your attention on your feeling'? How does someone who is not yet master of the concept of pain know what it is that he is supposed to be concentrating his attention on? The question raised here is what role 'concentrating your attention on your feeling' plays in our coming to grasp the meaning of our ordinary word 'pain'. There is a great temptation to think that we understand what the word 'pain' means on the basis of being presented with a *sample* or a *specimen* of pain, which we fix in our minds by concentrating our attention on our feeling. For 'once you know *what* the word stands for, you understand it, you know its whole use' (*PI* 264). Even if introspection cannot by itself determine what a sensation is (define an expression referring to sensations), we are still tempted to think that when we have a sensation language, introspection plays a vital part in our coming to understand the concepts of this language. Thus, 'it seems to us as though ... the instructor *imparted* the meaning to the pupil – without telling him it directly; but in the end the pupil is brought to the point of giving himself the correct ostensive definition' (*PI* 362).

In *PI* 265, Wittgenstein begins his attack on the idea that introspection, or private ostensive definition, has any role to play in defining our ordinary sensation concepts. He introduces the following analogy:

Let us imagine a table (something like a dictionary) that exists only in our imagination. A dictionary can be used to justify the translation of a word X by a word Y. But are we also to call it a justification if such a table is to be looked up only in the imagination? – "Well, yes; then it is a subjective justification." – But justification consists in appealing to something independent. – "But surely I can appeal from one memory to another. For example, I don't know if I have remembered the time of a departure of a train right and to check it I call to mind how a page of the time-table looked. Isn't it the same here?" – No; for this process has got to produce a memory which is actually *correct*. If the mental image of the time-table could not itself be *tested* for correctness, how could it confirm the correctness of the first memory? (As if someone were to buy several copies of the morning newspaper to assure himself that what it said was true.)

Looking up a table in the imagination is no more looking up a table than the image of the result of an imagined experiment is the result of an experiment.

In constructing this analogy, Wittgenstein is no longer concerned with the question of whether there could be such a thing as a private language, but has turned his attention to the question whether teaching someone our ordinary concept of pain involves indirectly bringing him to the point of giving himself the correct ostensive definition. What Wittgenstein is attempting to show is that there is something essentially problematic in this idea of a speaker's understanding the word 'pain' on the basis of his possessing his own private specimen of pain, or on the basis of his giving himself a private exhibition of what pain is. When we try to apply the concepts of pointing or exhibiting, or the concepts of a sample or a specimen, in this way, we are thinking of a kind of pointing that we do 'in our imagination', or of a sample that we point to 'with our imagination'. The difficulty is that while we understand pointing as an action that we perform (e.g.) with a finger, and while we have clear (though complex) criteria of what, in this case, has been pointed to, we have no grasp of what it is to point to something 'inwardly' or 'with the imagination'. On analogy with the final paragraph of *PI* 265: pointing to something in the imagination is no more pointing to something than the image of ostensively defining a word is an ostensive definition of it.

It is not that being able to point to appropriate samples is not part of our mastery of the concept of pain, but these samples, like samples of 'red' or 'square' or 'table', will be ones that we point to with our fingers. For example, in teaching a child the word 'pain' I might well use a picture to point, or to ask him to point, to a person who is in pain. Thus, 'I can exhibit pain, as I exhibit red, and as I exhibit straight and crooked trees and stones. – *That* is what we *call* "exhibiting"' (*PI* 313). In all these cases of exhibiting, what is exhibited will depend upon the use of the word that surrounds the act of pointing; it is how we ordinarily use the word 'pain' that determines that what I've pointed to when I say, 'Here is someone in pain', is an example of someone who is undergoing a particular sensation. Wittgenstein is not, therefore, suggesting that there is anything special or peculiar about the word 'pain'. What is peculiar is merely the idea, which we get while doing philosophy, that our grasp of the meaning of the word 'pain' involves us in a different sort of 'exhibiting', a sort that is not done with the finger but 'with the imagination'.

In order to get us to see that 'pointing to a sample in (or with) the imagination' is not an instance of pointing to a sample, Wittgenstein also offers a number of other comparisons. We would not want to say that looking up a table in the imagination is looking up a table, nor that the imagined result of an experiment is the result of an experiment. And nor would we want to say that looking up a clock in the imagination is a way of determining the time. Nor that imagining justifying the choice of dimensions for a bridge is a way of justifying a choice of dimensions. In all these cases we can see that although something does no doubt go on, what goes on does not constitute an instance of *performing* the imagined act. In the same way, pointing to an object with (in) the imagination is not an instance of pointing to an object. Looking up a table, finding out the result of an experiment, justifying the choice of dimensions for a bridge, pointing to an instance of a colour, a shape, a kind of object, a mood, etc. are all forms of *action*. Sitting still and either imagining something or saying something to yourself is not another way of doing these things; it is, at best, a way of imagining doing them. Thus the very idea that pointing to a sample with (or in) the imagination is an instance of pointing to a sample is completely idle or empty. All that actually happens when someone tries to point to something with his imagination is that he stands very still and pulls a strange expression.

In *PI* 268, Wittgenstein continues the investigation of whether the act of turning our attention inwards has any role to play in our coming to understand the meaning of our sensation words:

> Why can't my right hand give my left hand money? – My right hand can put it into my left hand. My right hand can write a deed of gift and my left hand a receipt. – But the further

practical consequences would not be those of a gift. When the left hand has taken the money from the right, etc., we shall ask: "Well, and what of it?" And the same could be asked if a person had given himself a private definition of a word: I mean, if he has said a word to himself and at the same time has directed his attention to a sensation.

What he is trying to get us to see is that the act of looking inwards, which we are tempted to think is vital to our understanding of the word 'pain', is in fact idle in respect of either achieving or displaying mastery of this concept. What matters for mastery of our concept of pain is an ability to use the relevant expression in accordance with our ordinary practice. The question is, How does the ceremony of saying the word 'pain' while directing my attention to what is going on inside me connect with this ability? Could what I do when I pull a face and 'direct my attention inwards' amount to my giving the word 'pain' a definition? If someone performs this act of 'private definition', don't we still want to ask 'Well, and what of it?', for we still don't know whether the speaker has understood the word 'pain', i.e. whether he has mastered the technique for using this word in accordance with our ordinary practice. The act of private definition, which seems so vital when we're doing philosophy, has no connection with our ordinary criteria for mastery of the concept of pain; the performance of this ceremony tells us nothing about whether the speaker has understood the concept.

In *PI* 270, Wittgenstein reintroduces the example of someone who is keeping a diary that records the occurrence of a particular sensation, 'S', only now he imagines that the use of 'S' is connected with the speaker's detecting a rise in his blood-pressure. The question is, What role does a private act of identifying what is introspected as 'the same again' play in this language-game? In order to get us to see that it plays no role, Wittgenstein asks us to imagine that the private ceremony of identification comes adrift from the public practice of the speaker's ascribing a rise in blood-pressure to himself. The point is not that the meaning of 'S' is exhausted by its connection with a rise in blood-pressure, but that its meaning derives from its use in the language-game, and not from its connection with anything that is identified by 'turning the attention inwards'. Deciding whether 'S' names a sensation is not a matter of conjecturing about what is going on inside the speaker when he uses 'S', or of speculating on the kind of object that he points to inwardly when he defines 'S', but of discerning, in the way that 'S' is used, the distinctive grammar of sensation words: 'And what is our reason for calling "S" the name of a sensation here? Perhaps the kind of way this sign is employed in this language-game' (*PI* 270). It is, for instance, the fact that 'S' displays the characteristic asymmetry of first-person and third-person use, that questions of duration and intensity make sense, that the question of pretence can arise, and so on, that warrants our calling 'S' the name of a sensation. Likewise, the question of whether 'S' names a *particular* kind of sensation – that is, the same kind every time – does not depend upon the truth of a hypothesis about what is occurring unseen inside the speaker, but upon the grammar of the language: 'Well, aren't we supposing that we write "S" every time?' (*PI* 270). Wittgenstein makes the same point elsewhere as follows:

> We imagine sometimes as though they were so many different things in a box – colour, sound, pain. But it makes no sense to say "I have this", pointing within myself. 'I am inclined to say' that pain is a sensation – but I can't justify this by a noticeable similarity among the contents of a box – colour, sound, pain. The similarity must be in the *concept*.
>
> (*WLPP*, p. 62)

In *PI* 271, Wittgenstein writes:

> "Imagine a person whose memory could not retain *what* the word 'pain' meant – so that he constantly called different things by that name – but nevertheless used the word in a way fitting in with the usual symptoms and presuppositions of pain" – in short he uses it as we all do. Here I should like to say: a wheel that can be turned though nothing else moves with it, is not part of the mechanism.

The above reading of *PI* 263–70 removes any temptation to read this as an implicit endorsement of logical behaviourism. The point that Wittgenstein is making here is simply that the unity of our concept of pain – its meaning the same thing over time and across speakers – does not depend upon our each correctly identifying objects in a private space as 'the same again'; our concept of pain serves as a name of one particular kind of sensation just insofar as there exists a stable, unified language-game within which the word 'pain' is employed, and within which it exemplifies the distinctive grammar of a sensation concept. Wittgenstein is not suggesting, quite absurdly, that what a speaker feels is irrelevant to our concept of pain; the fact that the word 'pain' describes what the speaker feels is revealed by the distinctive grammar of this concept. It is rather that there is nothing independent of this grammar that serves to fix what we mean by the word 'pain'; and there is nothing over and above our all using this word in the same way that constitutes our meaning the same thing by it. The scenario that the interlocutor describes is an illusion, for what the word 'pain' means is not fixed by speakers looking inward and identifying 'the same again'; it is fixed by the use that it has in our language-game, by the way we all use it.

In the paragraphs that follow, Wittgenstein's emphasis is on ridding us of the illusion that our understanding of psychological concepts depends upon fixing our attention on what is going on inside us: 'as if when I uttered the word I cast a sidelong glance at the private sensation, as it were in order to say to myself: I know all right what I mean by it' (*PI* 274). Consider, for example, the case of colour concepts. It simply doesn't occur to us outside of philosophy that we know what the word 'red' means on the basis of 'pointing into ourselves', or 'that really you ought not to point to the colour with your hand, but with your attention. (Consider what it means to "point to something with the attention".)' (*PI* 275). It never normally occurs to us that, apart from the public use of the word 'red', there is an act of private ostensive definition that tells me what I *really* mean by the word; this private act, which seems essential only while we're doing philosophy, is simply not part of our ordinary language-game. Not only that, but we've come to see that this private act is idle in respect of our mastery of our ordinary linguistic techniques. If someone says 'I call THIS "pain"', or 'I call THIS "green"', and at the same time directs his attention inwards, we shall ask 'Well, and what of it?' These ceremonies do not show us that he has mastered the concepts of pain or green; knowing what the words 'pain' or 'green' mean consists in nothing other than the ability to use these words in accordance with our ordinary language-game. The distinctive nature of the qualities that these concepts describe does not derive from the fact that we look inwards when we define these words, but from the particular nature of the technique that we learn in mastering them. What we wrongly attempt to capture through the illusion of private exhibition is already fully secured by the grammar of our concepts.

The underlying theme of all the remarks I've looked at in this chapter, from *PI* 243 to *PI* 275, is, first, that introspection plays no role in defining psychological concepts, and second, that the distinction between psychological states and behaviour, which the appeal to introspection is designed to capture, is a grammatical distinction which is properly understood through a careful attention to the differences in how we use the relevant concepts. The remarks on the idea of a private language represent no more than one element in a critique of introspection whose ultimate target is our tendency to misrepresent the role of private ostensive definition in fixing the meaning of our ordinary psychological concepts. In getting us to see that private ostensive definition is an illusion, and to accept that introspection plays no role in our coming to understand sensation words, we do not thereby resign ourselves to a behaviourist analysis of these concepts. Rather, we come to recognize that it is grammar, and not where we look, which shows us that our psychological concepts describe what subjects feel, or see, or intend, and which marks the undeniable distinction between the psychological states of a subject and the behaviour that expresses them. In the next chapter we will explore the distinctive grammar of our psychological concepts more fully, in a wider investigation of the temptation to interpret the distinction between psychological and behavioural concepts by reference to the notion of a private object or process that we know by introspection, each of us on the basis of his own case. The question we will now address is whether the idea that the notion of a private object is somehow vital to the functioning of our ordinary psychological concepts actually fits the grammar of our language-game of ascribing psychological states to ourselves and others.

References and further reading

Binkley, T., *Wittgenstein's Language* (The Hague: Martinus Nijhoff, 1973).

Budd, M., *Wittgenstein's Philosophy of Psychology* (London: Routledge, 1989).

Cavell, S., *The Claim of Reason: Wittgenstein, Skepticism, Morality and Tragedy* (Oxford: Oxford University Press, 1979).

Fogelin, R. F., *Wittgenstein* (London: Routledge, 1987).

Grayling, A., *Wittgenstein* (Oxford: Oxford University Press, 1988).

Hacker, P. M. S., *Insight and Illusion* (Oxford: Oxford University Press [1972], 1986).

—— *Wittgenstein: Meaning and Mind*, vol. 3 (Oxford: Blackwell, 1990).

James, W., *The Principles of Psychology* (Cambridge, Mass.: Harvard University Press, 1981).

Johnston, P., *Wittgenstein: Rethinking the Inner* (London: Routledge, 1993).

Kenny, A., *Wittgenstein* (Harmondsworth: Penguin, 1973).

Kripke, S. A., *Wittgenstein on Rules and Private Language* (Oxford: Blackwell, 1982).

McGinn, C., *Wittgenstein on Meaning* (Oxford: Blackwell, 1984).

Malcolm, N., 'Wittgenstein's *Philosophical Investigations*', in *Knowledge and Certainty* (Englewood Cliffs, NJ: Prentice-Hall, 1963).

Mulhall, S., *On Being in the World* (London: Routledge, 1990).

Nagel, T., 'What is is like to be a bat?', *Mortal Questions* (Cambridge: Cambridge University Press, 1979).

Pears, D. F., *The False Prison*, vol. 2 (Oxford: Oxford University Press, 1987).

Wright, C., 'Does *Philosophical Investigations* 258–60 Suggest a cogent argument against private language?', in P. Petit and J. H. McDowell, eds, *Subject, Thought and Context* (Oxford: Oxford University Press, 1986).

—— 'Wittgenstein's Later Philosophy of Mind: Sensation, Privacy, and Intention', *Journal of Philosophy*, vol. 86, 1989.

Chapter 5

The inner and
the outer
Philosophical
Investigations
281–307, pp. 227–8

Introduction

Wittgenstein's critique of introspection focused on
the temptation to picture the difference between the
concept of pain and the concept of crying as a distinction between terms that are defined by private, and
terms that are defined by public, ostensive definition.
We've seen Wittgenstein respond to this temptation by
showing, on the one hand, that the idea of private
ostensive definition is an illusion, and on the other,
that the distinction it was intended to explain is actually grounded in grammar, i.e. in the differences in the
use of the words 'pain' and 'crying'. Thus our sense
that we capture what is special or distinctive about
sensation concepts by appeal to the role that introspection plays in defining them is shown to be a false
lead. We actually come to understand the difference in
meaning between pain and crying through a reflective
awareness of the contrasts between the different
regions of our language that these concepts represent.

In this way, the discussion of *PI* 243ff. serves to bring about an acknowledgement of the role of grammar in marking the distinctions which our mastery of language prompts us to make, but which our urge to explain conceptual distinctions by reference to something independent of language makes us misunderstand. The position we've been brought to might be captured by the slogan: 'Back to grammar.' Achieving a clearer grasp of the grammar of our psychological concepts is the central task of the current chapter.

The focus on the question of the role of introspection in defining sensation words has meant that we have been more concerned with what is involved in teaching or coming to understand psychological concepts than with achieving an overview of how our pyschological concepts function. Thus, we have not yet looked in any detail at the grammar of the language-game of ascribing psycho-logical states to ourselves and others. Looking at the functioning of the wider language-game undoubtedly raises difficulties that we have not yet touched on. In particular, the ascription of psychological states to others raises questions that relate to the concept of perception and the notion of what is seen. These issues will be looked at in detail in the next chapter. However, much of the discussion of the problems which surround the use of our psychological concepts in describing the feelings, moods, beliefs, intentions, and so on, of ourselves and others is no more than a continued investigation of questions that have already been raised in the previous chapter. The question of the role of introspection in defining sensation words arose, I sug-gested, in the intuition of a distinction between pain and pain-behaviour, which we feel is captured by the picture of the pain as inner and the crying as outer. The application that we now make of this picture leads us into trying to explain the intuitive difference between pain and crying by appeal to the role of private ostensive definition in fixing the meaning of the concept of pain. But while the critique of introspection may have done the work of showing that we do not define sensation concepts by looking inwards and saying 'THIS', it has left unanswered the question, raised in *PI* 244–5, of how the relation between our ordinary concept of pain and the behaviour that expresses it is to be understood. As we shall see, our tendency to misunderstand this relation also has its roots in the misapplication of the picture of the inner and the outer.

A major concern of the current chapter, then, is to disperse some more of the fog that has come, through a misapplication of the picture of the inner and the outer, to surround our sensation concepts. In particular, the aim is to show how a misapplication of this picture leads us to misunderstand the connection between our ordinary concept of pain and the natural expression of pain in pain-behaviour. The question of the connection between the concept of pain and pain-behaviour has already been touched on in the discussion of Wittgenstein's remarks on how we use contexts in which the child has hurt himself to teach him words with which to express his pain. As we saw, the interlocutor's suggestion that this amounts to a claim that the definition of the word 'pain' connects it purely with outward behaviour is countered by the grammatical observation that the technique the child is trained in is one that allows him to *express* his feeling, not only in crying and groaning, but in articulate language: 'the verbal expression of pain replaces crying and does not describe it' (*PI* 244). The point of Wittgenstein's remark is that the connection between the word 'pain' and what a subject feels is achieved by the grammar – i.e. the use – of the linguistic technique that the child is being trained to employ. This observation marks the beginning of Wittgenstein's description of the use of our ordinary sensation language and of its intricate relations with human behaviour; there are a number of reasons – all of them connected with the misunderstanding of the distinction between inner and outer – why it is very difficult for us to see this relation clearly.

The fact that it is possible to pretend to be in pain, that others may hide what they are feeling, that we cannot point to the pain in the same way as we can point to the crying, that it is possible to imagine that someone who is behaving normally is really in pain, and so on, all invite us to picture pain as something that is 'inside us'. I have continually emphasized that, insofar as this picture is an attempt to capture the difference between sensation concepts and concepts that describe behaviour, Wittgenstein acknowledges its aptness. At the moment it is nothing more than a picture. And while it seems to sum up the grammatical difference between pain and crying, it has not yet been shown how it is to be *applied*. The problems arise when we come to apply the picture, for it is in the application which we are inclined to make of the picture that misunderstandings and confusions arise. There is a continual temptation to suppose that the application of the picture is much more straightforward than it is, and this can lead us to misunderstand the grammar of sensation concepts, and in particular, to misunderstand the relation between these concepts and behaviour. What begins as a picture of an important grammatical distinction comes to stand in the way of our achieving a clear view of the grammar of our concepts, so that it prevents us from seeing how our concepts actually function, and thus from appreciating the real nature of the distinction it was originally intended to capture. It is only by attending carefully to the clash between the application which we are inclined to make of the picture and the grammar of our ordinary language-game that we can escape from the confusions it invites, and achieve the understanding that it purports, but fails, to yield.

Wittgenstein expresses these points clearly as follows. First of all, our psychological concepts inevitably invite the thought that they describe thoughts and feelings which are 'inside us' in a way that our behaviour is not:

> *Certainly* all these things happen in you. – And now all I ask is to understand the expression we use. – The picture is there. And I am not disputing its validity in any particular case. – Only I also want to understand the application of the picture.
>
> (*PI* 423)

> The picture is *there*; and I do not dispute its *correctness*. But *what* is its application?
>
> (*PI* 424)

> In numberless cases we exert ourselves to find a picture and once it is found the application as it were comes about of itself. In this case we already have a picture which forces itself on us at every turn, – but does not help us out of the difficulty, which only begins here.
>
> (*PI* 425)

Wittgenstein now suggests that one of the reasons why the picture of sensations and thoughts as things that occur inside us has a tendency to mislead is that it is so much less ambiguous than the grammar of the language it is meant to represent:

> A picture is conjured up which seems to fix the sense *unambiguously*. The actual use, compared with that suggested by the picture, seems like something muddied.

> (*PI* 426)

The picture invites us to form the image of an internal realm of determinate states and processes. The uncertainty and indeterminacy which characterizes our ordinary psychological language-game – e.g. that it makes sense to doubt whether someone is really in pain, to wonder what someone really thinks, to be uncertain whether a smile is friendly, and so on – comes to look like a defect that does not afflict the reality it describes. Thus the picture of sensations as inner suggests that a god who could see into human consciousness might know what we, whose eyes cannot penetrate to what lies behind behaviour, can only guess at. By comparison with this god's use of psychological expressions, our own use seems indirect, and we begin to feel a certain sort of dissatisfaction with our ordinary language-game. The picture that was originally designed to capture the distinctive grammar of our psychological language-game ends by making us feel that 'in the actual use of expressions we make detours, we go by side-roads. We see the straight highway before us, but of course we cannot use it, because it is permanently closed' (*PI* 426). Our ordinary language-game comes to seem indirect and disconnected from the phenomena it is meant to describe; 'we are tempted to say that our way of speaking does not describe the facts as they really are' (*PI* 402). What we really need is not to abandon the distinction which makes the picture of the inner and the outer apt, but to be shown what is wrong with the application we make of this picture. In this way, we may be led away from the temptation to interpret 'the inner' as a quasi-spatial realm of inner states and processes, and to a proper appreciation of the real nature of the distinction that the picture of the inner and the outer was originally felt to capture. What Wittgenstein tries to show us is that the only real sense attaching to the distinction between inner and outer connects this distinction with the grammar of our concepts, that is, with the differences in how the concepts of pain and crying function. Our mistake is to suppose that the picture of the inner and the outer *explains* these differences, when all it really does is *describe* them: 'The question is not one of explaining a language-game by means of our experiences, but of noting a language-game' (*PI* 655); 'Look on the language-game as the *primary* thing' (*PI* 656).

Pain and pain-behaviour

Let us return, then, to the task of describing the way our ordinary sensation language functions. We have already seen how Wittgenstein's description of the grammar of our sensation concepts draws our attention to the link between our ordinary language-game and the natural expression of sensations in behaviour. In *PI* 281, his interlocutor asks: ' "But doesn't what you say come to this: that there is no pain, for example, without *pain-behaviour*?" '

The question can be seen as an attempt to reformulate Wittgenstein's grammatical observation as a general claim, about the connection between pain and pain-behaviour, which is at odds with our ordinary practice; for, of course, we do often speak of someone's being in pain but not showing it. Wittgenstein responds as follows:

> It comes to this: only of a living human being and what resembles (behaves like) a living human being can one say: it has sensations; it sees; is blind; hears; is deaf; is conscious or unconscious.
>
> (*PI* 281)

Wittgenstein's rejection of the interlocutor's generalization does not deny that there is some sort of a link between the concept of pain and pain-behaviour, but it suggests that the link has been oversimplified. There is a grammatical connection between pain and pain-behaviour, but the language-game we play with this concept is much more complex, and much more subtle, than the interlocutor's generalization suggests. Our sensation concepts are used to describe only those things (living human beings and what resembles them) that are seen to express pain, to look, to listen, to attend, and so on, but there is a complexity in the forms and possibilities which this region of our language presents that the interlocutor's generalization entirely obscures. Thus the possibilities for pretence, for suppression of the expression of pain, for doubting whether an expression is genuine, for acting, and so on, are all an essential part of our language-game. Our description of how our concepts function must not make this region of our language look more determinate or more certain than it actually is, or make what is actually an essential and distinctive part of it look like an embarrassing appendage. It is, in part, these very aspects of our language-game that make the picture of the inner and the outer so apt, and which give this picture its real content. Yet the application we are now tempted to make of the picture creates the seductive idea of a determinate inner realm of states and processes, which prompts us to regard this essential complexity in our ordinary language-game as a defect, or as a sign of the indirectness of our access to the psychological states of another.

In *PI* 282, the interlocutor appears to object even to Wittgenstein's weakened claim that *some* grammatical connection exists between psychological concepts and characteristic forms of behaviour: ' "But in a fairy tale the pot too can see and hear! " ' Doesn't this show that the concepts 'see' and 'hear' can function independently of behaviour? Isn't it just a question of what *experiences* the pot is having? But how does the fairy-tale achieve its imaginative aim of describing a pot in a way that allows us to see it as a pot which sees and hears? Isn't it by describing a pot which has come, in certain vital ways, to resemble a living human being? Don't we imagine the pot seeing and hearing by imagining it talking and responding to what goes on around it? And do we here imagine something that is simply false (as a matter of fact pots don't talk) or nonsensical (we don't know what it means to describe a pot as 'talking')?

Wittgenstein suggests that it is neither false nor nonsensical, for the fairy-tale description of the pot belongs to a fictional language-game which functions in a quite different way from ordinary discourse. Thus, the fairy-tale is akin to the kind of play-acting in which we imagine that a doll feels pain, or that we have magic powers, or that we are trains, and so on. In all these cases we use our knowledge of the real world to create an imaginary one, without ever having to ask ourselves under what circumstances we should actually say of a pot that it talks, of a doll that it is in pain, that a person has magic powers, or that we're applying the brake to a human body. This imaginative use of language represents a 'secondary' use of concepts; it shows us nothing about the boundary between sense and nonsense which governs their primary use. It is no doubt revealing that the fairy-tale has to imagine the pot *acting* in a certain way, but it is in the investigation of the primary use of psychological concepts that we must uncover the grammatical connections between these concepts and human behaviour.

In the primary use of psychological concepts, we apply them only to particular sorts of *thing*, namely living human beings and other animals. But why do we ascribe these concepts only to a kind of *thing*? 'Is it', Wittgenstein asks, 'that my education has led me to it by drawing my attention to feelings in myself, and now I transfer the idea to objects outside myself?' (*PI* 283). Here we have a particular application of the picture of inner and outer, in which pain and the things we ascribe it to are thought of as distinct kinds of object that stand in a particular relation to one another. Thus, the pain is a kind of private object (known from one's own case) which is somehow 'inside' the body, and the body itself is a kind of public object; the pain belongs to 'the psychological sphere' and the body to 'the physical sphere'. Thus, the pain and the things we ascribe it to are not linked conceptually, but belong to quite different 'realms' which exist in a purely empirical relationship to one another: one (somehow!) inside the other. Part of this application of the picture – the idea that the word 'pain' could be defined by introspecting a sample – has already come under scrutiny in the previous chapter, but here we approach it from a different angle. The focus is now on the idea that the concept of pain has no essential, or conceptual, ties with the objects we ascribe it to, but functions as the name of a 'something' – a kind of *object* – which is only empirically linked with a body. In order to get us to see what is wrong with this application of the picture of inner and outer, Wittgenstein asks the following, rather strange, question: 'Couldn't I imagine having frightful pains and turning to stone while they lasted?' (*PI* 283).

We can begin to see why Wittgenstein asks this question when we realize that our picture of the relation between pain and the body is one that effectively conceives the latter as in itself an insentient thing; the pain is merely (somehow!) *linked* with the physical body; in itself the pain is THIS, a particular phenomenal presence that we each know from our own case. So when he asks, 'Well, how do I know, if I shut my eyes, whether I have not turned into stone?' (*PI* 283), he is merely bringing out that, as we've pictured matters, the essence of pain has no connection with my physical body; everything could, conceptually speaking, remain psychologically – i.e. phenomenally – just as it seems, while profound physical changes take place. If pain is just a particular sort of object whose identity is fixed phenomenally, by its being THIS, then how can I simply dismiss the question of whether my body has turned to stone while I go on feeling pain, without actually checking? For the presence of THIS is, on this picture, conceptually unconnected with my body, and therefore with the kind of body I have. Suppose, then, that it has actually happened that I have turned to stone while feeling pain. Wittgenstein now asks: '[I]n what sense will *the stone* have the pains? In what sense will they be ascribable to the stone?' (*PI* 283). If we can imagine the pain going on while the body changes, then in what sense does the body have the pain? Why do we connect pain with a body at all? Indeed, 'why need the pain have a bearer at all here?!' (*PI* 283). As we've conceived matters, the concept of pain functions independently of the concept of the body, and, conceptually speaking, does not even require a body to bear it; it is just THIS. Thus, if we conceive of the relation between pain and the human body as an empirical relation between two kinds of object – so that pain occurs in the human body like a pearl in an oyster shell – then the body cannot be regarded as the real bearer of pain; it just exists alongside it.

Thus, by asking us to imagine having frightful pains and turning to stone while they lasted, Wittgenstein has presented us with a vivid picture of the way we are inclined to apply the picture of the inner and the outer, or to conceive of the relation between pain and the body. In this way he brings us to see that we have a picture of pain on which it is not actually ascribable to a body at all. Perhaps we will respond to this by saying that the pain does not belong to a body, but to a soul. But then what has this soul to do with a body? Wittgenstein now asks: 'And can one say of a stone that it has a soul and *that* is what has the pain? What has a soul, or pain, to do with a stone?' (*PI* 283). If we conceive of the body as in itself a thing, and of pain as a kind of private object whose essence is purely phenomenal, then we can put neither pain nor a soul in relation to the body; we have two discrete existences that are out of play to one another. Thus, the human body (the stone) becomes altogether lost to pain. But this clearly goes entirely against the grammar of our ordinary language-game. For our ordinary concept of pain has just the sort of link with bodies that this picture seems to make incomprehensible; our concept is used to ascribe pain *only* to living human beings and what resembles them:

> Only of what behaves like a human being can one say that it *has* pains.
>
> For one has to say it of a body, or, if you like of a soul which some body *has*.

> (*PI* 283)

The grammatical connection that exists in our language-game between the concept of pain and living beings as the bearers of pain shows that the picture of inner and outer cannot be given the sort of application we have tried to give it. But if the relation between pain and the body which has the pain cannot be conceived as an empirical relation between two distinct kinds of object, how is it to be conceived: '[H]ow can a body *have* a soul?' (*PI* 283).

Wittgenstein begins to answer this question in *PI* 284. He first of all repeats the observation that it makes no sense to say that the bearer of pain is a thing:

> Look at a stone and imagine it having sensations. – One says to oneself: How could one so much as get the idea of ascribing a *sensation* to a *thing*? One might as well ascribe it to a number! – And now look at a wriggling fly and at once these difficulties vanish and pain seems able to get a foothold here, where before everything was, so to speak, too smooth for it.

The application we are inclined to make of the picture of the inner and the outer leads us to make an ontological cut somewhere deep inside the body. Thus the body is seen as belonging to the realm of outer things, while the pain belongs to a psychological realm, inside the body, within which conscious experiences occur. The reflections of *PI* 283 bring home to us that, given this application of the picture, we can no longer connect pain and the human body. In assigning the human body to a category of physical things which lack any conceptual connection with sensation concepts, we have put it entirely beyond the reach of the concept of pain; it would make no more sense to ascribe pain to this body than it would to a stone or to a number. When we look at how our psychological concepts actually function, then we begin to see that the cut which our language makes does not lie *within* the body – is not between the private pain and the public body – but *between* bodies of quite different kinds: those that are accessible to the concept of pain and those that are not. The boundary between the stone and the fly is not an empirical one (we have 'discovered' ('conjectured') that stones do not have pains inside them, and that flies do), reflecting an empirical relation which exists between some physical objects and the special category of private objects. Rather, it is a conceptual one, which reflects the conceptual connection that exists in our language between sensation concepts and bodies of a quite particular kind: living human beings and what resembles them. Thus it makes no sense to say that a stone feels pain, but it makes sense to say it of a fly. The false distinction between a 'physical realm' and a 'psychological realm', which the misapplication of the picture of the inner and the outer leads us to make, is replaced by a distinction between the living and the non-living, whose roots lie deep in the grammar of our language.

PI 284 continues: 'And so, too, a corpse seems to us quite inaccessible to pain.' The death of a human being does not leave us with the 'thing' half of the previously coexisting body and mind, but at death the human body *becomes* a thing, an object that is inaccessible to psychological description. The difficulty is in recognizing how profound this difference is. It is not merely a difference in how we describe things, what we *say* of them. For the division between the living and the non-living which is drawn in our language enters into the fundamental structure of our form of life; it represents the form of our world. It is tied up, not merely with what we say, but with all our ways of acting and responding to the world. Thus: '[o]ur attitude to what is alive and to what is dead is not the same. All our reactions are different' (*PI* 284). When the interlocutor responds, '"That cannot simply come from the fact that a living thing moves about in such-and-such a way and a dead one not"', he shows that he is inclined to think that the body and the stone are the same kind of objects (material objects, say) which simply *behave* differently. Wittgenstein replies by pointing out that this difference in behaviour grounds a much deeper cut than this suggests. We have here two distinct categories of thing; a 'transition from quantity to quality' (*PI* 284).

In *PI* 285, Wittgenstein explores an aspect of my experience of living things which reveals something of the nature of this 'qualitative transition':

> Think of the recognition of *facial expressions*. Or of the description of facial expressions – which does not consist in giving the measurements of the face! Think, too, how one can imitate a man's face without seeing one's own in a mirror.

Recognizing a face as friendly, bored, aggressive, or hurt amounts to recognizing the *significance* or *meaning* of the other's look. The descriptions that we give of facial expressions are rich in terms which ascribe a particular significance to them: 'a friendly smile', 'a hostile stare', 'a shocked expression'. 'a shameful look', and so on. We do not see or describe physical features disposed in a physical relation to one another, but human faces whose expressions have a significance to which we have become attuned. Imitating a man's face does not require me to look in the mirror and arrange my features in the same way as his. I understand the meaning of his look and I now act out this meaning in my own face. It is not merely 'that a living thing moves about in such-and-such a way and a dead one not', for the movements of a living thing have a significance that the movements of a physical object do not have. The difference may be seen as analogous to that between a spoken or written sentence and random sounds or marks. Thus, the series of marks 'Keep off the grass' is distinguished from '@£$!^&%|-/' insofar as the former possesses a significance which is an essential part of our description of it, and which is entirely alien to the series of random marks; human language and meaningless marks enter into our form of life in such fundamentally different ways that we do not hesitate to recognize them as distinct categories of thing. Likewise, the movements of living things are distinguished from the movements of physical objects insofar as they have a meaning which enters essentially into our description of them, and which marks off the living from the non-living as a distinct category of phenomena.

The living body, then, is not of the same category as a stone. The body is alive, not merely in the sense that it moves about, but in the sense that the continual play of its movements and gestures have a particular meaning or significance. Thus there is no gap between the concept of intention, say, and the movements of a cat stalking a bird; the intention is not merely "associated" with this intent look, these cautious movements, this readiness to spring, etc., but is the meaning of all of these things. It is in this sense that 'the human body is the best picture of the human soul' (*PI*, p. 178): the concepts of intention, expectation, grief, pain, and so on are grounded in the forms of expression of the living bodies of humans and other animals. In mastering our psychological language-game we are not being trained to identify processes in an inner realm, but to participate in, and identify the significance of, ever more complex patterns of acting and responding that are woven into our intricate form of life. Our psychological concepts connect with the distinctive patterns in the complex form of life of living things, and not with a hidden realm of inner states and processes. Thus, when Wittgenstein remarks that 'an "inner process" stands in need of outward criteria' (*PI* 580), he is not drawing a behaviourist conclusion from an argument against the possibility of private language. Rather, he is making a grammatical observation on the essential connection that exists in our ordinary language between our psychological concepts and the distinctive patterns that are discernible within the form of human and animal life; the remark is purely descriptive, not prescriptive.

Thus our concept of pain does not describe a 'something' that exists hidden inside the physical body, but connects with the living body as such, in the sense that it expresses or describes the meaning of its cries and gestures. In *PI* 286, Wittgenstein remarks: 'But isn't it absurd to say of a *body* that it has a pain?' We do not, for example, say that my hand feels pain, 'but I in my hand' (*PI* 286). Our psychological concepts are grammatically linked with the concept of a subject, and that subject is not my body but 'I'. There is once again a great temptation to think that this shows that there is another object besides the body (a soul, say) that is the real subject of the pain. What Wittgenstein wants us to see is that this move from 'the body' to 'the subject who feels the pain' (to 'I') is not a movement between entities, but a *grammatical movement*, a movement between language-games. Thus:

> What sort of issue is: Is it the *body* that feels pain? – How is it to be decided? What makes it plausible to say that it is *not* the body? – Well, something like this: if someone has a pain in his hand, then the hand does not say so (unless it writes it) and one does not comfort the hand, but the sufferer: one looks into his face.
>
> (*PI* 286)

We do not decide the issue by introspection, by discovering that there is something in *addition* to the body, but by reference to the grammar of our language-game. When we look at our practice of describing living human beings, then we find that the human body enters our language-game, not merely as an object of physical and physiological description, but as an embodied subject: a unified centre of psychological ascription. What looks at first sight like a shift between entities – from the physical body to the soul – is in fact a shift between two language-games. As we've seen, this duality in our language between the objective language of behavioural and physiological description and the language of psychological description invites, not only the picture of the inner and the outer, but also a particularly disastrous application of it. Wittgenstein is once again attempting to show that the urge to use the picture of the inner and the outer to explain the grammatical distinction between behavioural and psychological concepts misfires. All we have done is construct a mythical entity – the disembodied soul – that we can do nothing with, when all along the distinction we are struggling to make is already there, right before our eyes, in the grammatical differences between our language-games that reveal the nature of the phenomena we describe.

The idea of the private object

In the quotation from Augustine's *Confessions*, with which the *Investigations* begins, Augustine thinks of the soul of the infant as in no way different from that of an adult: the child cannot yet speak, yet it thinks; it cannot yet say 'I wish . . .', yet it has wishes; it cannot yet ask for anything's name, yet it grasps the concept of naming; and so on. The picture that emerges from a grammatical investigation of our psychological concepts is quite different. Although our language-game is rooted in the natural human responses of hunger, fear, anger, happiness, and their expression, the effect of training in the use of language is to initiate the child into complex forms of human life whose patterns are laid down in the language-games of intending, expecting, wishing, dreaming, and so on. As the child acquires the characteristic modes of our complicated form of life, he gradually takes on the distinctive form of a human soul. The process is long and drawn out and involves the child in learning both to use the words 'I intend . . .', 'I expect', 'I hope', 'I dreamt', 'I'm irritated', 'I'm in pain', and so on in appropriate contexts, and also to recognize and respond in appropriate ways to characteristic forms of expression in others. The child is not taught to identify private objects that are inside him, but is trained to use language in a way that is essential to our distinctive form of life. He is not taught that others have inside them what he has inside himself, but is trained to notice and to respond, not only to the other's use of language, but to the characteristic patterns of movement, gesture, facial expression, and so on against which our psychological concepts function.

The discussion of Wittgenstein's remarks on private ostensive definition, in the previous chapter, has already revealed that there is something deeply problematic in the idea that we introduce a criterion of identity for pain by turning our attention inwards and saying '*this*'. The aim of this discussion was to show that it is how the word 'pain' is used in our ordinary language-game that fixes what kind of thing pain is, and not an act of inner ostension. In *PI* 288, Wittgenstein covers this same ground from a different angle: he shows that the grammar of our ordinary language-game simply doesn't fit Augustine's picture of an inner world in which psychological states exist like so many objects in a box. He reintroduces this picture by means of his vivid metaphor for how the picture conceives of the relation, e.g. between pain and the body: 'I turn to stone and my pain goes on.' The pain is once again being thought of as a 'something' which exists in a mere empirical relation to the body, and which we identify by looking inwards. In that case, the question arises whether I have identified the correct 'something' as pain: 'Suppose I were in error and it was no longer *pain*?' (*PI* 288). But this question is not one that can arise in our ordinary language-game: 'it means nothing to doubt whether I am in pain!' (*PI* 288). The tension shows once again how inclined we are to give the wrong application of the picture of inner and outer. There is something in our use of the concept of pain that makes the picture of 'the inner' apt, yet the application we then make of this picture is completely at odds with how the word 'pain' is used in our ordinary language. For if we apply the picture in a way that ignores the grammatical links which exist in our language, between the concept of pain and the living human body, then we have described a concept for which a doubt whether a correct identification has been made would be possible, when in fact the possibility of doubt does not exist.

On this interpretation of Wittgenstein's remarks, he is not offering a proof that the intelligibility of the concept of pain depends upon there being behavioural criteria of application against which a first-person use of the word can be checked. The point is a purely grammatical one. If we apply the picture of the inner in a way that neglects the grammatical connections which exist in our language between the concept of pain and the living human body, then we can no longer make sense of the way this concept actually functions, in particular, we cannot make sense of the fact that 'the expression of doubt has no place in the language-game' (*PI* 288). If we cut the grammatical links and picture pain as an inner object that we each identify when we look inwards, then 'it looks as if I might *legitimately* begin to doubt afresh' (*PI* 288). It is not that human behaviour provides an essential check, but that the absence of any grammatical link between the concept of pain and the behaviour that expresses it would indicate a use of the word quite different from the one it actually has: 'if I assume the abrogation of the normal language-game with the expression of a sensation, I need a criterion of identity for the sensation; and then the possibility of error also exists' (*PI* 288).

It may, however, be hard for us to abandon the picture of an act of inner identification which guides my use of the word 'pain', for it might seem that without some such act the use of the word pain would be arbitrary; there would be nothing by reference to which its use on a particular occasion could be justified. Thus, we want to say: ' "When I say 'I am in pain' I am at any rate justified *before myself*" ' (*PI* 289). Wittgenstein responds by asking:

> What does that mean? Does it mean: "If someone else could know what I am calling 'pain', he would admit that I was using the word correctly?"
>
> (*PI* 289)

In that case, we don't actually justify the use of the word, but merely *imagine* justifying it. We carry out the act of justifying the use of the word 'in our imagination', but this, as we've seen, is not to justify the use of a word. This act which we think must be essential to a rule-governed use of the word 'pain' is actually completely idle.

If these reflections seem to make our use of the word 'pain' look arbitrary, then we should remember that 'to use a word without a justification does not mean to use it without right' (*PI* 289). When my training in the language results in a mastery of the use of an expression, I do not look for reasons, but unreflectively employ the language in accordance with the practice in which I've been trained. It is my mastery of the language-game that is played with the word 'pain' that gives me the right to use it as I do, and not an inner act of justification. Thus, there is no act of 'identify[ing] my sensation by criteria' (*PI* 289). I simply use the words 'I am in pain', as I've been trained to, as an instrument for giving expression to what I feel. We may call this 'describing my sensation', or 'describing my state of mind'. However, we must not be misled by the fact that we use the word 'describing' here and also speak of 'describing my room' into supposing that there is a single language-game of 'describing'. The word 'describing' is like the word 'naming'; it is a generic term that elides grammatical differences. Thus, '[w]hat we call "*descriptions*" are instruments for particular uses' (*PI* 291). If we are not to be misled into picturing all these instruments on the basis of one particular kind of description ('describing my room'), then we 'need to call to mind the differences between . . . language-games' (*PI* 290).

Thus, when we look at how our concepts are actually used, we begin to see how various this thing we call 'describing' really is: 'Think how many different kinds of thing are called "description": description of a body's position by means of its co-ordinates; description of a facial expression; description of a sensation of touch; of a mood' (*PI* 24). In all of these cases we do something quite different: in the first, we measure out a position on a grid and the distinction between correct and incorrect description is clear-cut; in the second, how we respond to the face is bound up with our description of it and there is scope for disagreement; in the third, we may look for comparisons ('It feels like silk'); in the fourth, we may give ourselves up to the mood and just let the words come. Calling them all cases of 'description' 'cannot make the uses themselves any more like one another. For, as we've seen, they are absolutely unlike' (*PI* 10). Saying 'I describe my state of mind' and 'I describe my room' tells us nothing; it is only by looking at language-in-use that we begin to discern the grammatical distinctions that reveal the nature of these two quite different language-games.

The difference between these language-games can also be observed in the way the concept of truth functions within each. If we think of the criteria for the truth of a confession of a motive, or of the report of a dream, then we can see that they function quite differently from the criteria for the truth of a description of a process which someone is observing, or of the contents of a box which I cannot see into. It is not only that the criteria for the truth of the report are much more straightforward in the latter cases, but there is also room for a distinction between the speaker giving a truthful account of what he sees and the account being true. Thus it makes sense to suppose that we can correct a speaker's sincere report of the contents of a box by comparing the report with what our own inspection of the box reveals, and finding that the speaker has misidentified one or more objects. The same distinction cannot be made in the case of a truthful report of a motive, a mood, or a dream. In this case, the questions that arise are quite different. Supposing we accept a report of a motive as sincere, we may wonder whether the speaker isn't self-deceived; or, if the report relates to events that happened a long time ago, we may question whether he has remembered correctly. But neither of these questions is settled by a comparison between the report and an inner process. Even if these questions are raised by the speaker himself – which also makes perfect sense – they will be settled by looking at the wider context of the speaker's actions, by trying out alternative interpretations of what has been said and done, and so on. And whoever asks these questions, the speaker's sincere assent to the account of a motive always has a special significance; it is only in very special circumstances that we can discount it. What Wittgenstein wants us to see is that these contrasts in how the different regions of our language function is not something that either requires or can be given an explanation. Rather it is the contrasts in how our concepts function that ground the distinctions between categories of phenomena; there is no route to a grasp of the distinction that we want to make between psychological and behavioural concepts other than that which is provided by the distinctive grammar of our language-games.

In *PI* 293, Wittgenstein responds to the picture of pain as a private object whose essence consists simply in its being 'THIS' with the following parable:

> Suppose everyone had a box with something in it: we call it a "beetle". No one can look into anyone else's box, and everyone says he knows what a beetle is only by looking at *his* beetle. – Here it would be quite possible for everyone to have something different in his box. One might even imagine such a thing constantly changing. – But suppose the word "beetle" had a use in these people's language? – If so it would not be used as the name of a thing. The thing in the box has no place in the

> language-game at all; not even as a *something*: for the box
> might even be empty. – No, one can 'divide through' by the
> thing in the box; it cancels out, whatever it is.

The opening image of the parable presents a physical analogy of the
idea that we each know what pain is on the basis of identifying an
inner object. Just as I picture myself as deriving a knowledge of what
pain is by identifying a 'something' that is inside my body and accessible only to me, so Wittgenstein pictures a speaker deriving his
knowledge of what a 'beetle' is by looking inside a box which no
one else can look into. The first thing he observes is that we can
make no assumptions about whether everyone has the same kind of
object in his box, or even about the stability of these objects over
time. However, we are also to suppose that the word 'beetle' does
have a use within the language of these people. Wittgenstein does not
say what this use is, but we are clearly intended to imagine that the
word 'beetle' is used within a stable, unified language-game in which
all the speakers of the language participate. Thus he creates a situation in which two things go on. On the one hand, there is each
speaker's act of looking into his box and saying 'THIS is a "beetle"';
on the other, there is the established technique of using the word
'beetle' within a stable language-game. The question is: How do these
two things connect? What the parable is meant to get us to see is
that they do not connect at all. The language-game that is played with
the word 'beetle' can be taught, learnt and participated in independently of what the speaker discovers when he opens his box, for,
as we've seen, we can imagine that this is something different in
everyone's case, or that what is in the box is constantly changing, or
even that there is nothing in the box at all. It is by seeing that there
is no connection between the use that the word 'beetle' has in the
language-game – i.e. between the meaning of 'beetle' in these people's
language – and what each of them has in his box, that we come to
appreciate that the ceremony which is described at the beginning of
the parable is completely idle in respect of the meaning that the word
'beetle' has in these people's language. As far as the meaning of the
word 'beetle' is concerned, 'we can "divide through" by the thing in
the box; it cancels out whatever it is.'

The point of the parable of the beetle in the box is not, on this interpretation, to show that our psychological concepts must possess public criteria of application. The point is rather this: if we are tempted, by the sense of a distinction between pain and crying, to suppose that the word 'pain' functions as the name of an object that each of us identifies when we look inwards, then this object cannot connect with the use of the word 'pain' in our ordinary language. For we can imagine that this private object, like the object in the physically private box, is different in everyone's case, or that it constantly changes, or even that there is nothing there at all. But that only shows that our ordinary language-game can be taught, learnt and participated in whatever this object is: 'the object drops out of consideration as irrelevant' (*PI* 293). The conclusion we are meant to draw is that it is a mistake to attempt to capture the distinction between pain and crying by means of the idea that 'pain' names a private object that we each know from our own case; the picture of the inner and the outer, which the distinction between pain and crying invites, simply cannot be applied in this way. Our sense of a difference in what the words 'pain' and 'crying' mean cannot be captured in terms of the idea of a private object known to each of us versus a public object accessible to all. For 'if we construe the grammar of the expression of sensation on the model of "object and designation" the object drops out of consideration as irrelevant' (*PI* 293).

Yet it may seem that, without the idea of the private object, we are once again in danger of losing the distinction between pain and the behaviour that expresses it. The interlocutor gives expression to this anxiety as follows:

> "Yes, but there is *something* there all the same accompanying my cry of pain. And it is on account of that that I utter it. And this something is what is important – and frightful."
>
> (*PI* 296)

Wittgenstein responds:

> Only whom are we informing of this? And on what occasion?

That the concept of pain describes (gives expression to) the feeling that prompts me to cry out, and not the cry itself, is not something of which we can *inform* anyone who understands the concept of pain; the expressiveness of the words 'I'm in pain' is intrinsic to the use that we make of them, and is thus an essential part of our mastery of the concept. That the feeling, rather than the cry, is the important thing, and that it is something frightful, are likewise intrinsic aspects of the use of the concept of pain; they belong to the form of our language-game; they are not observations which I make subsequent to learning the use of the word 'pain', on the basis of inspecting and describing my particular private object. The interlocutor's words do not tell us about something he has 'got' and I have not; they tell us nothing that is not already there in the characteristic grammar of our language-game, i.e. in the way we all use the concept of pain. However, his sense of a need to say these things suggests that he is no longer satisfied with a mere grammatical distinction among our concepts; everything has come to look like surface to him, and to get to the *vital* thing – the pain behind the cry – he feels he must resort to an act of inner attention. It is as if he were to look for an inside behind that which is defined by the distinction between the grammar of the concept of pain and that of the concept of crying.

Wittgenstein tries to expose the sheer pathology of this sudden sense of dissatisfaction with distinctions that are drawn within the grammar of our language by means of the following analogy:

> Of course, if water boils in a pot, steam comes out of the pot and also pictured steam comes out of the pictured pot. But what if one insisted on saying that there must also be something boiling in the picture of the pot?

(*PI* 297)

The analogy presents us with two distinct categories of phenomena that are connected with two quite different language-games. On the one hand, there is a physical pot of boiling water, in which the boiling liquid causes steam to come out of the pot. On the other hand, there is a picture of a pot with steam coming out of it. In the one case, we have a language-game that is woven into our practice of using pots, water, heat, etc. in connection with cooking and various other activities. In the other case, we have a language-game that is woven into a practice of using pictures in illustration, in instruction, in story-telling, and so on. The language-game of using pictures, like that of cooking, is part of our human natural history: it just is the case that human beings use and respond to pictures as representations of aspects of their everyday world. How this language-game of representing the world in pictures actually functions may not be immediately clear, but however it functions, it is clearly very different from the language-games that are woven in with the reality that our pictures represent.

We can now begin to see that someone who insists that there must also be something boiling in the picture of the pot is led by a sense of the inadequacy of what lies on the surface into confusing these two language-games. Struck by the fact that the picture is not merely a picture of steam and a pot, but of a boiling pot, it seems that there must be more to the picture than strikes the eye; for a boiling pot is more than just a pot and steam. Seeing that the boiling pot does not appear in the picture in the same way that the steam and the pot do, the speaker is tempted into thinking that there must be something behind what lies on the surface, something that is hidden inside the picture of the pot in the way that boiling water is hidden inside the physical pot. Thus, it has come to seem that if we are to have more than a picture of steam and a pot, then there must actually be something boiling in the pictured pot. The strength of the analogy is that it allows us to see clearly that something has gone wrong: it is not the case that the picture is a picture of a boiling pot in virtue of something (somehow!) boiling inside it. It is rather that the juxtaposition of the steam and a pot in the picture has a certain *significance* for us; we *respond* to this juxtaposition in a particular way; the meaning of the picture enters into our experience of it in such a way that, without in any sense going beyond what is presented in the picture, we unselfconsciously describe it as 'a picture of a boiling pot'.

The person who insists 'there is *something* there all the same accompanying my cry of pain' makes an analogous mistake. Seeing that the pain is not public in the way that the cry is, he is led to feel dissatisfied with what lies on the surface and to use a mistaken analogy – the analogy of an object hidden inside a container – in an attempt to understand how the cry is not merely a cry, but a cry of *pain*. So it seems that if we are to have more than a cry (more than mere behaviour), then there must be something behind the cry – the private object – in virtue of which it is a cry of pain. What we need to recognize is that it is not the case that a cry is a cry of pain in virtue of something hidden inside the body, in the way that a box is a gift in virtue of what is hidden inside it. In picturing things this way, we have been misled by a false analogy into misunderstanding the way this language-game functions. It is true that the pain is not public in the way the cry is, but the pain enters into the language-game insofar as this cry is woven into a pattern that has a particular significance; the significance of this pattern enters into our experience of the cry, and figures in our unreflective description of what we hear. We don't hear a cry and conjecture that it is accompanied by a particular kind of private object ('THIS'); we hear a cry of pain, a shriek of fear, a hoot of delight, and so on. The pain, the fear, and the delight are not public in the way that the cry, the shriek or the hoot are; but insofar as we experience these sounds as having a particular significance or meaning, these feelings are an intrinsic element in our description of what we hear.

The indeterminacy of our psychological language-game

Thus Wittgenstein has tried to get us to see that the meaning of a gesture, a sigh, a grimace, made in a particular context, is not merely connected with it in the sense of being something conjectured, something that we infer on the basis of observed correlations. I can no more perceive a sigh of resignation without perceiving its meaning than I can hear the words 'It's cold in here', on a particular occasion of their utterance, without understanding them. The meaning of the sigh is not laid over it, but written into it:

> It is possible to say "I read timidity in his face" but at all events the timidity does not seem to be merely associated, outwardly connected, with the face; but fear is there, alive, in the features. If the features change slightly, we can speak of a change in the

fear. If we were asked "Can you think of this face as an expression of courage too?" – we should, as it were, not know how to lodge courage in these features.

(*PI* 537)

However, facial expressions, like words, are notoriously ambiguous. Wittgenstein wants us to see that the ambiguity or indeterminacy that characterizes our use of psychological concepts is not a defect, but an essential part of our language-game, something which characterizes the essence of human psychological phenomena. Even the timid face described above might allow for different reactions. Thus, Wittgenstein suggests, we might respond to the question of whether we cannot think of the face as courageous as follows: ' "Yes, now I understand: the face as it were shews indifference to the outer world." So we have somehow read courage into the face. Now once more, one might say, courage *fits* this face' (*PI* 537). But what do we do to make courage fit this face? We tell ourselves a story, perhaps, or fit the expression into a different pattern of behaviour, or into a different set of expectations concerning future responses, and so on. The meaning of a facial expression, like the meaning of the words we utter, changes with the context, and a change in my perception of the context of an expression can alter its significance. Thus:

> I see a picture which represents a smiling face. What do I do if I take the smile now as a kind one, now as malicious? Don't I often imagine it with a spatial and temporal context which is one either of kindness or malice? Thus I might supply the picture with the fancy that the smiler was smiling down on a child at play, or again on the suffering of an enemy.

(*PI* 539)

This is not to say that in ordinary life we do, without special reason, revise our first sight response to a situation and interpret it differently by putting it in a wider context: 'If no special circumstances reverse my interpretation I shall conceive a particular smile as kind, call it a "kind" one, react correspondingly' (*PI* 539). I may, of course, engage in this sort of reinterpretation idly, e.g. if I try to imagine that the people in the street are automata, or if I imagine that someone whom

I see laughing is really in terrible pain. But this takes a special act of imagination which I must self-consciously perform, perhaps, as Wittgenstein says, with a slight sense of uncanniness. These acts of imagination cannot become the grounds of a real (lived) doubt, for they do not impinge upon responses which my training has made second nature to me, and which are tied up with my sincere description of what I see. We simply cannot keep hold of these ideas in the midst of our ordinary intercourse with others; our natural reactions assert themselves and we respond in the normal way to the characteristic patterns of our human form of life:

> But can't I imagine that the people around me are automata, lack consciousness, even though they behave in the same way as usual? – If I imagine it now – alone in my room – I see people with fixed looks (as in a trance) going about their business – the idea is perhaps a little uncanny. But just try to keep hold of this idea in the midst of your ordinary intercourse with others, in the street, say!
>
> (*PI* 420)

The role of our reaction in how we conceive a situation does, however, open up a possibility for disagreement and uncertainty, which is characteristic of our psychological language-game. Someone who is naturally trusting may, for example, see a smile quite differently from someone who is naturally suspicious. It is a characteristic feature of our complex form of life that 'there is in general ... no agreement over the question whether an expression of feeling is genuine or not' (*PI*, p. 227). It may be the case that 'I am sure, *sure*, that [someone] is not pretending; but some third person is not' (*PI*, p. 227). Is it always the case, Wittgenstein asks, that I can convince the other? And if I cannot convince him, does this mean that one of us is mistaken in his observations? The interlocutor remarks: ' "The genuineness of an expression cannot be proved; one has to feel it" ' (*PI*, p. 228). The cues that one picks up on here are immensely subtle. Wittgenstein characterizes them as 'imponderable evidence', which 'includes subtleties of glance, of gesture, of tone' (*PI*, p. 228). Thus 'I may recognize a genuine loving look, distinguish it from a pretended one ... But I may be quite incapable of describing the difference'

(*PI*, p. 228). In this case, there may be quite concrete confirmation of my judgement, but in other cases matters may be much more diffuse, and it may be hard to establish anything clear. In some cases we may never come to a final agreed judgement, so that we are left with a situation in which one person embraces a judgement which another holds back from. If we are tempted to think that there must nevertheless be a fact of the matter, we have only to reflect that the subject himself may feel the same uncertainty ('Do I really love her?', 'Am I really sorry?'). In this case, the subject, like everyone else, will have recourse to looking for a special pattern of action and response to motivate his judgement, and the account of his motives which he constructs will likewise be constrained by the need to provide a coherent story concerning what was actually said and done.

Wittgenstein tries to capture the distinctive subtlety and indefiniteness of our psychological language-game as follows:

> Is there such a thing as 'expert judgment' about the genuineness of expressions of feeling? – Even here, there are those whose judgment is 'better' and those whose judgment is 'worse'.
>
> Correcter prognoses will generally issue from the judgments of those with better knowledge of mankind.
>
> Can one learn this knowledge? Yes; some can. Not, however, by taking a course in it, but through '*experience*'. – Can someone else be a man's teacher in this? Certainly. From time to time he gives him the right *tip*. – This is what 'learning' and 'teaching' are like here. – What one acquires here is not a technique; one learns correct judgments. There are also rules, but they do not form a system, and only experienced people can apply them right. Unlike calculating rules.
>
> What is most difficult here is to put this indefiniteness, correctly and unfalsified, into words.
>
> (*PI*, p. 227)

It is, as we've seen, in part this possibility of asking whether someone's expression of feeling is genuine that makes the picture of the inner so apt. In a case where a doubt arises, it is natural for us to express this as a question about 'what is really going on inside him'. We feel that we should like to see inside his head and find out what is really going on in there. But really this is no more than a vivid picture. What we mean by it is 'what elsewhere we should mean by saying we should like to know what he is thinking' (*PI* 427). The picture is a natural one, but it is the application that is obscure to us. If we feel that someone is not giving candid expression to his thoughts, then we do say that he is hiding something, that he is keeping his feelings bottled up inside him, and so on. But these pictures are just another way of saying that he isn't telling us what he feels. Confusion arises only when we are led by a mistaken analogy with things that are physically hidden, or physically kept locked up in a bottle, into making an inappropriate application of the picture. And we see that this application is inappropriate when we observe how at odds the application is with the way our psychological concepts actually function.

Pain is not a something, but not a nothing either

It is, however, hard to overcome our sense, when doing philosophy, of a need to insist that when we describe someone with the words 'He is in pain', we do not merely describe his behaviour, but also his pain. Wittgenstein expresses this continuing temptation at the beginning of *PI* 300:

> It is – we should like to say – not merely the picture of the behaviour that plays a part in the language-game with the words "he is in pain", but also the picture of the pain. Or, not merely the paradigm of the behaviour, but also that of the pain.

He now works to uncover the confusions that this philosophical temptation expresses. First of all, in our anxiety not to deny the feeling, we fail to observe a grammatical distinction between pain and the behaviour that expresses it:

> It is a misunderstanding to say 'The picture of pain enters into the language-game with the word "pain".' The image of pain is not a picture and *this* image is not replaceable in the language-

game by anything that we should call a picture. – The image of pain certainly enters into the language-game in a sense; only not as a picture.

(PI 300)

It makes no more sense to speak of a 'picture of pain' than it does to speak of a picture of a number or a sound; the grammar of the concept is such that it makes sense to speak of *imagining* pain, but not of picturing or visualizing it. Thus I can form an image of pain, as I can of a sound (though not of a number), and I can do this without imagining behaving in any particular way. And what I imagine is indeed the feeling that our language-game describes. Insofar as the grammar of the concept of pain connects it with a feeling, it connects it with something that can be imagined but not pictured or visualized. Once again, we do justice to the distinction between pain and pain-behaviour, not by trying to make them equal partners – here the picture of the behaviour, there the picture of the pain – but by observing the grammatical distinctions between the concepts: a picture can correspond to my image of pain-behaviour, but not to my image of pain. It is through these grammatical distinctions that we grasp the real ground of our intuition of the differences in the kinds of phenomena our concepts describe.

The temptation which is expressed in the opening words of *PI* 300 is linked with another, namely the temptation to suppose that understanding the word 'pain' requires us to imagine something in connection with it. The idea that we know what the word 'pain' means from our own case and then transfer the idea to others assigns a special role to the imagination in our understanding of sensation concepts. We have already looked at the role of the imagination in coming to understand the concept of pain in connection with Wittgenstein's remarks on the notion of a private exhibition, but in *PI* 302 Wittgenstein considers the role of imagination from another perspective:

If one has to imagine someone else's pain on the model of one's own, this is none too easy a thing to do; for I have to imagine pain which I *do not feel* on the model of pain which I *do feel*. That is, what I have to do is not simply to make a transition in imagination from one place of pain to another. As, from pain in the hand to pain in the arm. For I am not to imagine that I feel pain in some region of his body. (Which would also be possible.)

Here Wittgenstein's concern is not with the emptiness of the idea that we define the word 'pain' by pointing to a feeling 'with our imagination', but with the illusion that understanding the third-person use of the concept of pain involves my forming an image of pain, which I then transfer to other people. How can the imagination play the role that we here attempt to assign to it? How can my image of pain be a model for someone else's pain? To form an image of a feeling is just to imagine feeling something. To transfer my image of pain to another I would have to imagine a feeling which I do not imagine feeling, but this is nothing short of a contradiction. The application that we make of the picture of the inner and the outer ignores the grammatical connection between the concept of a sensation and that of a subject who feels the sensation. I cannot just imagine the feeling without a subject who feels, and then add either he has it or I have it. Either I imagine my feeling pain (form an image of pain), or I imagine someone else feeling pain. The latter does not involve me in forming an image of pain, but nor need it involve me in imagining the other behaving in any particular way. I might, for example, imagine someone being in pain without expressing it. This might require me to tell a rather elaborate story, but it does not involve my imagining his pain on the model of my own. Our desire to distinguish pain and pain-behaviour by making our image of pain fundamental to our understanding of the concept goes against a grammatical asymmetry which runs throughout the language-game. What we have to see is that it is by attending to this characteristic asymmetry, without attempting to explain it, that we reveal the essence of the distinction which we wish to make.

The difficult thing is to accept that it is the distinctive grammar of our sensation concepts which lends the picture of the inner and the outer whatever sense it has: What we mean by describing the pain as inner and the cry as outer is exhausted by the grammatical differences in how these concepts function. The picture of the inner and the outer invites an application which leads us to neglect the distinction which is there before our eyes, in the grammar of our concepts, and to think of the sensation itself as something that is hidden behind what we originally captured with the notion of the inner. In rejecting this application of the picture, it can look as if Wittgenstein is denying the inner, when all he is doing is reminding us of the real nature of the distinction that our picture was meant to capture, and exposing our nonsensical applications as nonsensical. Thus, when the interlocutor asks: ' "But you will surely admit that there is a difference between pain-behaviour accompanied by pain and pain-behaviour without any pain?" ' (*PI* 304), Wittgenstein responds: 'Admit it? What greater difference could there be?' (*PI* 304). This is a distinction which is there in the grammar of our language-game. It is characteristic of this region of our language that someone can lie about what he feels, that someone can pretend to be in pain, that someone can act the part of a man in pain, and so on. Learning the language-game involves, both becoming master of these different performances, and coming to recognize and understand these distinctions in the actions of others. In the latter case, this involves our detecting and responding appropriately to subtle and complex patterns of behaviour, which we have a nose for but which we cannot always make explicit. The distinction which the interlocutor feels he must insist on has not been denied, for it is intrinsic to the structure of our language-game. But then why does the interlocutor believe that Wittgenstein has denied the distinction?

The interlocutor expresses his concern as follows: ' "And yet you again and again reach the conclusion that the sensation itself is a *nothing*" ' (*PI* 304). Wittgenstein responds: 'Not at all. It is not a *something*, but not a *nothing* either!' (*PI* 304). He is not suggesting that there is nothing behind the cry of pain, that all there is is behaviour. It is rather that if we conceive of sensations as objects which we each know from our own case, then 'a nothing would serve just as well as a something', for this private object does not connect with the use (i.e. with the meaning) of the word 'pain'; it is 'a something about which nothing can be said' (*PI* 304). Wittgenstein's response is not to deny the existence of pain, but to reject 'the grammar which tries to force itself on us here' (*PI* 304). For 'the paradox disappears only if we make a radical break with the idea that language functions in one way, always serves the same purpose: to convey thoughts – which may be about houses, pains, good and evil, or anything else you please' (*PI* 304). It is through an appreciation of the differences in the way these different regions of our language function that we free ourselves from the urge to make the inappropriate application of the picture of the inner and the outer, which lies behind the interlocutor's sense that something has been denied, and that we grasp the real nature of the distinction which he feels he must insist upon. The impression that Wittgenstein is out to deny something 'arises from our setting our faces against the picture of the "inner process". What we deny is that the picture of the inner process gives us the correct idea of the use of [our psychological concepts]. We say that this picture with its ramifications stands in the way of our seeing the use of [these expressions] as it is' (*PI* 305). Thus, when the interlocutor asks ' "Are you not really a behaviourist in disguise? Aren't you at bottom really saying that everything except human behaviour is a fiction?",' Wittgenstein responds, 'If I do speak of a fiction, then it is of a *grammatical* fiction' (*PI* 307).

In this chapter, I have tried to describe how Wittgenstein uses the techniques of grammatical investigation to show that the application we are inclined to make of the picture of the inner and the outer is completely empty. We have gradually been brought to see that this tempting application of the picture not only makes no contact with the way our psychological concepts are actually used, but is a vain attempt to elucidate a distinction which is already fully revealed in the grammar of our language. It is not only that this application of the picture of the inner is empty, but the very idea that hidden psychological facts provide something *vital*, something without which we are mere things, is shown to be grounded in a fundamentally mistaken idea of the relation between our psychological concepts and the characteristic forms of movement, gesture and expression of the living bodies of humans and other animals. The division which we are mistakenly inclined to draw between public and private objects is shown to be one that is actually grounded in the grammatical distinctions between the concepts which describe the phenomena that constitute our world. Yet all this might leave us with a sense of a problem. Throughout this exposition of Wittgenstein's remarks, I have spoken of the meaning or significance of the movements, gestures, sounds, etc. that a living thing makes as entering into our experience of them, so that in describing a cry as a cry of pain, a smile as friendly, or a look as hostile, I do not go beyond what is perceptually given or speculate about the nature of what is hidden behind them. But how can this be? How can the meaning of a cry or a smile or a look enter into our experience of it? If someone sees a smile and does not know it for a smile, it is not because there is something wrong with his eyesight, no more than someone's failure to grasp the meaning of a sentence spoken in a foreign language he doesn't understand is a result of something's being wrong with his hearing. The idea that we *see* the smile as friendly, or *hear* the cry as a cry of pain, is at odds with the appealing idea that a perceptual quality is one that can be detected by anyone with the appropriate perceptual equipment. It is to this problem that I now turn.

References and further reading

Budd, M., *Wittgenstein's Philosophy of Psychology* (London: Routledge, 1989).

Cavell, S., *The Claim of Reason: Wittgenstein, Skepticism, Morality and Tragedy* (Oxford: Oxford University Press, 1979).

Fogelin, R., *Wittgenstein* (London: Routledge, 1986).

Hacker, P. M. S., *Wittgenstein: Meaning and Mind*, vol. 3 (Oxford: Blackwell, 1990).

Hertzberg, L., 'The kind of certainty is the kind of language game', in L. Hertzberg, *The Limits of Experience*, *Acta Philosophica Fennica*, vol. 56, 1994.

Johnston, P., *Wittgenstein: Rethinking the Inner* (London: Routledge, 1993).

Kenny, A., *Wittgenstein* (Harmondsworth: Penguin, 1973).

McDowell, J. H., 'Criteria, Defeasibility and Knowledge', *Proceedings of the British Academy*, vol. LXVIII, 1982.

Mulhall, S., *On Being in the World* (London: Routledge, 1990).

Pears, D. F., *The False Prison*, vol. 2 (Oxford: Oxford University Press, 1987).

Schulte, J., *Experience and Expression: Wittgenstein's Philosophy of Psychology* (Oxford: Oxford University Press, 1993).

Wright, C., 'Wittgenstein: Later Philosophy of Mind: Sensation, Privacy and Intention', *Journal of Philosophy*, vol. 86, 1989.

Chapter 6

Seeing and seeing aspects *Philosophical Investigations* 398–401: Part II, section xi

Introduction

In the previous two chapters, we have seen how Wittgenstein works to overcome the idea that the notion of a private object explains the difference between psychological and non-psychological concepts, or between subjects and non-subjects. Central to his overcoming of the philosophical myth of the private object is an acknowledgement of the qualitative difference between our experience of human beings and other animals, on the one hand, and our experience of machines and other inanimate objects, on the other. The ontological cut that our language-games reveal is not between an inner and an outer realm, but between bodies whose form of life makes them accessible to psychological description and objects that are out of play to psychological concepts. One important aspect of this fundamental division between the categories of phenomena that make up our world is the qualitative difference in how

we experience them: the words and cries, the gestures, movements and facial expressions of other living things have a significance for us that enters into our experience of them and figures essentially in our descriptions of what we see and hear. However, while these shifts in how we see matters may help us to counter the temptation to form a mythological picture of the essence of psychological states, they may also seem to conflict outright with some strong intuitions that arise from a different region of our language-game, namely, from the region that centres on the concept of perception. Surely, we might feel, all that is *really seen* when we look at an object is what can be explained as an immediate sensory effect of the objective world of matter, namely the shapes, colours, textures and movements of objects. Likewise, all that is *really heard* are sounds of different pitch, frequency and loudness. Any further properties that are attributed to an object must somehow be inferred from those that are actually perceived.

Wittgenstein expresses this intuition clearly as follows:

> "What I really *see* must surely be what is produced in me by the influence of the object" – Then what is produced in me is a sort of copy, something that in its turn can be looked at, can be before one; almost something like a *materialization*.
>
> And this materialization is something spatial and it must be possible to describe it in spatial terms. For instance (if it is a face) it can smile; the concept of friendliness, however, has no place in an account of it, but is *foreign* to such an account (even though it may subserve it).
>
> (*PI*, p. 199)

This conception of visual perception pictures seeing, at least in part, as an awareness of a field of spatially related coloured shapes that is produced in the perceiving subject by the influence of physical objects on his sensory surfaces. Physical objects are thought of as producing something in the subject – a visual impression – that only he is aware of, and which characterizes his experience as a *visual* experience of the world. This picture of perception tempts us to think of the content of perceptual experience in terms of the properties of an object that such a visual impression of a physical object might conceivably be supposed to record: the colours, shapes, the spatial relations between shapes, textures, and so on. And it is this idea of the content of perception – of 'what is really seen' – that now makes us want to say: 'You speak of *seeing* that the face is friendly, but how can you *see* the friendliness?' Suddenly, a whole class of what look like perceptual reports comes to seem puzzling, for it is as if we everywhere talk of seeing what our picture of perception now makes us think cannot *really* be seen.

Where does this idea of visual perception as awareness of an impression of spatially related coloured shapes come from? There is clearly a strong temptation to think that our idea is grounded in a theory of perception, which draws on a scientific understanding of the eye and the patterns· of light that stimulate it. However, Wittgenstein wants to trace the roots of this picture back to an unclarity about how the concept of 'visual experience' actually functions, and to a temptation to suppose that we will come to understand the nature of visual experience by thinking very hard about what it is like to see. This picture of perception then determines the form of our enquiry and generates a series of puzzles which we believe can be solved only by means of a further elucidation of what visual experience consists in. What Wittgenstein wants us to see is that the problems that our picture of the essence of visual experience generates are not ones that can be resolved by means of a theory of perception, for the problem lies in the very first steps in which this picture of visual experience and of what is seen gets a grip on our imagination. Our problems, he believes, will only be solved if we return to the roots of our trouble and clarify how the concepts of seeing, of what is seen, and of visual experience, actually function. For he believes that there is no route to an understanding of the nature or essence of visual experience except through a description of the grammar of the concepts that figure in our language-game of ascribing visual experiences to ourselves and others, of representing what is seen, and so on. Here we have just another case of that special class of questions which express a puzzlement about the form of the phenomena of our world – those things which we know when no one asks us, but which we no longer know when we are asked to give some sort of account – and which are answered by means of a grammatical investigation.

A grammatical investigation will not only give us the understanding we seek, but it will also show how the pictures of the state of seeing and of what is seen that we are inclined to construct simply don't fit the phenomena of human perception, as these are revealed in the grammar of our language:

> What we have ... to do is to *accept* the everyday language-game, and to note *false* accounts of the matter *as* false. The primitive language-game which children are taught needs no justification; attempts at justification need to be rejected.
>
> (*PI*, p. 200)

Wittgenstein's discussion of how this region of our language functions occurs in a small number of remarks scattered through Part I, and in the longest section of Part II, of the *Investigations*. The remarks in Part I are mostly linked with the concerns of the previous two chapters, in that they are addressed to the temptation to construct the idea of a visual impression, as something that occurs in the subject when he perceives an object, and which we know only by introspection, on the basis of our own case. The remarks in Part II, which date from a later period than those in Part I, focus more on looking at how the concept of 'seeing' actually functions within our ordinary language-game. Wittgenstein's aim in the latter remarks is to disperse the fog that surrounds the concept of perception, by means of a careful attention to the detailed workings of our language-game. Thus he focuses on a wide range of particular cases of our use of the concepts of seeing, seeing-as and description of what is seen, in an attempt to make us recognize how differently the concept of visual experience functions from the way we are inclined to imagine when doing philosophy:

> [D]o not think you [know] in advance what the '*state* of seeing' means here! Let the use *teach* you the meaning.
>
> We find certain things about seeing puzzling, because we do not find the whole business of seeing puzzling enough.
>
> (*PI*, p. 212)

The visual room

Let us begin by looking at a few of the remarks from Part I of the *Investigations*, which focus on the temptation to picture visual experience in terms of the occurrence of a visual impression which only the perceiving subject has access to. The remarks I want to look at closely are those that occur between *PI* 398 and *PI* 401. These are notoriously difficult passages which centre on the discussion of the concept of the 'visual room'. The aim of the passages is to show that the idea of a visual impression, as something occurring within the consciousness of the perceiving subject, breaks down as soon as we attempt to apply it in detail. If we hold that visual experience depends upon the existence of certain visual impressions within the mind of the perceiver, then we need to say more precisely what kind of thing these impressions are and what our relationship to them is. What Wittgenstein tries to show in the discussion of the visual room is that we have no grammatical model that applies in the current case; when we're pressed to make the notion of 'my visual impression' more precise, we find that we do not know how we are to conceive either it or our relation to it.

PI 398 begins with an expression of the temptation to think of visual experience in terms of having certain private images or sense data:

> 'But when I imagine something, or even actually *see* objects, I have *got* something which my neighbour has not.'

Here the interlocutor presents us with a picture: perceiving an object or physical scene involves my having certain visual impressions which I can describe to another, but which only I am aware of or have access to. The following reflection may help to make this picture compelling. If someone who is normally sighted and someone who is red–green colour blind both look at a scene incorporating a number of red and green objects, what they see will be different in each case. But since they are looking at a single scene, the difference must reside in their experiences of it, and not in anything objective. Thus we are led to picture each of them as aware of his own visual impressions, which the other can only know by description, as if each were privy to something from which the other is eternally shut out. Wittgenstein is very well aware of the attractions of such a picture, and he responds to the interlocutor as follows:

> I understand you. You want to look about you and say: "At any rate only I have got THIS."

(*PI* 398)

However, he now goes on to question what we might mean when we feel that we have to say these things: 'What are these words for? They serve no purpose' (*PI* 398). He goes on:

> Can one not add: "There is here no question of a 'seeing' and therefore none of a 'having' – nor of a subject, nor therefore of 'I' either"?

Why does Wittgenstein say that there is no question of a 'seeing'? If we mean by 'seeing' that relation in which I stand to the physical objects in my environment, then clearly I do not stand in the same relation to my alleged visual impressions. I do not have an inner eye that stands to these impressions as my ordinary eye stands to the physical scene that I am contemplating. Whatever relation I have to the alleged visual impression, it cannot, in this sense of 'see' at least, be one of seeing it. Thus, my visual impressions are not an object for visual consciousness in the same way that a physical object or a material picture might be. But in that case, Wittgenstein asks, in what sense can I be said to 'have' these impressions; in what sense is there a 'something' to which I stand in a relation of 'having'? We are tempted to think of visual experience in terms of my having certain visual images, and the most natural way to interpret this is in terms of these images being an *object of consciousness*. But we don't have any clear model of what sort of 'object of consciousness' we're speaking of here or of what our relationship to it consists in, for we do not literally see these images in the way that we might see a material representation of a scene.

Wittgenstein follows this up with a further grammatical attack on the idea that we should think of visual experience in terms of our each having access to images that no one else is privy to:

> Might I not ask: In what sense have you *got* what you are
> talking about and saying that only you have got it? Do you
> possess it? You do not even *see* it. Must you not really say that
> no one has got it? And this too is clear: if as a matter of logic
> you exclude other people's having something, it loses its sense
> to say that you have it.
>
> *(PI* 398)

What does the interlocutor mean when he says that he has 'got' something his neighbour has not? In what sense does he 'possess' it? It
makes no sense to speak of my 'having a visual impression' (in the
sense of 'possessing an object'), for this use of the concept of having
requires a grammatical object whose identity is not dependent on
ownership, and possession of which can therefore be transferred from
one individual to another. This notion of a grammatical object does
not fit the concept of a visual image or visual impression, for, unlike
a physical object that I see, my visual impression is not something
that can be detached from the act of experiencing it. In that case, talk
of my 'having a visual impression' cannot denote my standing in a
relation to a special kind of sensory object; the concept of an object
simply doesn't apply in this case. What we're beginning to see is that
when we try to apply the picture of a visual impression as something
that I have whenever I see something – which initially seems so intuitive and unproblematic – we cannot make it connect with anything,
for there is nothing that is both an object of consciousness and accessible to the subject alone.

What is it, then, that the interlocutor was speaking of when he
said that when he sees something he has 'got' something that his
neighbour has not? 'It is true', Wittgenstein allows, '[that] I said that
I knew within myself what you meant' *(PI* 398). However, he now
gives this remark the following gloss:

> But that meant that I knew how one thinks to conceive this
> object, to see it, to make one's looking and pointing mean it.
> I know how one stares ahead and looks about one in this case
> – and the rest. I think we can say: you are talking (if, for
> example, you are sitting in a room) of the 'visual room'.
>
> *(PI* 398)

The concept of the 'visual room' is introduced as a term to describe my visual impression of the material room, which the material room allegedly produces in me. The visual room is not the material room, but the visual impression of the material room; it is conceived as something that arises or occurs in me when I look at the latter. The reflections of the previous paragraph have already shown that it makes no sense to think of the visual room as an object that I *have* or *own*: 'The "visual room" is the one that has no owner' (*PI* 398). As we've seen, it is not something I look at, or see, or point to: 'I can as little own it as I can walk about it, or look at it, or point to it. Inasmuch as it cannot be anyone else's it is not mine either' (*PI* 398). Yet when we do philosophy we are drawn into thinking of the visual room as a quasi-material thing, as an image or experience that I have, as something which I have access to but which no one else can know directly. We want to assign a grammar to this concept – the grammar of an object term – which is simply inappropriate, or which it cannot be made to fit.

Wittgenstein now points out that the mere fact that we are tempted to think and talk in this way about our visual impression – i.e. as if it were a kind of object – does not make what we want to say intelligible: '[the visual room] does not belong to me *because* I want to use the same form of expression about it as about the material room in which I sit' (*PI* 398). I want to think of the visual room as a visual impression that I have when I look at the material room. But this, as we've seen, requires me to treat the visual room as if it were an object of consciousness, as something that is – grammatically speaking – on a par with the material room, or with a material representation of it, but which is accessible to me alone. Yet when we look more closely, we see that this grammar cannot be made to fit. Not only is the material room something I can walk about in, look at, point to, and so on, but also '[t]he description of the [material room] need not mention an owner, in fact it need not have any owner. But then the visual room *cannot* have any owner. "For" – one might say – "it has no master outside or in"' (*PI* 398). We want to think of the visual room as a visual impression that is present to my consciousness when I see a material room, but when we try to apply this picture of a special sort of object of experience, it crumbles in our hands, for we cannot find anything that is both an object of consciousness and that only I have access to.

But why does Wittgenstein say that the visual room 'has no master, outside or in'? To answer this question we need to look at the use Wittgenstein now makes of a comparison between the visual room and material pictures. He asks us to 'think of a picture of a landscape, an imaginary landscape with a house in it' (*PI* 398). The point of introducing this comparison is clear, for we want to think of the visual room as a sensory projection of the material room, which arises in, and is only accessible to, the consciousness of the perceiving subject. The visual room is an analogue of a picture of the room, insofar as both can be thought of as representations of the material room. We've already seen that the analogy cannot be applied strictly, for, unlike the material picture, we cannot think of the visual room as itself a kind of object. However, this might still leave room for the idea that, although the visual room is not a psychological analogue of a picture of a room, it is still (somehow!) a visual representation that is mine. Wittgenstein now uses the comparison with material pictures to show that this idea is also an illusion. Thus, he goes on:

> Someone asks "Whose house is that?" – The answer, by the way, might be "It belongs to the farmer who is sitting in the bench in front of it". But then he cannot for example enter his house.

> (*PI* 398)

If we think of how we might answer this question about ownership of the represented house, then we see clearly that the only possible answer must refer to something that is part of the same pictorial representation. Moreover, any answer that appeals to such a pictorial element will not be describing a genuine relation, but will be based on a story that surrounds the picture, or which the picture is illustrating, for the criteria that define ownership in ordinary life have no application to pictured objects ('[the farmer] cannot for example enter his house'). If we think of the visual room not as an object – a psychological analogue of a material picture – but simply as a representation of the material room, then, Wittgenstein suggests, 'surely the owner of the visual room would have to be the same kind of thing as it is'. If we shift from talk of objects that represent to representations, then the grammar shifts too, and this grammatical shift means that we still have no model of how we are to conceive of the relation between a subject and his visual impression. For the new grammar no more fits the case than the old one did: the visual room has no owner outside or in.

If we try to conceive of visual impressions as private, sensory representations of the material world, then we find that we cannot begin to specify either what sort of thing they are or what our relationship to them is. There is no psychological analogue of a material picture which is accessible only to me; and it makes no sense to speak of a human subject 'having' or 'owning' a mere representation. When we're asked to say more precisely how a subject stands in relation to his alleged visual impression, we find that we cannot provide a satisfactory model of the relation. What Wittgenstein wants us to see is that it is a mistake to think that talk of 'my visual impression' or of my 'having such-and-such a visual impression' introduces us to a new kind of entity, something that exists in me whenever I see an object and that is causally correlated with the latter. Talk of visual impressions is, at bottom, no more than another way of saying 'I see ...': 'The visual room seemed like a discovery, but what its discoverer really found', Wittgenstein suggests, 'was a new way of speaking, a new comparison' (*PI* 400).

The 'new comparison' that Wittgenstein refers to here is that between my visual experience of the room and a picture of it. The comparison seems to us peculiarly apt, for a picture draws our attention to something distinctive about the visual experience that we are not normally aware of, namely its characteristically perspectival nature. It is, in part, this discovery that invites us to separate out the objective room from my visual impression of it. For while a table that I see, say, is square, if I want to draw what I see, I would have to draw something asymmetrical. My visual impression seems, therefore, to have objective features which are not features of the objects that I see. The temptation is now to divide my visual experience up into a visual impression, whose objective features mirror those of a pictorial representation of the scene, and what my experience is an experience *of*, namely the material room that causes the visual impression to occur in me. What Wittgenstein has tried to show is that in creating the idea of the private visual impression, we have thereby created a chimera. There is no new object – the visual impression – discovered here; we have simply found a new way of representing what we see.

Wittgenstein expands on these points in *PI* 401 as follows:

> You have a new conception and interpret it as seeing a new object. You interpret a grammatical movement made by yourself as a quasi-physical phenomenon which you are observing. (Think for example of the question: "Are sense-data the material of which the universe is made?")
>
> But there is an objection to my saying you have made a 'grammatical' movement. What you have primarily discovered is a new way of looking at things. As if you had invented a new way of painting; or, again, a new metre or a new kind of song.

Wittgenstein questions the justice of calling this a 'grammatical movement', for this would suggest that we have invented a new language-game, or a new way of conceiving of visual experience, when really all we have done is think of a new way of representing what we see: 'a new way of looking at things. As if [we] had invented a new way of painting.' Representing our visual experience in a two-dimensional picture, composed entirely of coloured shapes, impresses us because it seems to abstract exactly what it is like to view a scene from a particular point of view, but we must not be misled by this into thinking that there is some psychological analogue of the picture, whose objective features are depicted in the latter. This way of representing visual experience is just one way of describing what I see, but it has no special claim to have uncovered a new kind of object that lies at the heart of visual experience even though we never normally notice it.

It is clear that in offering this critique of the concept of my visual impression Wittgenstein does not mean to deny that visual experience has a distinctive sensational content. However, this idea of the distinctive sensational content of visual experience is to be linked, not with the notion of something that is accessible only to me, but with the sensible properties of objects that are uniquely available to vision. The sensible properties characteristic of vision do not, in any sense, belong only to me; the concept of 'red', for example, does not point in two directions, both to something public and to something in me that I know through introspection. We must not, Wittgenstein warns, 'detach the colour-*impression* from the object, like a membrane' (*PI* 275). And he wonders how it is 'even possible for us to be tempted to think that we use the word to *mean* at one time the colour known to everyone – and at another the 'visual impression' which *I* am getting *now*' (*PI* 277). It is, he suggests, when we cease to attend to what we see and try to focus on our experience of colour as such, when 'I immerse myself in the colour' (*PI* 277) – it's then that we create the philosophical illusion of 'my red'. It is not, therefore, that Wittgenstein denies that visual experience has a distinctive sensational content, but like every other feature of visual perception it refers us to an intersubjective world of physical objects, and not to something that is occurring in me.

All these points are entirely negative. They show that if we approach the problem of understanding visual experience by concentrating hard on what it is like, for example, to see a room, then it is virtually inevitable that we will be led into thinking of visual experience in terms of images that the perceiver knows directly and which no one else has access to. We are led into thinking of visual experience in the way that introspection seems to present it: as a conscious presentation of the purely visible, as a distinctive quality of experience that we each know from our own case, and which we try to indicate by staring before us and saying '*this*'. The remarks on the visual room reveal that this idea of a visual impression as a phenomenon of consciousness is empty, we cannot begin to say either what this special object of consciousness is or what our relationship to it might be; the visual impression as a private object of experience is a philosophical illusion. Characteristically, Wittgenstein approaches the problem of understanding the concept of 'visual experience' in a quite different way: through a grammatical investigation of how the concepts in this region of our language actually function. He takes up this grammatical enquiry in earnest in Part II, section xi of the

Investigations. The principal aim of these remarks is, first of all, to overcome the exaggerated sense of the importance of introspection in understanding the nature of visual experience, and second, to reveal the grammatical links that exist between the concept of visual experience and behaving and responding in particular ways, or being able to *do* something.

Seeing and seeing-as

Part II, section xi opens with a distinction between two uses of the word 'see':

> The one: "What do you see there?" – "I see *this*" (and then a description, a drawing, a copy). The other: "I see a likeness between these two faces".
>
> (*PI*, p. 193)

It is clear that the distinction between these two uses of the word 'see' relates to the problem which we set out at the opening of this chapter, for in the second of these uses we have another case in which we speak of 'seeing' something that philosophical reflection makes us want to say we cannot really see. For one thing, a failure to see a likeness, like a failure to recognize a smile as friendly, does not imply that a subject's sight is defective or that there is anything wrong with his eyes. Indeed, Wittgenstein observes, someone might draw two faces very accurately and fail to see a likeness that someone else notices at once. Thus there is simply no place for the idea of 'seeing' a likeness in our picture of visual experience as a kind of sensory imprint that is caused by the influence of physical objects on our sensory surfaces. Are we, then, *wrong* when we speak of 'seeing' the likeness? Should we deny that the person who notices the likeness and the one who doesn't 'see' the faces differently? Wittgenstein suggests, instead, that we need to recognize a 'difference of category between the two "objects" of sight' (*PI*, p. 193). It is through an investigation of examples of the second use of the word 'see' that Wittgenstein tries to reveal that the concept of perception functions quite differently from the way we are inclined to think when we approach it by reflecting on what it is like to see.

The discussion begins with the following case: 'I contemplate a face, and then suddenly notice its likeness to another' (*PI*, p. 193). Wittgenstein notes that in such a case 'I *see* that it has not changed; and yet I see it differently' (*PI*, p. 193). He labels this phenomenon – in which I both see that an object hasn't changed and yet see it differently – 'noticing an aspect' (*PI*, p. 193). The example takes us to the heart of the problems with which we began, for it presents us with a case in which we appear to draw a distinction between visual experiences – i.e. to recognize a difference in what is seen – while acknowledging that, in another sense, the object hasn't changed. How are we to understand the use of the word 'see' when I say that I 'see' the object differently but yet, in another sense, I see it hasn't changed? What goes on when I suddenly notice an aspect? If the object itself doesn't change, then what is it that changes? By investigating this region of our language-game, Wittgenstein gradually brings about the essential shift in our understanding of the concept of visual experience that is required to weaken the grip of the picture of perception as a visual image that is produced in me by the influence of objects on my sensory surfaces.

In order to investigate the phenomenon of aspect seeing further, Wittgenstein asks us to consider the following figure, which he derives from Jastrow's duck-rabbit (*PI*, p. 194):

The picture is ambiguous: it can be seen either as a duck or as a rabbit. If I look at the picture and see it now one way and now the other, then it is clear that we have another example in which I want to say that I see the picture differently, and yet I also see that the picture doesn't change. Is it right to talk about 'seeing' in the first case? Well, isn't it possible, Wittgenstein asks, that the picture has been shown to me and I have never seen it as anything other than the picture of a rabbit, that the other way of seeing the picture has never struck me? He labels this 'continuous aspect seeing' in order to distinguish it from the 'dawning of' an aspect. In this case, asked what I see I should unhesitatingly reply: 'I see a picture of a rabbit'. We might find exactly such a picture used in a cartoon drawing, or to illustrate a story, or to instruct someone, or to inform others of the presence of rabbits; seen in these contexts the duck-aspect of the picture will probably remain unnoticed. Wittgenstein calls these pictures 'picture-objects', and he observes that we 'stand towards' them in somewhat the way we stand towards the objects they represent. Thus:

> Here it is useful to introduce the idea of a picture object. For instance

> would be a 'picture-face'.
>   In some respects I stand towards it as I do towards a human face. I can study its expression, can react to it as the expression of the human face. A child can talk to picture-men or picture-animals, can treat them as it treats dolls.

(*PI*, p. 194)

Let us suppose, then, that I have always seen Jastrow's duck-rabbit as a picture-rabbit. If I were asked 'What is that?' I should have replied 'A picture-rabbit', and would have responded to further questions by talking about rabbits: describing them and their habits, showing other pictures of them, imitating them, and so on. In this case, Wittgenstein notes, I would *not* describe what I see by saying 'Now I am seeing it as a picture-rabbit' or 'I see it as a picture-rabbit', but would simply 'have described my perception: just as if I had said "I see a red circle over there"' (*PI*, p. 195). Nevertheless, someone who knows that the figure is ambiguous might say of me 'She is seeing it as a picture-rabbit'. The expression 'seeing-as' is not used in circumstances in which we are simply reporting a perception or describing what we see; 'I am seeing it as . . .' is not a simple report of what is seen:

> It would have made as little sense for me to say "Now I am seeing it as [a picture-rabbit]" as to say at the sight of a knife and fork "Now I am seeing this as a knife and fork". This expression would not be understood. – Any more than: "Now it's a fork" or "It can be a fork too".
>
> (*PI*, p. 195)

> If you say "now it's a face for me", we can ask: "What change are you alluding to?"
>
> (*PI*, p. 195)

Seeing the Jastrow duck-rabbit and responding to the question 'What is it?' with the reply 'It's a rabbit' is, then, an indication that the ambiguity of the picture has escaped me: I am simply reporting my perception. If, however, I know that I am being presented with an ambiguous figure, then I may respond to the question in one of two different ways. I may say 'It's the duck-rabbit'. This too, Wittgenstein suggests, would be a perceptual report, i.e. a report of what (in the first sense of 'objects' of sight) it is that I see. But I may also respond by saying: 'Now I am seeing it as a rabbit'. And this, as we've seen, cannot be understood simply as a report of my perception, or as a description of the object that I see. Yet if the aspect now changes, I may report the change as follows: 'The picture has changed. Now I am seeing it as a duck'. I describe the change in what I see 'quite as if the object had altered before my eyes' (*PI*, p. 195), as if I am actually seeing something different each time. Yet the words I use to describe the change also contain an acknowledgement that the figure itself (the object) has not altered: the picture is altogether different, and yet it is the same. If we feel disinclined to speak of 'seeing' at all here, then we should recall the connection with the case of continuous aspect seeing; in that case 'It's a rabbit' is a straightforward perceptual report that describes the object that is seen. Wittgenstein also asks us to imagine a case in which 'I see two pictures, with the duck-rabbit surrounded by rabbits in one, by ducks in the other. I do not notice that they are the same. Does it *follow* from this that I *see* something different in the two cases? – It gives us a reason for using this expression here' (*PI*, p. 195). But if what I see is different, and given that the object itself doesn't change, just *what* is it that is different? Is it 'my impression? my point of view? – Can I say?' (*PI*, p. 195).

One temptation is to try to *explain* the change that occurs when an aspect switches, by appeal to some quasi-objective alteration in what is seen. For example, suppose I am looking at a puzzle picture and trying to find the human face that is 'hidden' in a pattern of branches. Suddenly I see the face. Where before I saw only a disorganized tangle of branches, I now recognize the characteristic outline and features that depict a human face. This may tempt us into explaining the change that takes place in terms of an alteration in the 'organization' of the picture. Thus, when I see the face in the puzzle picture, I see not merely a collection of particular shapes and colours, but also a particular organization of them. In this way, we try to make organization a quasi-objective property of what I see, on a par with colour and shape. But now suppose I am asked to draw what I see before and after I have seen the solution to the picture. If my drawing is accurate, then surely I will have to draw *the same thing* both times. The idea of a particular organization, which we are tempted to appeal to in order to explain the difference in my visual experience, does not actually help us here, for I do not know how to make the organization an objective property of what I see. It is not that the concept of a change in organization doesn't, in some sense, describe the experience I have when I suddenly see the face in the puzzle picture, but rather that this concept cannot be applied in the way we now want to apply it: as a description of an objective property of the picture on a par with colour and shape.

Since the organization of the picture cannot be recorded as an objective aspect of it, there is now a temptation to think of the visual impression of the picture as something that is distinct from the picture itself, as something only I have access to: 'After all my visual impression isn't the *drawing*; it is *this* – which I cannot show to anyone' (*PI*, p. 196). Having failed to record the change that we experience in the outer picture, we are here tempted to construct an 'inner picture', which we model on the outer picture, but which we also imagine incorporates the elusive property of 'organization' as one of its objective features. But, Wittgenstein objects, we still have no idea of how to represent this difference that leaves everything unchanged as a visual property of the 'inner picture'; what we couldn't make part of the objective drawing is now just stipulated to be a constitutive element of inner pictures. In our embarrassment, we have simply created 'a chimera; a queerly shifting construction' (*PI*, p. 196) that absorbs rather than solves our difficulty. It is true that my visual impression is not the drawing, but, Wittgenstein observes, 'neither is it anything of the same category, which I carry within myself' (*PI*, p. 196). The appeal to an inner picture which is both like and unlike an outer one does not get us any further; it is nothing more than a philosophical illusion which appears to solve our problem only because we don't examine it carefully enough. As soon as we look closer, we see that there is no inner analogue of the outer picture; and even if there were, we still don't know how to make the organization an objective feature of it.

I cannot, then, capture the difference between the visual experience I have when I say 'Now it is a rabbit' and the one I have when I say 'Now it is a duck' in terms of two distinct objects of sight, in the sense of objects that can be distinguished by pointing to two different things, or by drawing two different pictures. Here we have a case in which there is a difference between visual experiences that cannot be recorded in a straightforward perceptual report, or in a picture of what is seen. We have a case of the second category of an 'object' of sight. What Wittgenstein wants us to see is that we can only begin to understand this second use of the word 'see' – and thereby the distinction between visual experiences that the duck-rabbit brings to our attention – if we stop thinking about the concept of 'perception' in terms of something that is *given* or that is *caused* to occur in us by objective features of the material world, and connect it with the subject's way of *responding* to what he sees. Thus:

> If I saw the duck-rabbit as a rabbit, then I saw: these shapes and colours (I give them in detail) – and I saw besides something like this: and here I point to a number of different pictures of rabbits.

> (*PI*, pp. 196–7)

The difference in the two visual experiences does not arise from an objective alteration in the object itself, but from a difference in how the subject places the picture in two different contexts: 'I see something like this' (pointing to other pictures of rabbits) or 'I see something like that' (pointing to other pictures of ducks). The difference between the two experiences cannot be recorded by pointing to two different objects, but only by reference to the subject's way of responding to the picture, by putting it now in relation to these objects, now in relation to those: 'what I perceive in the dawning of an aspect is not a property of the object, but an internal relation between it and other objects' (*PI*, p. 212). Wittgenstein believes that this difference in how we are to understand the distinction between the two visual experiences reveals that 'seeing' and 'seeing-as' are two different, though related, concepts: ' "Seeing as . . ." is not part of perception. And for that reason it is like seeing and again not like' (*PI*, p. 197). Both are concepts of visual experience, but they are importantly different. The difference, moreover, provides a corrective to our temptation to think of visual perception purely introspectively, and prompts us to recognize the internal link that exists between what is seen and the subject's way of responding. In this way, the case of seeing-as works against our inclination to think of perception in terms of the influence of objects on a receptive faculty, and draws our attention to the role of an active, responding subject in determining the nature of visual experience, or in fixing what is seen.

Seeing and responding

Wittgenstein now draws our attention to a different distinction between visual experiences that we make within our ordinary language-game:

> I look at an animal and am asked: "What do you see?" I answer: "A rabbit". – I see a landscape; suddenly a rabbit runs past. I exclaim "A rabbit!".
>
> (*PI*, p. 197)

In the first case, Wittgenstein suggests, my words are a straightforward report of what I see; in the second, my words also represent an exclamation or cry, something that I let out almost involuntarily, as an immediate response to something which surprises or delights me. 'Both things', he believes, 'are expressions of perception and of visual experience. But the exclamation is so in a different sense from the report' (p. 197). He characterizes the difference further as follows:

> If you are looking at an object, you need not think of it; but if you are having the visual experience expressed by the exclamation, you are also *thinking* of what you see.
>
> (*PI*, p. 197)

In this case, as in the case of seeing-as, there is an aspect of the visual experience that is not recorded in the bare idea of an accurate report or picture of the object of sight, understood as something that we might point to. Thus we cannot make the distinction between the visual experience that is expressed by the report and that expressed by the exclamation in terms of an objective difference in the objects of sight; the difference in the form in which the two experiences are expressed – i.e. the difference between the exclamation and the report – is an essential element in the distinction that we make between them, and is not something merely incidental to it. Here again we have a case in which a distinction between two visual experiences is seen to have an internal connection with ways of responding to what is seen. The criteria for having the visual experience that is expressed in the exclamation 'A rabbit!' reveal a grammatical connection between this particular experience and *behaving* in a particular way. Our grasp of the distinction between the visual experience expressed by the report and the one expressed by the exclamation is rooted in the difference in how they are expressed in behaviour, and not in an objective difference in the objects experienced.

Alongside the cases of seeing aspects and of suddenly noticing an object, Wittgenstein also asks us to consider a range of cases in which we suddenly recognize an object we have been looking at for some time. Here too we may have the experience of a sudden change in our visual experience, which takes place even though we see that, in another sense (in the sense of the first kind of object of sight), nothing has changed:

Someone suddenly sees an appearance which he does not recognize (it may be a familiar object, but in an unusual position or lighting); the lack of recognition perhaps lasts only a few seconds. Is it correct to say he has a different visual experience from someone who knew the object at once?

I meet someone whom I have not seen for years; I see him clearly, but fail to know him. Suddenly I know him, I see the old face in the altered one.

(both from *PI*, p. 197)

In these cases too, Wittgenstein believes, we capture the difference in our experiences by reference to a change in how we respond to the object, e.g., in how we would describe or draw it before and after the act of recognition. Thus, in the first case, although the object before my eyes doesn't change, the change in my experience is expressed in the fact that I would now draw or describe what I see much more confidently and accurately, and there are certain mistakes in description that I would no longer make. In the second case, the change in experience that goes along with my new understanding of the face might be expressed in my making a quite different portrait of it, if I could paint. The differences in visual experience connected with sudden recognition are not linked with any objective alteration in the object, but with a change in how the subject is situated, or disposed to act, towards the object, i.e. with a change in what Wittgenstein calls 'fine shades of behaviour' (*PI*, p. 207). As in the example of suddenly noticing, Wittgenstein believes we are tempted to think of the phenomenon of recognition as something that is not purely visual, but is part perception and part thought. Thus, we think that the words in which we describe these experiences are not perceptual reports, but something else as well: 'a cry of recognition' (*PI*, p. 198). The important thing to see, however, is that if we try to separate out the recognition from the visual experience, then we can no longer capture the difference between the visual experience – i.e. the difference in what is seen – of someone who knows the object straight away and someone who recognizes it only after a moment.

Wittgenstein now makes explicit the essential complexity in the concept of visual experience that these examples have served to reveal. Each of the examples is similar to the one with which Wittgenstein began, in that they all involve what I have been calling the second sense of ' "objects" of sight'. In all of the examples, Wittgenstein has tried to show that the concept of seeing is forced on us here: they all involve a change in visual experience – i.e. a change in what is seen – even though, in another sense, the object that is seen doesn't alter. This use of the word 'see' is then used to reveal an internal connection between the concept of visual experience and the concept of responding or behaving in a certain way. For we cannot draw the distinctions between visual experiences that the examples require without an appeal to criteria that relate to differences in the subject's response, rather than to objective changes in the scene. The use of the word 'see' in connection with the first category of objects of sight – i.e. in straightforward descriptions that might be used in reply to the question 'What do you see?' – tempts us to think of visual experience purely in terms of something's being given to a perceiving consciousness. However, the change in visual experience that occurs when an aspect changes, or when I suddenly notice or recognize something, shows that there is more to our concept of visual experience than this suggests. The examples show that the idea that differences in visual experience always correspond to objective differences in what is presented is a mistake; this is only one kind of difference in visual experience, and it does not cover all the distinctions that we draw. Thus we find that our concept of visual experience does not function in the way we've imagined; the concept is much more closely tied to distinctive ways of behaving than the picture of visual experience as the passive reception of 'visual data' suggests.

This complexity in our concept of visual experience goes along, Wittgenstein suggests, with an 'elasticity' in our concept of a representation of what is seen:

> The concept of a representation of what is seen, like that of a copy, is very elastic, and so *together with it* is the concept of what is seen. The two are intimately connected. (Which is *not* to say that they are alike.)
>
> (*PI*, p. 198)

Our concept of what is seen is intimately connected with the concept of a representation of what is seen, in that one criterion of what a subject sees is the representation or description that he gives of what he sees. But how do we represent those aspects of our visual experience that are connected with our way of responding to the object, rather than with any objective feature of it? It is here that we need to acknowledge an elasticity in our concept of a representation of what is seen. It does not cover only exact copies or bare physical descriptions of what we see, but also portraits, rich and evocative verbal descriptions, gestures, facial expressions, comparisons, mimicking, and so on. Wittgenstein suggests that we can see this elasticity in our concept of a representation of what is seen, if we ask ourselves how we know that human beings see three-dimensionally, or how this aspect of their visual experience might be represented or captured. The most natural way to represent it does not attempt to produce a representation of 'what it is like to see three-dimensionally', but uses gestures, which exploit our own insertion in space, to represent what we see. In this case the response to what is seen, which is naturally expressed in gestures, becomes itself a representation of what is seen, so that what is seen is mirrored in the movements of the body:

> How does one tell that human beings *see* three-dimensionally?
> – I ask someone about the lie of the land (over there) of which he has a view. "Is it like *this*?" (I shew him with my hand) – "Yes" – "How do you know?" – "It's not misty, I see it quite clear." He does not give reasons for the surmise. The only thing that is natural to us is to represent what we see three-dimensionally; special practice and training are needed for two-dimensional representation whether in drawing or in words. (The queerness of children's drawings.)
>
> (*PI*, p. 198)

At the beginning of the chapter, I suggested that Wittgenstein's discussion of seeing aspects would shed light on the source of any dissatisfaction we might feel with our earlier talk of seeing the friendliness in a smile. Take the case of a picture of a smiling face. We may imagine that someone looking at the picture may fail to recognize the smile as a smile. Does he, Wittgenstein asks, see the face (or the picture-face) differently from someone who sees it and understands it as smiling? If so, then clearly we have another example of the second category of objects of sight, for both perceivers are looking at the very same picture of a face. The difference in their visual experiences cannot be captured by means of two different visual representations of what is seen, for these would both have to reproduce the original picture. What they each see is represented in a different way: 'He mimics it differently, for instance' (*PI*, p. 198). When we allow that our concept of the representation of what is seen possesses this additional richness or elasticity, then the criteria that distinguish the content of these two visual experiences become clear. Our earlier sense that a facial expression – e.g. the friendliness of a face – cannot strictly be part of our visual experience, but must involve an 'interpretation' of it, can be seen to be connected with our tendency to think only of the first kind of object of sight, and to suppose that all differences in visual experience (as opposed to the interpretation of it) must be traceable to some objective change in what is presented to consciousness. By making us aware of an unforeseen complexity in our concepts of visual experience and the representation of what is seen, Wittgenstein works to overcome the prejudices that stand in the way of our accepting a form of description that is part of our ordinary language-game.

The following reflection, however, might still tempt us to think that a facial expression cannot strictly be seen: if we hold a drawing of a face upside down, we can no longer recognize what is expressed by it. Yet the picture that we have turned round is still an accurate visual representation of a face. If the expression is part of the content of our visual experience of the face, then surely it cannot be made to disappear simply by giving the figure a new orientation. To see what is wrong in this, Wittgenstein asks us to consider the following pairs of examples:

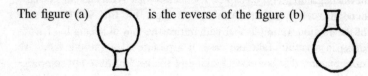

The figure (a)   is the reverse of the figure (b)

As (c) *Pleasure* is the reverse of (d) *Pleasure*

(*PI*, p. 198)

He now observes that, not only is the change between (c) and (d) more dramatic than that between (a) and (b), but 'there is a different difference between my impressions of (c) and (d) and between those of (a) and (b)' (*PI*, p. 198). Although what has been done to the object is exactly the same in each case, the reversal has an impact on the second pair of figures that it does not have on the first. Clearly, this difference in impact is not connected with a greater objective alteration, for the two pairs bear exactly the same relation to one another. Rather, the difference between the two cases is linked with the presence, in the second pair, of changes in how we respond to the figures. Thus, '(d), for example, looks neater than (c). . . . (d) is easy, (c) hard to copy' (*PI*, p. 198); it is these differences in our reactions to the reversed figures that ground the qualitative change in our experience of (d) and (c). The change in visual experience connected with the reorientation of a figure is not a simple product of an objective alteration in the visual array. For changes in orientation may have an unpredictable impact on visual experience that is linked with a change in how we react to the figure. The change in the content of our experience when the picture of a face is turned upside down – the fact that we see the smile in the one case but not in the other – is not something that can be conveyed by appeal to the alteration in the visual array, but is shown or expressed only in the changes in 'fine shades of behaviour'. For example, when you hold the drawing upside down, 'you cannot imitate the smile or describe it more exactly' (*PI*, p. 198).

Let us accept, then, that when we find the face in a puzzle picture, we see the picture in a new way: 'Not only can you give a new kind of description of it, but noticing the [face] was a new visual experience' (*PI*, p. 199). Are we to conclude from this that 'the copy of the figure [is] an *incomplete* description of my visual experience?' (*PI*, p. 199). Wittgenstein clearly wants us to draw no such conclusion, for there is something distinctly suspect in the implication that there is such a thing as the *complete* description or representation of a visual experience. Whether a description that I give of my visual experience is incomplete depends upon whether the person I am giving the description to understands what I want to convey. A drawing of the figure '*may* be an incomplete description, if there is still something to ask' (*PI*, p. 199). If someone asks me what I saw, then I may be able to make a drawing that will satisfy his curiosity. If I can, then we would not call the drawing 'incomplete', even though it will not record, for example, the way my glance ranged over the scene, focusing on one detail and then another, in a pattern which I will mostly be unable to recollect. What Wittgenstein wants us to see is that there is an indefinite number of descriptions of what is seen – think, e.g., of how the movements of someone's gaze might be represented on film, or the way in which one might represent the fact that a particular object is one's principal focus of interest, or that an unidentified object has just moved swiftly across one's visual field – each one serving a different purpose, and none of which qualify as the '*one genuine* proper case of such description – the rest being just vague, something which awaits clarification, or which must be swept aside as rubbish' (*PI*, p. 200).

In this way, Wittgenstein works to reveal how our picture of visual experience as a special kind of presence to consciousness, which I try to indicate by staring fixedly ahead of me, is grounded in the mistaken idea of the grammar of the concept of visual experience. What Wittgenstein's grammatical investigation has revealed is not only that visual experience is not just a passive reception of visual data, but that the link between the concept of visual experience and certain patterns of response is much closer than we think. The idea, which we have when doing philosophy, that all differences in visual experience must be traceable to objective differences in the objects themselves proves to be an illusion. The criteria of what is seen are much more complex, and much more closely tied to ways of *responding*, than our philosophical idea of the essence of visual experience makes us suppose.

In the remarks that follow, Wittgenstein looks at a wide range of examples of seeing and seeing-as that work further to reveal connections between the content of visual experience and the response we have to an object, the context in which it is seen, the attention we give to it, the attitude we take towards it, the use of the imagination or conceptual abilities that we apply in respect of it, and so on. The complexity in how our concept of visual experience functions that emerges in this discussion, on the one hand, works against the temptation to rely on introspection to reveal the essence of visual experience, or to think of visual experience in terms of a subject's passive reception of what is given to a perceiving consciousness. On the other hand, it also works to underline the grammatical connections that exist between our use of the concepts of seeing and seeing-as and forms of behaviour – including gestures, verbal descriptions, abilities to draw or mimic, and so on – in which seeing and seeing-as are expressed. What we find is that, as in the case of all other psychological concepts, what the concept of visual experience describes is not clarified by introspection, or by trying to imagine something, but by uncovering the patterns of employment that characterize its use in the language-game. What these patterns of employment reveal is a concept that is internally linked with doing, or being able to do, something, rather than with having something that we each of us know only from our own case. It is not that there is no distinction between having a visual experience and expressing it, for, as with every other psychological concept, the possibilities for concealment and pretence are an essential part of our ordinary language-game. But none of this detracts from the fact that the language-game we play with the words 'seeing' and 'seeing-as' links these concepts with forms of behaviour in which the experiences that these concepts describe are expressed.

Once this shift in our understanding of the concept of visual experience is achieved, then, as we've seen, the problem with which we began this chapter disappears. Once we recognize the complexity in our ordinary criteria for seeing and for what is seen, and the connection between these criteria and 'fine shades of behaviour', then we are freed from the idea that 'it must be possible to describe [visual experience] in spatial terms' (*PI*, p. 199). Thus, we are no longer tempted to insist that all we can really see is what can be represented in a spatial pattern of coloured shapes. For our concept of visual experience is seen not to denote a special quality of experience, or a certain sort of presence to consciousness, but to connect with a wide range of characteristic forms of movement, gesture, expression, and abilities that constitute our criteria for someone's seeing something, noticing or recognizing something, watching or looking at something, seeing something as something, and so on. The criterion of what is seen – our notion of the content of visual experience – is no longer fixed by a speculative account of what constitutes the essence of visual perception; we are now able to accept our ordinary, complex language-game of describing or representing what is seen. Our sense that we do not really *see* the friendliness in a face, or that 'He gave a friendly smile' is not really a perceptual report, is seen to lie in nothing more than a mistaken idea of how the concept of visual experience functions.

References and further reading

Anscombe, G. E. M., 'The Intentionality of Sensation', in R. J. Butler, ed., *Analytical Philosophy*, 2nd series (Oxford: Blackwell, 1965).

Budd, M., *Wittgenstein's Philosophy of Psychology* (London: Routledge, 1989).

Fogelin, R. F., *Wittgenstein* (London: Routledge, 1987).

Hacker, P. M. S., *Wittgenstein: Meaning and Mind*, vol. 3 (Oxford: Blackwell, 1990).

Mulhall, S., *On Being in the World* (London: Routledge, 1990).

Schulte, J., *Experience and Expression: Wittgenstein's Philosophy of Psychology* (Oxford: Oxford University Press, 1993).

Scruton, R., *Art and Imagination* (London: Methuen, 1974).

Strawson, P. F., 'Imagination and Perception', in *Freedom and Resentment and other Essays* (London: Methuen, 1974).

Bibliography

Aidun, D., 'Wittgenstein's Philosophical Method and Aspect-Seeing', *Philosophical Investigations*, vol. 5, 1982.

Anscombe, G. E. M., 'The Intentionality of Sensation', in R. J. Butler, ed., *Analytical Philosophy*, 2nd series (Oxford: Blackwell, 1965).

—— 'On the Form of Wittgenstein's Writing', in R. Kiblansky, ed., *Contemporary Philosophy: A Survey*, vol. 3 (Firenze: La Nuova Italia, 1969).

—— 'Wittgenstein: Whose Philosopher?', in A. Phillips Griffiths, ed., 1992.

Arrington, R. L. and Glock, H.-J., eds, *Wittgenstein's Philosophical Investigations: Text and Context* (London: Routledge, 1991).

Saint Augustine, *Confessions* (Harmondsworth: Penguin, 1961).

Baker, G., 'Following a Rule: The Basic Themes', in S. H. Holtzman and C. M. Leich, eds, 1981.

—— *Wittgenstein, Frege and the Vienna Circle* (Oxford: Blackwell, 1988).

—— '*Philosophical Investigations* section 122: Neglected Aspects', in R. L. Arrington and H.-J. Glock, 1991.

Baker, G. and Hacker, P. M. S., *Wittgenstein: Understanding and Meaning, An Analytical Commentary on the Philosophical Investigations*, vol. 1 (Oxford: Blackwell, 1983).

—— *Wittgenstein: Rules, Grammar and Necessity: An Analytical Commentary on the* Philosophical Investigations, vol. 2 (Oxford: Blackwell, 1985).

—— *Scepticism, Rules and Language* (Oxford: Blackwell, 1984).

Barnett, W., 'The Rhetoric Of Grammar: Understanding Wittgenstein's Method', *Metaphilosophy*, vol. 21, 1990.

Bartley, W. W., *Wittgenstein* (London: Quartet, 1977).

Binkley, T., *Wittgenstein's Language* (The Hague: Martinus Nijhoff, 1973).

Birsch, D. and Dorbolo, J., 'Working with Wittgenstein's Builders', *Philosophical Investigations*, vol. 13, 1990.

Boghossian, P. A., 'The Rule Following Considerations', *Mind*, vol. 98, 1989.

Bouveresse, J. ' "The Darkness of This Time": Wittgenstein and the Modern World', in A. Phillips Griffiths, ed., 1992.

—— *Wittgenstein Reads Freud* (Princeton, NJ: Princeton University Press, 1995.

Budd, M., 'Wittgenstein on Meaning, Interpretation and Rules', *Synthèse*, vol. 58, 1984.

—— *Wittgenstein's Philosophy of Psychology* (London: Routledge, 1989).

Cavell, S., 'The Availability of Wittgenstein's Later Philosophy', in G. Pitcher, ed., 1966.

—— *The Claim of Reason: Wittgenstein, Skepticism, Morality and Tragedy* (Oxford: Oxford University Press, 1979).

—— 'Declining Decline: Wittgenstein as a Philosopher of Culture', *Inquiry*, vol. 31, 1988.

—— *Conditions Handsome and Unhandsome: The Constitution of Emersonian Perfectionism* (London: University of Chicago Press, 1990).

—— *Philosophical Passages: Wittgenstein, Emerson, Austin, Derrida* (Oxford: Blackwell, 1995).

Engelmann, P., *Letters from Ludwig Wittgenstein with a Memoir* (Oxford: Blackwell, 1967).

Fann, K. T., *Wittgenstein's Conception of Philosophy* (Oxford: Blackwell, 1969).

—— ed., *Ludwig Wittgenstein: The Man and his Philosophy* (Hassocks: Harvester Press, 1978).

Fogelin, R. F., *Wittgenstein* (London: Routledge [1976], 1987).

French, P. A, Uehling, T. E. and Wettstein, H. K., eds, *The Wittgenstein Legacy, Midwest Studies in Philosophy*, vol. XVII (Notre Dame, Indiana: University of Notre Dame Press, 1992).

Gaita, R., 'Language and Conversation: Wittgenstein's Builders', in A. Phillips Griffiths, ed., 1992.

Gasking, D. A. T. and Jackson, A. C., 'Wittgenstein as Teacher', in K. T. Fann, ed., 1978.

Genova, J., *Wittgenstein: A Way of Seeing* (London: Routledge, 1995).

Goldfarb, W. D., 'I Want You To Bring Me A Slab: Remarks on the Opening Sections of the *Philosophical Investigations*', *Synthèse*, vol. 26, 1983.

—— 'Wittgenstein, Mind and Scientism', *Journal of Philosophy*, vol. 86, 1989.

—— 'Wittgenstein on Understanding', in P. A. French, T. E. Uehling and H. K. Wettstein, eds, 1992

Grayling, A. C., *Wittgenstein* (Oxford: Oxford University Press, 1988).

Griffiths, A. Phillips, ed., *Wittgenstein Centenary Essays* (Cambridge: Cambridge University Press, 1992).

Hacker, P. M. S., *Insight and Illusion* (Oxford: Oxford University Press [1972], 1986).

—— *Wittgenstein: Meaning and Mind, An Analytical Commentary on the* Philosophical Investigations, vol. 3 (Oxford: Blackwell, 1990).

Haller, R., *Questions on Wittgenstein* (London: Routledge, 1988).

Heal, J., 'Wittgenstein and Dialogue', in T. Smiley, ed., *Philosophical Dialogues: Plato, Hume, Wittgenstein*, Proceedings of the British Academy (Oxford: Oxford University Press, 1995).

Heller, E., 'Wittgenstein: Unphilosophical Notes', in K. T. Fann, ed., 1978.

Hertzberg, L., 'The kind of certainty is the kind of language game', in D. Z. Phillips and P. Winch, eds, 1989.

—— 'Language, Philosophy and Natural History', in L. Hertzberg, 1994.

—— *The Limits of Experience, Acta Philosophica Fennica*, vol. 56, 1994.

Hilmy, S., *The Later Wittgenstein: The Emergence of a New Philosophical Method* (Oxford: Blackwell, 1987).

—— ' "Tormenting Questions" in *Philosophical Investigations* section 133', in R. L. Arrington and H.-J. Glock, 1991.

Holtzman, S. H. and Leich, C. M., eds, *To Follow a Rule* (London: Routledge, 1981).

Hughes, J., 'Philosophy and Style: Wittgenstein and Russell', *Philosophy and Literature*, vol. 13, 1989.

James, W., *The Principles of Psychology* (Cambridge, Mass: Harvard University Press, 1981).

Janik, A. and Toulmin, S., *Wittgenstein's Vienna* (London: Weidenfeld and Nicolson, 1973).

Johnston, P., *Wittgenstein: Rethinking the Inner* (London: Routledge, 1993).

Kenny, A., *Wittgenstein* (Harmondsworth: Penguin, 1973).

—— 'Wittgenstein on the Nature of Philosophy', in B. McGuiness, ed., 1982.

—— *The Legacy of Wittgenstein* (Oxford: Blackwell, 1984).

Kripke, S. A., *Wittgenstein on Rules and Private Language* (Oxford: Blackwell, 1982).

Malcolm, N., *Ludwig Wittgenstein: A Memoir With a Biographical Sketch by George Henrik von Wright* (Oxford: Oxford University Press [1958], 1984).

—— 'Wittgenstein's *Philosophical Investigations*', in *Knowledge and Certainty* (Englewood Cliffs, NJ: Prentice-Hall, 1963).

—— *Nothing is Hidden: Wittgenstein's Criticism of his Early Thought* (Oxford: Blackwell, 1986).

—— 'Language Game (2)', in D. Z. Phillips and P. Winch, eds, 1989.

McCulloch, G., *The Mind and its World* (London: Routledge, 1995).

McDowell, J. H., 'Criteria, Defeasibility and Knowledge', *Proceedings of the British Academy*, vol. LXVIII, 1982.

—— 'Wittgenstein on Following a Rule', *Synthèse*, vol. 58, 1984.

—— 'Meaning and Intentionality in Wittgenstein's Later Philosophy', in P. A. French, T. E. Uehling and H. K. Wettstein, eds, 1992.

McGinn, C., *Wittgenstein on Meaning* (Oxford: Blackwell, 1984).

McGuiness, B., ed., *Wittgenstein and his Times* (Oxford: Blackwell, 1982).

—— *Wittgenstein: A Life. Young Ludwig 1889–1921* (London: Duckworth, 1988).

Minar, P., 'Feeling at Home in the Language (What makes reading the *Philosophical Investigations* possible?), *Synthèse*, vol. 102, 1995.

Monk, R., *Ludwig Wittgenstein: The Duty of Genius* (London: Jonathan Cape, 1990).

Mulhall, S., *On Being in the World: Wittgenstein and Heidegger on Seeing Aspects* (London: Routledge, 1990).

Nagel, T., 'What is it like to be a bat?', in *Mortal Questions* (Cambridge: Cambridge University Press, 1979).

Pears, D. F., *Wittgenstein* (London: Fontana, 1971).

—— *The False Prison*, vol. 2 (Oxford: Oxford University Press, 1987).

Phillips, D. Z. and Winch, P., eds, *Wittgenstein: Attention to Particulars. Essays in Honour of Rush Rhees (1905–1989)* (London: Macmillan, 1989).

Pitcher, G., ed., *Wittgenstein: The* Philosophical Investigations (New York: Doubleday, 1966).

Redpath, T., *Ludwig Wittgenstein: A Student's Memoir* (London: Duckworth, 1990).

Rhees, R., ed., 'Wittgenstein's Builders', in K. T. Fann, ed., 1978.

—— *Ludwig Wittgenstein: Personal Recollections* (Oxford: Blackwell, 1981).

Rowe, M. W., 'Goethe and Wittgenstein', *Philosophy*, vol. 66, 1991.

—— 'Wittgenstein's Romantic Inheritance', *Philosophy*, vol. 69, 1994.

Savickey, B., 'Voices in Wittgenstein's *Philosophical Investigations*', M.Phil thesis, Cambridge University, 1990.

—— 'Wittgenstein's Method of Grammatical Investigation', D.Phil. thesis, University of York, 1995.

Savigny, E. Von, 'Common behaviour of many a kind: *Philosophical Investigations* section 206', in R. L. Arrington and H.-J. Glock, eds, 1991.

Schulte, J., *Experience and Expression: Wittgenstein's Philosophy of Psychology* (Oxford: Oxford University Press, 1993).

Scruton, R., *Art and Imagination* (London: Methuen, 1974).

Staten, H., *Wittgenstein and Derrida* (London: University of Nebraska Press, 1986).

Strawson, P. F., 'Imagination and Perception', in *Freedom and Resentment and other essays* (London: Methuen, 1974).

Thompkins, E. F., 'The Money and the Cow', *Philosophy*, vol. 67, 1992.

Walker, M., 'Augustine's Pretence: Another Reading of Wittgenstein's *Philosophical Investigations*', *Philosophical Investigations*, vol. 13, 1990.

Wright, C., 'Does *Philosophical Investigations* 258–60 suggest a cogent argument against private language?', in P. Petit and J. H. McDowell, eds, *Subject, Thought and Context* (Oxford: Oxford University Press, 1986).

—— 'Wittgenstein's Later Philosophy of Mind: Sensation, Privacy and Intention', *Journal of Philosophy*, vol. 86, 1989.

Wright, G. H. Von, 'The Origin and Composition of the *Philosophical Investigations*', in *Wittgenstein* (Oxford: Blackwell, 1982).

—— 'The Wittgenstein Papers', in *Wittgenstein* (Oxford: Blackwell, 1982).

Index